The
Literature of Change

STUDIES IN THE NINETEENTH-CENTURY PROVINCIAL NOVEL

JOHN LUCAS

Professor of English, Loughborough University

THE HARVESTER PRESS, SUSSEX

BARNES & NOBLE BOOKS, NEW JERSEY

This second edition published in Great Britain in 1980 by
THE HARVESTER PRESS LIMITED
Publishers: John Spiers and Margaret A. Boden
16 Ship Street, Brighton, Sussex

and in the USA by
BARNES & NOBLE BOOKS
81 Adams Drive, Totowa, New Jersey 07512

First published in 1977 by The Harvester Press Limited
and in the USA by Harper and Row Publishers Inc.,
Barnes and Noble Import Division
Revised and with new material, 1980

© John Lucas 1977, 1980

British Library Cataloguing in Publication Data
Lucas, John, *b. 1937*
    The literature of change. – 2nd ed.
    1. Hardy, Thomas, *b. 1840* – Criticism and interpretation
    2. Rutherford, Mark – Criticism and interpretation
    3. Gaskell, Elizabeth Cleghorn – Criticism and interpretation
    I. Title
    823'.8'09   PR871
    ISBN 0–85527–233–3
    ISBN 0–85527–243–0 Pbk

Barnes & Noble Books
ISBN 0–389–20020–4 (cloth)
      0–389–20021–2 (pbk)

Printed in Great Britain by
Redwood Burn Limited, Trowbridge and Esher

FOR
CARL PIDGEON
AND
LAURIE FINCHAM

Contents

Introduction to the Second Edition

IN this new edition of *The Literature of Change* I have corrected a number of literal errors which appeared in the first edition. I haven't, however, made any other alterations. This is not out of indifference to the criticisms made by, for example, Barbara Hardy and William Myers. It is simply because I couldn't have re-cast the book without weakening such coherence as it now has. Barbara Hardy is perhaps right to complain that my chapter on Hardy simplifies his novels; but I was trying to isolate a major concern of those novels, and although I can see that the danger of this is that it may leave out of account their complexity as artistic wholes, the corresponding advantage is that it may direct attention towards areas of the novels which haven't been much noticed, but which ought to be.

William Myers thinks that I am insufficiently concerned with my novelists' theoretic or intellectual positions. I am not sure that I fully understand his objection, but I am certain that the only way one can judge the adequacy or otherwise of a novelist's theoretical position *qua* novelist, is through the novels themselves. And it was with the novels that I was primarily concerned. I know there is a danger in this, because it allows, perhaps encourages, one to read the novels as signs or symptoms of cultural distress, in other words as fictions not fully controlled by their authors; as works which betray as much as, or more than, they reveal. It is a matter of great importance, and it links with another, very proper, criticism made of *The Literature of Change*: that I nowhere attempt to explain what I mean by 'provincial.' It is so, and I am much more aware of the real nature of that flaw than I was when I wrote the book. I can only say that in the book I am now working on, a study of Elizabeth Gaskell, I hope to repair that error. I shall also be trying to deal with the problem of novel as 'symptom.'

JOHN LUCAS

Introduction

THIS book is about nineteenth-century provincial novels. Not all of them, and in particular not those of George Eliot. The reason for this is simple. So much has already been said about her, and said so well – by, among others, John Goode, Barbara Hardy, John Harvey and William Myers – that for me to add my piece would inevitably require me to go over ground they have already covered. It would also take up space that I think is better given over to the three novelists on whom I've chosen to concentrate. To be sure, George Eliot hovers over many of the pages that follow. It could hardly be otherwise. Mrs Gaskell knew and admired her work, Hale White was deeply impressed by it and, some would say, directly indebted to it; and there are obvious links between her fictions and those of Hardy's. So the references are there and the comparisons also. But there it stops. I want to leave as much room as possible to discuss the work of these other, less well regarded writers.

The main purpose of the present book is to show that the provincial novel in the nineteenth century is not only concerned with the nature of social change but uniquely well placed to record and explore how it happened, note its effects on individual lives, on patterns of living, on communities. Above all, I am concerned with processes of separation: what it means for a person to find himself – or, more usually and significantly, herself – struggling to retain an undivided sense of selfhood. And failing. For a sense of self isn't finally separable from a sense of community or family, and yet change enforces separations from both. Which means that the sense of self changes, suffers, becomes fractured.

Put it another way. It seems to me that my three chosen novelists are in their different ways keenly alert to pressures

that the social process puts on the individual and to how all the
pressures combine to defeat the possibility of unhampered
continuity, of contentment, of an unproblematic, untaxed sense
of selfhood. Indeed Hale White almost seems to place his hope
for survival of self in self-transcendence, in a deliverance from
self through duty, political action, altruism. And with both
Mrs Gaskell and Hardy survival becomes scarred with tragic
probabilities; it is fought for and secured at the expense of a
breaking of an integral self.

For survival in and cooperation with the social process comes
to much the same thing as accepting as inevitable the fact of
separation: from family, friends, community. And from self.
Such an acceptance is radically new, a reading of experience utterly different from the way in which, for example, Jane
Austen handles what seem to be experiences of a similar kind.
To take an obvious example: in *Mansfield Park* Fanny Price
pays a belated visit home to her parents' house in Portsmouth,
and is appalled at what she finds.

> She was at home. But alas! it was not such a home, she had not such
> a welcome, as – she checked herself; she was unreasonable. What right
> had she to be of importance to her family? She could have none, so
> long lost sight of! . . . Yet to have so little said or asked about herself –
> to have scarcely an enquiry made after Mansfield! It did pain her to
> have Mansfield forgotten; the friends who had done so much – the
> dear, dear friends! But here, one subject swallowed up all the rest.
> Perhaps it must be so. The destination of the Thrush must now be
> pre-eminently interesting. A day or two might shew the difference. *She*
> only was to blame. Yet she thought it would not have been so at
> Mansfield. No, in her uncle's house there would have been a con-
> sideration of times and seasons, a regulation of subject, a propriety, an
> attention towards every body which there was not here [vol. iii, ch.
> vii].

When you read that, you realize that Fanny feels utterly
separated from her parents and desires chiefly to return to
Mansfield. And you also realize that she feels no sense of tug-
of-war between her loyalties to the two houses. Simply Mansfield contains her 'dear, dear friends'. Admittedly, we have
been shown that it also houses those who are viciously opposed
to her, and it is tempting to suppose that Jane Austen is being
ironic at Fanny's expense here. Perhaps she has become a snob,
incapable of seeing the truth of her situation, and perhaps also

she has become a querulously vain person ('to have so little said
or asked about herself')? But of course it won't do. The fact of
the matter is that Jane Austen is on Fanny's side, and especially
in favour of a house in which there is regulation of subject and
propriety. Fanny gravitates naturally to that and, so it seems,
ensures its continuing health (the blood of the Bertrams needs
an injection of Fanny's resilient integrity).

And by and large Jane Austen's fiction endorses the idea of
continuity, of acceptance of the right 'house'. There is an important moment in *Emma* when the heroine gazes at Donwell
Abbey and feels:

> . . . all the honest pride and complacency which her alliance with the
> present and future proprietor could fairly warrant, as she viewed the
> respectable size and style of the building, its suitable, becoming,
> characteristic situation, low and sheltered – its ample gardens stretch-
> ing down to meadows washed by a stream, of which the Abbey, with
> all the old neglect of prospect, had scarcely a sight – and its abundance
> of timber in rows and avenues, which neither fashion nor extravagance
> had rooted up. – The house was larger than Hartfield, and totally un-
> like it, covering a good deal of ground, rambling and irregular, with
> many comfortable and one or two handsome rooms. – It was just what
> it ought to be, and it looked what it was – and Emma felt an increasing
> respect for it, as the residence of a family of such true gentility, un-
> tainted in blood and understanding [vol. II, ch. VI].

Donwell is the very model of order, of continuity. It resists improvement, prospects, fashion and extravagance; and it even
suggests a kind of naturalness that is surely intended to lay to
rest awkward questions about where the money for its upkeep
comes from. 'Rambling and irregular.' Those epithets disarm,
as do the earlier 'suitable, becoming, characteristic'. No wonder
Emma should feel an 'honest pride and complacency' in her
alliance with such a house.

But the fact is that such alliances become problematic in later
fiction, because they involve the process of separation that
really doesn't much enter Jane Austen's fiction. (The only painful separations in her novels are those of the outcasts, and such
pain has to be assumed; it isn't dwelt on.) I suppose the most
spectacular example of this is *Wuthering Heights*, and what happens to Cathy when she chooses Linton and Thrushcross Grange
and so renounces Heathcliff. But the process is played out in
different ways and at different levels in the work of the three

novelists who take up the present book. Sometimes it is seen mainly in terms of community, sometimes of family, sometimes of self; but it is always there. And it is typically centred on women. For in the work of all the novelists I am concerned with (and in George Eliot and the Brontës, too, for that matter) women come to occupy the centre of interest, provide the means by which the significance of choice, separation and exclusion can be most fully explored. It is hardly surprising that this should be so. In an obvious sense women in love and/or marriage are more likely to experience a sense of separation from family and community. That's the way it happens.

And it also happens that they experience an accompanying sense of uncertainty, of indecision and agony about where and to what they belong, and therefore what they identify with, what gives them their identity. One of the things that seems to me of increasing importance in the fictions of Hale White and Hardy is how they regard the problematic sexual nature of their heroines and how their heroines regard themselves, and how this is bound to be expressed in terms of confusion, contradiction, separation.

The confusions and contradictions aren't only in the heroines, but frequently in their creators as well. Indeed in all three novelists there seem to me to be splits, anarchic tendencies that fight against conventionalities and out of which important literature comes. Not always. Mrs Gaskell does lapse into cosy liberalism, Hale White occasionally uses his narrator, Mark Rutherford, as a way of muddying and protecting him from his own troubling insights; and Hardy sometimes sinks into banalities about nature's inexorable laws, which save him the trouble of doing much more than shrugging off as hopeless the problems that he himself has been exploring.

The flaws matter and I hope that in what follows I don't sweep them under the carpet. _The Literature of Change_ isn't meant to be a work of hagiography. But it equally isn't written in a mean or carping spirit (or so I hope). Mrs Gaskell, Hale White and Hardy are all marvellous writers, and at least two of them still haven't had their proper due.

Mrs Gaskell and the Nature of Social Change

I

IT is obvious enough that Mrs Gaskell is a novelist much concerned with the nature of social change. Her famous social-
problem novels, *Mary Barton* and *North and South*, are, among
other things, studies of the effects of industrialization on working-
class and middle-class families. They also offer a vision of
'reconciliation'. Mrs Gaskell is clearly alert to the problems that
accompany and in some ways are industrialization. Equally
clearly, she hopes that the problems can somehow be detached
from their context and so made to appear contingent rather
than inevitable. The result is that two otherwise fine novels are
weakened by their author's readiness to slacken her realistic grip
on probabilities in order to make room for some convenient
liberal pieties; we are offered an entirely ahistorical view of
change as being able to accommodate and reconcile conflicting
interests and energies. At its crudest (and such a view hardly
ever rises above such crudeness) this comes down to suggesting
that master and man will learn to understand, respect and even
love one another. Barton and Carson, Higgins and Thornton:
they are to stand as a general and generous statement about
enlightened relationships in an industrialized society. (I note in
passing that Mrs Gaskell's desire to convert class-antagonism
into a pattern of reconciliation is discoverable in many of her
short stories, especially *The Heart of John Middleton*.)

But it will not do. In the novels themselves Mrs Gaskell has
to fudge the important issues she herself has raised. It may of
course be that Higgins and Thornton will come to understand
one another – though Mrs Gaskell is a good deal more convincing when she writes of their misunderstandings, and it may

be that Margaret will come to understand the North. But such understanding amounts to little more than an impotent recognition that this is the way things are – master stays master, man stays man; and for Mrs Gaskell to suggest that it amounts to any more than that is silly. Besides, as soon as Thornton and Higgins arrive at their highly unlikely friendship they cease to be representative figures and drop into eccentricity. Limited and atypical reconciliations cannot be given the kind of representativeness that Mrs Gaskell desperately hopes will accompany the vast social changes many of whose effects she so finely studies.

So much by way of introduction. I am not going to say any more about the social-problem novels, partly because I have little to add to what I wrote about them in *Tradition and Tolerance in Nineteenth Century Fiction*,[1] and partly because the two novels have by now received quite enough critical attention to be going on with. (The best essays are by Arnold Kettle and Raymond Williams.)* My present concern is with three later works, which in their different ways reveal how Mrs Gaskell kept coming back to the nature and problems of social change and how she tried to find fictions to express her awareness of and puzzlement at these things. This does not mean that I think there is anything like a steady development in Mrs Gaskell's thought. On the contrary. Her last work, *Wives and Daughters*, has far more in common with the early *Cranford* than it has with what comes between. It is an idyllic novel and it is not difficult to see why *Cranford* and *Wives and Daughters* are held in such permanent affection by her readers. For they are both beautiful idylls (Martin Dodsworth's 'dark' reading of *Cranford* is simply fatuous), and they both minister to that particularly English love for remembrance of things past. *Morton Hall* and *My Lady Ludlow* are minor works in the same vein. *Morton Hall*, which was written in 1853, relates the history of a noble family fallen on hard times: 'There is no one living at Morton that knows the tradition of Sir John Morton and Alice Carr; yet the very first part of the Hall that the Drumble builder has pulled down is the old stone dining-parlour where the great dinner for the preachers mouldered away.' And *My*

* But see ch. 2.

Lady Ludlow, written some five years later, begins: 'I am an old woman now, and things are very different to what they were in my youth.' And the narrator goes on to tell of her years as companion to Lady Ludlow, an imperious gentlewoman, now dead. I do not think that we can feel quite the sympathy for Lady Ludlow that Mrs Gaskell seems to have intended (her liberal, middle-class pride typically gives way whenever she writes of 'old' families: they are nearly always seen in an exclusively favourable light), yet we are free to admire how fully and finely she registers Lady Ludlow's qualities and distinction, quite simply because she is dead, has become a part of the past that is sealed off from the present. Like much of Mrs Gaskell's fiction, *My Lady Ludlow* is about an irrecoverable moment in English life: 'Alas! alas! I never saw my dear lady again. She died in eighteen hundred and fourteen.' The tale is also something of a lament.

It is perhaps worth remarking that Hardy's novels have been made to stand for just such a series of laments. But to turn *The Woodlanders* and *Tess of the d'Urbervilles* into grievings over a lost pastoral world – soft primitives – is Procrustean and wilfully at odds with their true subject. Which can hardly be said of any such reading of *Cranford*, *Wives and Daughters* or *My Lady Ludlow*. Yet there are other fictions of Mrs Gaskell's which show that she had an historical imagination not very dissimilar from Hardy's, and at its finest not all that inferior to his. The least successful of these fictions is *A Dark Night's Work*. More successful is *Sylvia's Lovers*. More successful still, *Cousin Phillis*.

II

A Dark Night's Work is a story of novel length that was first published in 1863. There are serious objections to be made against it. It is clumsily told and far too long. More damagingly, but also more interestingly, it gives the impression of being out of focus, as though Mrs Gaskell is not quite sure why she is writing the story, or what she wants to say. At one level – the less rewarding – *A Dark Night's Work* is a tediously moral tale of retribution. A wealthy lawyer, Wilkins, takes on a partner, Dunster, who gradually comes to have near control of the business, while Wilkins takes to living beyond his means, threatens the well-being of their affairs and kills Dunster in a drunken rage when his partner dares to tell him as much. Wilkins buries the body in the garden of his house, helped by his daughter, Ellinor, and an old family servant, Dixon (very faithful, these servants). From then on all is decline. Wilkins degenerates into alcoholism, Ellinor falls ill and her engagement to a rising young lawyer, Ralph Corbet, is broken off. Wilkins dies, his business in ruins. The house is sold and Ellinor, who is by now resigned to a life of shabby-genteel spinsterhood, goes to live with old family friends at Chester. Years later a branch line is driven through what had been Wilkins's grounds. Dunster's body is dug up and Dixon, whose pocketknife had been found beside the body, is arrested, tried and convicted. Ellinor hears about this, dashes to London to intercede and discovers that the judge in the case is no other than her erstwhile lover, Ralph Corbet, now a middle-aged man with wealth and wife. She tells Corbet the truth and Dixon is released. End of story.

Now all this is tedious to a degree, and one might wonder why Mrs Gaskell, who by now had several fine short stories behind her, should so mismanage her tale as to swell what is essentially an anecdote into such ungainly proportions. But there is more to *A Dark Night's Work* than murder and retribution. For it is also much concerned with shifting social patterns, in ways that link it with other, greater works of nineteenth-century fiction. The concern is intermittent rather than constant, hence the blurring of focus. But its presence guarantees the story's real interest.

In the first place we are shown that Wilkins is a man of social ambition in a society where social gradations are inevitably subtle and complex. His father had given him 'an education and tastes beyond his position', with the result that

> . . . he could scarcely fancy bringing home any one of the young ladies of Hamley to the elegant mansion, so full of suggestion and association to an educated person, so inappropriate a dwelling for an ignorant, uncouth, ill-brought-up girl. Yet Edward was fully aware, if his father was not, that of all the young ladies who were glad enough of him as a partner at the Hamley assemblies, there was not one of them but would have considered herself affronted by an offer of marriage from an attorney, the son and grandson of attorneys [ch. 2].

Mrs Gaskell comments: 'The young man had perhaps received many a slight and mortification pretty quietly during these years, which yet told upon his character in after life . . . he took a secret pleasure in the power which his father's money gave him' (ch. 2). Not so secret, in fact. He marries the niece of a penniless Baronet, who 'said one or two bitter and insolent things to Mr Wilkins, even while giving his consent to the match' (ch. 3). And Mrs Gaskell adds that this was 'his temper, his proud, evil temper'. Which is worth quoting because it reveals how liable she is to see class attitudes in merely individual terms.

Wilkins is by now hastening up the social ladder. When his wife dies and leaves him with an infant daughter he determines to come the grand. He indulges in 'hunting, and all field-sports', and shares a moor in Scotland with one of the Baronet's family. The Baronet tells him that he is living beyond his means, they quarrel, and the two consequences of the quarrel are that: 'Mr. Wilkins advertised for a responsible and confidential clerk to conduct the business under his own superintendence: and he also wrote to the Heralds' College to ask if he did not belong to the family bearing the same name in South Wales – those who have since reassumed their ancient name of De Winton' (ch. 3). Dunster becomes Edward Wilkins's confidential clerk and the Heralds' College allow his claim to the De Winton name.

> Before the end of the year he went up to London to order a brougham to be built (for Ellinor to drive out in wet weather, he said; but as going in a closed carriage always made her ill, he used it principally himself in driving to dinner-parties), with the De Winton Wilkinses' arms neatly emblazoned on panel and harness. Hitherto he had always gone about in a dog-cart – the immediate descendant of his father's old-fashioned gig [ch. 3].

Wilkins's dissatisfaction with being 'merely' an attorney, the gathering cancer of class consciousness that gnaws at him, pushing him towards absurdity and ultimate disaster – all this is neatly sketched in.

Meanwhile Ellinor is growing up. She falls in love with Ralph Corbet, a young man of good family who has been taken in as pupil of the local cleric. He returns her love but wants to 'improve' her. Early on in their relationship we hear from Ellinor that Ralph 'had been giving me a lecture, and saying I

didn't do what his sisters did'; and we are told that he dis-
approves of her friendship with Dixon: 'He once or twice in-
sinuated that he did not think it was well to talk so familiarly as
Ellinor did with a servant – one out of a completely different
class – such as Dixon' (ch. 3).

As with the father, so with the daughter: she is being encouraged to develop 'an education and tastes', which are beyond her position. But unlike her father Ellinor has no desire to
rise. She feels awkward with Corbet and embarrassed by her
father's social pretensions. When she comes out we learn:

> Ellinor made her appearance at the Hamley assemblies, but with less
> éclat than either her father or her lover expected. Her beauty and
> natural grace were admired by those who could discriminate; but to
> the greater number there was (what they called) 'a want of style'. . . .
> Perhaps it was not a good place for a correct appreciation of Miss
> Wilkins; some of the old dowagers thought it a piece of presumption in
> her to be there at all – but the Lady Holster of the day (who remem-
> bered her husband's quarrel with Mr Wilkins and looked away when-
> ever Ellinor came near) resented this opinion. 'Miss Wilkins is
> descended from Sir Frank's family, one of the oldest in the county; the
> objection might have been made years ago to the father, but as he had
> been received, she did not know why Miss Wilkins was to be allowed to
> be out of her place' [ch. 5].

It is a witty, clear-eyed passage. And it touches on a familiar
subject, the raising and improving of a young girl. One finds it
operating at every level of society represented in nineteenth-
century fiction: from Lady Dedlock's maid, Rose, through to
Tess Durbeyfield; from Edith Skewton to Grace Melbury; from
Rosamund Vincy to Mark Rutherford's Catherine Furze. I do
not pretend that Mrs Gaskell's treatment is particularly original
or important. Yet it has its interest. She is good on Ellinor's
half-resentful, half-acquiescent attitude to what is being done
to (rather than for) her; she is finely understanding of the re-
sulting tensions in the girl's relationships with her father and
with Corbet; and she is brilliant on Ralph Corbet's growing
realization that for all his and Wilkins's efforts, Ellinor won't
really do as his wife. We are told that Ralph 'associated on
equal terms with magnates of the county, who were the employers of Ellinor's father, and spoke of him, always as "Wilkins"; just as they spoke of the butler as "Simmons" ' (ch. 9).
And so the engagement is broken off.

But of course Ralph has to have an excuse for this and he finds it in what is the most crucial scene in the story. By now Dunster is dead and Wilkins a near-drunkard. Ralph and Wilkins slide into argument, the latter thinking that he has been insulted. He ends by ordering Ralph out of the house, and one of Mrs Gaskell's special virtues emerges in the way she tracks the complexity of Ralph's response to this:

> 'You shall never have to say to me twice what you have said to-night. Henceforward we are as strangers to each other. As to Ellinor' – his tones softened a little in spite of himself – 'I do not think we should have been happy. I believe our engagement was formed when we were too young to know our own minds, but I would have done my duty and kept to my word; but you, sir, have yourself severed the connexion between us, by your insolence to-night. I, to be turned out of your house by your servants! I, a Corbet, of Westley, who would not submit to such threats from a peer of the realm, let him be ever so drunk' [ch. 9].

Class feeling and Ralph's certainties merge into, veer away from, personal feeling: he is still fond of Ellinor, but, 'I do not think we should have been happy.' For after all he is 'a Corbet, of Westley'. And therefore Wilkins has been 'insolent' to him. The word is central to my interest in *A Dark Night's Work*, the scene in which it occurs vitally important in revealing its range of meanings and class reverberations. But before I say more about it I must turn to the handling of Dunster.

We are not told a great deal about him:

> Mr. Dunster, the new clerk, was a quite-respectable looking man; you could not call him a gentleman in manner, and yet no one could say he was vulgar. He had not much varying expression on his face, but a permanent one of thoughtful consideration of the subject in hand, whatever it might be, that would have fitted as well with the profession of medicine as with that of law, and was quite the right look for either. Occasionally a bright flash of sudden intelligence lightened up his deep-sunk eyes, but even this was quickly extinguished by some inward repression, and the habitually reflective, subdued expression returned to the face [ch. 3].

Dunster is no Bartleby, nor is he a Carker – quite. Yet for all her efforts to be fair-minded, it is clear that Mrs Gaskell doesn't at all like the man. It is significant that both Dixon and Catherine detest him. Dixon tells Ellinor: '. . . that Dunster fellow is not to my mind', and Ellinor exclaims vehemently, 'I hate Mr.

Dunster!' (ch. 3). We are not meant to question the worth of
their remarks. The new clerk is allowed no such moment as the
one where Uriah Heep explains to David why he has taken to
being 'umble. One would love to know something more about
Dunster's flash of sudden intelligence and the inward repression,
but Mrs Gaskell keeps him pretty much of a mystery, a man
seen only from the outside. Why, then, the dislike for him?

The answer is that Dunster is very much one of the 'new' men
that we find in much nineteenth-century fiction, though it goes
without saying that such men are presented in very different
ways (as different as Carker and Farfrae, for example). What
they all have in common, however, is efficiency. Again and
again in Victorian novels one finds the new man, the outsider,
entering into a family business in order to safeguard its success
or ensure its survival. He is needed either because the head of
the business has decided that he is above business affairs or
because he cannot cope with new business methods (in general,
it is the earlier novels which deal in the former – *Dombey and
Son*, *A Dark Night's Work* – later novels which emphasize the
latter – *The Mayor of Casterbridge*, *Catherine Furze*). The outsider
is therefore inevitably viewed with suspicion by the family
whose unity he may seem to threaten, and often enough does.
Dombey and Son *can't* any longer be Dombey and Son once
Carker has moved in. Besides, the outsider is socially inferior
(Dunster is not 'a gentleman in manner') or *ought* to be inferior –
for what is the point of wanting to be above business if you
can't employ people whose proper level *is* business? and yet
his efficiency and therefore inevitable familiarity with the
family business guarantees him close knowledge of and acquain-
tanceship with the family. (Carker's elopement with Edith is a
striking instance of the playing-out of the middle-class fear of
being 'invaded' from below, a fear which often shows itself
in sexual terms: the new man may be more vital, more attractive than his master; Farfrae takes both Lucetta and Elizabeth-
Jane from Henchard; Tom Catchpole has to be sent away
from Catherine Furze. Even Agnes is not safe from Heep.)

It is important to note, however, that in the later novels all
the resentment and suspicion brought to bear on the new man
are customarily confined to the family on whom he intrudes.
They are unlikely to be shared by the author. Dickens and Mrs

Gaskell, on the other hand, feel as much distrust for the outsider as any character in their novels. This is not to deny that they see that the follies of the master create a need for an efficient man of business, but it is to suggest that their dislike of such men may well reveal important class hostilities. As a matter of fact, I think Dickens's treatment of Carker can be cleared of this charge, because he is so marvellously aware of the extent to which Dombey creates him and also because his hatred of Carker is an essential part of his anti-determinism (Carker didn't *have* to be like that). And Dunster? Well, consider the moment when we are told that Wilkins 'lay late in bed, and hated Mr Dunster for his significant glance at the office-clock when he announced to his master that such and such a client had been kept waiting for more than an hour to keep an appointment' (ch. 4). Aren't we there being invited to feel more sympathy with Wilkins than is justified? Of course, Mrs Gaskell does her best to play fair with the clerk. It is only after his death that Wilkins's business goes to pot and it is made quite clear that Dunster has been scrupulously proper in his handling of the business. Yet she cannot prevent herself from siding with Ellinor when the girl feels anger at Dunster 'who had seemed all along to be a thorn in her father's side, and had latterly gained some power and authority over him, the exercise of which, Ellinor could not help feeling, was a very impertinent line of conduct from a junior partner, so lately only a paid clerk, to his superior' (ch. 5). Ellinor's thoughts are not subjected to any kind of ironical scrutiny. On the contrary, they appear to do service for some kind of definitive statement about Dunster. And this is borne out by Wilkins's explanation of why he killed him. 'He taunted me – he was insolent, beyond my patience – I could not bear it. . . . Insolent.' We are reminded that Ralph has accused Wilkins of being insolent to him and that the penniless Baronet was insolent to Wilkins. In those cases our sympathies are meant to be mostly on Wilkins's side. This is the nub of the matter, as it reveals precisely how Mrs Gaskell's fiction betrays class bias for all her attempted and assumed impartiality. Distinctions between the gentry/aristocracy and her own class are not absolute. Distinctions between the middle class – *her* middle class – and anyone thought to be lower are. How dare Ralph accuse Wilkins of insolence. But how dare Dunster be insolent.

The OED has two important definitions of 'insolent', which make clear its class basis. On the one hand the insolent man is 'proud, disdainful, arrogant, overbearing; offensively contemptuous of the rights of others' (Ralph, the Baronet and, surely, Wilkins in his dealings with Dunster, though it is Dunster who is accused of insolence). On the other hand the insolent man is 'contemptuous of rightful authority; presumptuously contemptuous; impertinently insulting'. Dunster? Hardly, given all that we are shown. Yet obviously he can appear insolent to Wilkins, given the fact that Wilkins is obsessed with raising himself. But the most crucial point is that Dunster appears insolent to Mrs Gaskell as well.

I come back here to the flaw in her notion of reconciliation. In the end such a notion is intolerably complacent. The gentry must be reconciled to the middle class, must not be insolent to them. The lower classes must be reconciled to staying where they are, must not be insolent to those in 'rightful authority'. By way of enforcing the point I want to say a little about Mrs Gaskell's handling of Preston, the character in *Wives and Daughters* for whom she has a quite virulent dislike.

Preston is a 'new' man, of no known parentage (the sure indication of 'newness'), and all who come into contact with him readily admit his efficiency. He is manager to the estates of the Cumnors, a 'newish' Whig family, wealthy and fashionable. There is another landowner in the novel, Squire Hamley, who comes of a very 'old' family and is Tory. He is in financial difficulties, he cannot manage his estate and he rather despises the Cumnors. Mrs Gaskell is very much on his side (he is a male version of Lady Ludlow), and she is particularly sympathetic to him in an encounter he has with Preston. The manager is at this time supervising the draining of some Cumnor land which Hamley thinks encroaches on his estate (he wants to drain his land but cannot afford to do so). Throughout their interview Preston remains calm, while the Squire becomes increasingly outraged and, so it seems to me, outrageous. Finally, he burst out:

> 'I don't know who you are, but I've known land-agents who were gentlemen, and I've known some who were not. You belong to this last set, young man,' said the Squire, 'that you do! I should like to try to horsewhip you for your insolence.'

'Pray, Mr. Hamley,' replied Mr. Preston coolly, 'curb your temper a little, and reflect. I really feel sorry to see a man of your age in such a passion . . .'

Just at this moment Roger Hamley came close up. He was panting a little, and his eyes were stern and dark; but he spoke quietly enough. 'Mr. Preston, I can hardly understand what you mean by your last words. But, remember, my father is a gentleman of age and position, and not accustomed to receive advice as to the management of his temper from young men like you' [ch. 30].

There is no doubt that in this exchange we are meant to be on Roger's side. Yet Preston is totally in the right. The Squire is a hot-tempered, arrogant snob. Why on earth should Preston be deferential to him? The answer comes pat. Such men as Preston threaten the pattern of reconciliation that shows itself even in this idyllic novel. It is not merely that he is 'insolent'; he aspires to be on familiar terms with his 'superiors'. Which is not to be borne. We are told that he is furious at Roger's intervention. Indeed, he has 'an animal's instinctive jealousy and combativeness against all popular young men' (ch. 31). I do not wish to make too much of this; but quite apart from the fact that Mrs Gaskell has been betrayed into absurdity – as far as I know animals are not jealous of popular young men (are they even jealous of popular young animals?) – the very fact that she reaches instinctively for the word indicates a class bias of a very primitive kind. Preston is simply anathema to her. The word may seem excessively harsh to use of so even-tempered a novelist, but no other will do. Consider how he is spoken of by Lady Harriet, the only one of the Cumnors of whom we are thoroughly to approve. ' "I cannot bear that sort of person," said Lady Harriet, almost before he was out of hearing; "giving himself airs of gallantry towards one to whom his simple respect is all his duty. I can talk to one of my father's labourers with pleasure, while with a man like that underbred fop I am all over thorns and nettles" ' (ch. 14). There is no suggestion that it is Lady Harriet who is being insolent here, 'offensively contemptuous of the rights of others'. No, it is impossible to be insolent to Preston. True Mrs Gaskell does not ignore the fact that Squire Hamley and Lady Harriet are capable of insolence. For example, they are insolent to the Gibsons, the central, decently middle-class family of the novel. But the Gibsons forgive them, and we are meant to do likewise.

It is only a harmless quirk and does not indicate essential class
differences. Molly Gibson is the friend of Lady Harriet and
marries Roger Hamley.

But there is no forgiveness for Preston. He has the imperti-
nence to love Cynthia Kirkpatrick, Molly's half-sister, and
when Molly stumbles on one of their clandestine meetings:
'Molly came forward and took Cynthia's arm, her eyes steadily
fixed on Mr Preston's face. It was fine to see the fearlessness of
her perfect innocence. He could not bear her look . . .' (ch. 42).
Just like an animal, you see. And later, when he dares to question Lady Harriet's right to inquire into his private affairs,
there is a 'touch of insolence' in his way of speaking to her,
which 'put her mettle up; and she was not one to check herself,
in any course, for the opinion of an inferior' (ch. 49). Oh, good
for her. It is worth noting that Molly Gibson won't be put
down by Lady Harriet, and obvious that we are to admire her
sturdy independence in refusing to be condescended to or
treated as an inferior. But what is admirable in her – it forms
the subject of chapter 14, 'Molly Finds herself Patronised' – is
merely insolence in Mr Preston.

The word reverberates through *A Dark Night's Work* as it does
through *Wives and Daughters* and it may well lead us to conclude
that Mrs Gaskell's class consciousness is thoroughly complacent.
Yet this would be unfair. Because complacent though her
notion of reconciliation undoubtedly is, it competes against
something equally important in her work: her awareness of the
fact that class relationships are in flux, that class itself is the
product of social pressures, is not really fixed and immutable,
and that the strains on individuals involved in, responding to
and creating, the pressures may well be intolerable. Which
brings me to the final point I want to make about *A Dark
Night's Work*.

We might, however, approach it from a slightly different
direction by noting that both Dunster and Corbet can be
spoken of as 'intruder' figures, and by noting further that such
intruders are not arbitrary or novelistically wilful creations, but
perfectly proper means of dramatizing class attitudes in flux,
placed within history. The attitudes centre on Wilkins, of
course. Dunster and Corbet intrude on his life. They do so
because of his desire to rise, which includes the desire to have

much theory (and purpose) to it. Its determined positivistic slant requires the study of great or atypical individuals who are, if not above, then somehow apart from their society. Which in its turn requires George Eliot to fictionalize history in an impermissible way, for otherwise her characters would not triumph or be instructively defeated.

Now Mrs Gaskell is very far from wanting to write history with a purpose, let alone a theory. That is, she reveals no such desire when she is at her truest (at her worst theory shines through with a glaring obviousness that momentarily disconcerts but does not effectively harm her achievement). And this 'innocence' gives her a decided advantage over George Eliot. For in *Sylvia's Lovers* she produces an impressive historical novel which in its study of social conflict and change reminds one very strongly of Hardy. Whatever there is of heroic individualism in *Sylvia's Lovers* is seen as a response to an actual social situation; and it is ultimately defeated (as well as qualified by its own inadequacies and the different challenges to its worth). But Mrs Gaskell's essential concern is with the typical, which means the ordinary. And also with the past. And here I want to turn aside for a moment and offer what may seem to be a digression.

Like most of her contemporaries, Mrs Gaskell is obsessed with the past. In particular she broods over that which recedes and becomes remote, ways of life from which we feel ourselves to be cut off. Memory alone preserves such ways and there is no doubt that for nineteenth-century writers memory takes on a radically new significance. It is the only means by which some kind of continuity or link with the past can be established and, as a result of which, identity (familial, personal, social) can be grounded in more than simple assertion. Memory is activated by an entirely new awareness of what change *is*: disruptive, likely to fracture and destroy any sense of connection and continuity.

In *The Task* Cowper wrote with a certain phlegmatic resignation:

> We build what we deem eternal rock,
> A distant age asks where the fabric stood;
> And in the dust, sifted and searched in vain,
> The undiscoverable secret sleeps.

Cowper was much moved by the destruction of things he held

dear to himself, as 'The Poplar Field' eloquently demonstrates.
But these lines have an almost contented tranquillity about
them. The secret does, after all, 'sleep': it is still somehow alive,
and capable of being awoken. Move a few years forward, however, and we find Wordsworth speaking with altogether more
urgency in the great *Preface to the Lyrical Ballads*: 'In spite of
difference of soil and climate, of language and manners, in
spite of things silently gone out of mind and things violently
destroyed, the poet binds together by passion and knowledge
the vast empire of human society, as it is spread over the whole
earth, and over all time.' Unlike Cowper, Wordsworth sees the
poet's task as an essentially historical one. He must rescue all
that he can from time's injurious hand, there must be no un-
discoverable secrets. In fact Wordsworth is particularly liable
to be moved by what would have gone silently out of mind were
it not for the poet's power to preserve or restore. He restores –
in art at least – what otherwise would be irretrievably lost.
Hence *Michael*, which is not only one of the great poems in our
language, but a distinctively modern one (we can take the
measure of Wordsworth's insistence on the fact of loss and on
the poet's responsibility by noting that in the famous letter to
Fox in which he explained his purpose in writing *Michael*,
Wordsworth speaks of the 'statesmen' in the present tense,
whereas in the poem itself Michael is already dead, his way of
life violently destroyed).

   Though Wordsworth's insistence that the poet *does* bind
together the vast empire of human society gradually gives way
to the hope that a poet *may* effect such binding (and for poet
we can read novelist), it remains true that nineteenth-century
writers are deeply concerned with the past. Obviously such a
concern can, and frequently does, lead to a merely enervate
nostalgia or to the creation of those types of idyll which include
Cranford and *Wives and Daughters* (but emphatically not Hardy's
great novels, for all that critics have wanted to see in them a
celebration of a timeless past). It can also lead to that familiar
invention of an ideal, static, preindustrial world which appears
under various guises: merry England, feudalistic society, the
organic community (the world of Hayslope, for example). And
it can also lead to the kind of 'frozen' tabulating of a moment
of the past – smaller and clearer as the years go by – which

inevitably has its genuine if limited fascination. No wonder photography was a Victorian invention. As soon as the question, 'what was it *really* like then?' began to be current, a way of answering it was provided that would prove to be far more satisfying than the assertion 'I remember, I remember'. Here, for example, is a paragraph from Hale White's *The Revolution in Tanner's Lane*, where the narrator gives voice to his wish that he could recall the Cowfold (Bedford?) of his youth.

> Many of us have felt that we would give all our books if we could but see with our own eyes how a single day was passed by a single ancient Jewish, Greek, or Roman family; how the house was opened in the morning; how the meals were prepared; what was said; how the husband, wife, and children, went about their work; what clothes they wore, and what were their amusements. Would that the present historian could do as much for Cowfold! Would that he could bring back one blue summer morning, one afternoon and evening, and reproduce exactly what happened in Cowfold Square, in one of the Cowfold shops, in one of the Cowfold parlours, and in one Cowfold brain and heart. Could this be done with strictest accuracy, a book would be written, although Cowfold was not another Athens, Rome, nor Jerusalem, which would live for many years longer than much of the literature of this century [ch. 16].

Well, one might say, such books already existed: *Adam Bede*, for example, or *Cranford*. Perhaps neither possesses the 'strictest accuracy'. But it hardly matters. Or if it does, then go to the photograph. All of them tell you something about the past, 'reproduce exactly' a moment, a house, even a community. Yet they are not historical works. *Sylvia's Lovers* on the other hand is. It is about change, about how one small but typical society grows, alters, for better and for worse, gains and loses.

Loss is very important. As with Wordsworth and Dickens, Mrs Gaskell is keenly aware of the frailty of the present's connection with the past, its inheritances and continuities. Thus we have the loving delineation in the novel of market-day at the Butter-Cross and the Corney's New Year's Eve Party (it takes up all of the long chapter 12). And throughout *Sylvia's Lovers* Mrs Gaskell makes great use of dialect words and phrases, often pausing somewhat awkwardly to explain their meaning. More deeply, though, there is a sense in which she sees certain life-styles as hopelessly at odds with social pressures which are inferior to them in worth and yet defeat them. And against

that, the primly complacent official Mrs Gaskell occasionally
bestirs herself. One recognizes her entry by a brisk no-nonsense
air that comes over the prose, an insistence that the past is
after all merely quaint and that we ought to give thanks for
living in the present. 'It is astonishing to look back and find how
differently constituted were the minds of most people fifty or
sixty years ago; they felt, they understood, without going
through reasoning or analytic processes, and if this was the case
among the more educated people, of course it was still more so
in the class to which Sylvia belonged' (ch. 28). No irony there.

Such a passage reveals of course that Mrs Gaskell was very
conscious of George Elliot's approach to history and of her
positivistically derived belief in social evolution. But though
such an approach can sometimes be detected in *Sylvia's Lovers*
it isn't at all part of Mrs Gaskell's historical imagination. In
short that passage – and others are scattered among the novel's
pages – feels very much at odds with the novel's prevailing tone.
Sylvia's Lovers is set on the north Yorkshire coast. The time is the
1790s and much of the action of the novel has to do with repeated attempts of a press-gang to take away local men for the
war against France. The action serves a purpose: it dramatizes
the ways in which values of town and rural communities, of law
and freedom, collide, interlock, do battle; and how the battle
ends in defeat for some, victory for others.

One mustn't, however, set the matter out too schematically.
It would be quite wrong to suggest that Mrs Gaskell sets up the
kind of opposition that critics of Hardy used, wrongly, to find in
his novels: of an old 'stable' society confronting and losing out
to a new, aggressively rootless, one. It isn't so. The world of
rural values which is focused in Sylvia Robson's family is itself
complex and changing. Sylvia has two lovers. Her father
favours Charlie Kinraid, a romantic individualist, a man who
belongs to an older, less 'civilized' way of life; whereas her
mother greatly prefers the solid virtues of the townsman, Philip
Hepburn, who is in trade. And, as one might expect, Mrs
Gaskell won't allow us simply to praise one and damn the other.
Against Philip's grave and grey life one has to set Charlie's
fecklessness; against his *insouciant* courage and daring the other
man's steady loyalties.

There are two closely intertwined plots in *Sylvia's Lovers*. One deals with Sylvia's relationship with Philip and with Charlie. Philip loves her, she loves Charlie and they become unofficially engaged. But Charlie has to go to rejoin his whaling ship and on the way is captured by the press-gang. Philip sees it all happen but will not tell Sylvia about it; instead he allows her to believe that Charlie has been drowned (he genuinely believes that Charlie is a bad man and will do Sylvia harm). Eventually Sylvia accepts Charlie's death as fact and marries Philip, who takes her to Monkshaven (Whitby) where she pines for her former life of rural freedom and for Charlie. After some three years Charlie turns up again, Philip is forced to confess the truth and, in an agony of remorse, runs off to enlist as a soldier. He is hideously wounded and returns to Monkshaven to die. Charlie marries well and goes to live in the south of England. Sylvia is left to live out a lonely life.

The other plot concerns the doings of the press-gangs and the resentment they arouse. Eventually, there is a popular riot against them. Sylvia's father, Daniel Robson, is one of the leaders, and he is taken up, imprisoned and finally executed (his death and the consequent loss of Haytersbank Farm have much to do with Sylvia's reluctant agreement to marry Philip).

The two plots are linked because nearly all the characters are caught up in the conflicts of feeling which the press-gangings cause. Daniel and Charlie are dead against the gang's activities, and it would be possible to sketch in their hostility so as to suggest that they represent an old, romantic set of values against the newer, heartless legalism which argues for the gang's existence and its ways. But Mrs Gaskell will not allow for such stark divisions. She notes that the whalingmen would quickly become rich and set up as shipowners; and she goes on:

> . . . at the time of which I write, the Monkshaven ship-owners were growing so wealthy and consequential, that the squires, who lived at home at ease in the old stone manor-houses scattered up and down the surrounding moorland, felt that the check upon the Monkshaven trade likely to be inflicted by the press-gang, was wisely ordained by the higher powers . . . to prevent overhaste in getting rich, which is a scriptural fault, and they also thought that they were only doing their duty in backing up the Admiralty warrants by all the civil power at their disposal, whenever they were called upon, and whenever they could do so without taking too much trouble in affairs which did not after all much concern themselves [ch. 1].

It is worth comparing the way Mrs Gaskell sets down the squires' utterly cynical attitude to the law with her recording of Philip's candid and simple respect for it, which shows itself in a spirited argument that he has with Daniel Robson. We are told that Daniel had been a 'sailor, smuggler, horse-dealer, and farmer in turns'; and he has an instinctive hatred for and deep-rooted suspicion of law. Philip claims that the press-gang is needed if England is to be saved from the threat of a French victory and even invasion.

> 'For my part, when I read o' the way those French chaps are going on, I'm thankful to be governed by King George and an English Constitution.'
> Daniel took his pipe out of his mouth at this.
> 'And when did I say a word against King George and the Constitution? I only ax 'em to govern me as I judge best, and that's what I call representation. When I gived my vote to Measter Cholmley to go up to t'Parliament House, I as good as said, "Now yo' go up theer, sir, and tell 'em what I, Daniel Robson, think right, and what I, Daniel Robson, wish to have done." Else I'd be damned if i'd ha' gi'en my vote to him or any other man. And div yo' think I want Seth Robson (as is my own brother's son, and mate to a collier) to be cotched up by a press-gang, and ten to one his wages all unpaid? Div yo' think I'd send up Measter Cholmley to speak up for that piece of work? Not I.'
> 'But, asking pardon, laws is made for the good of the nation, not for your good or mine.'
> Daniel could not stand this. He laid down his pipe, opened his eyes, stared straight at Philip before speaking, in order to enforce his words, and then said slowly –
> 'Nation heere! nation theere! I'm a man and yo're another, but nation's nowheere. If Measter Cholmley talked to me i' that fashion, he'd long look for another vote frae me. I can make out King George, and Measter Pitt, and yo' and me, but nation! nation, go hang' [ch. 4].

There is little doubt that Daniel comes out of this exchange much better than Mrs Gaskell intended. The official Mrs Gaskell, that is. But it is only proper to remark how typical it is of her to let the 'wrong' man have the better of it. As with John Barton and Nicholas Higgins, so with Daniel Robson: each is allowed the opportunity to speak out for individual human needs and rights against the 'rights' of the nation. Just how much justification there is for Daniel comes out a little later, when a young man is shot by the press-gang as he struggles to escape its clutches. The Anglican vicar of Monkshaven, 'a vehement Tory', preaches the funeral sermon.

> The Darley who had been killed was the son of the vicar's gardener, and Dr. Wilson's sympathies as a man had been all on the bereaved father's side. But . . . Darley had been resisting the orders of an officer in his Majesty's service. What would become of due subordination and loyalty, and the interests of the service, and the chances of beating those confounded French, if such conduct as Darley's was to be encouraged?

Caught in this dilemma, the vicar merely mumbles: 'In the midst of life we are in Death,' though when his eyes 'caught the up-turned, straining gaze of the father Darley, seeking to find a grain of holy comfort in the chaff of words, his conscience smote him.' But there is nothing he can do. It is simply 'beyond his power' to see a way out of his dilemma. Such a moment seems to me typical of Mrs Gaskell at her best, registering the way in which people find themselves caught up in intolerable conflict. And it is typical of her at her worst that she should try to evade the implications which the scene sets up. So we are informed that although some of the vicar's listeners feel disappointment and anger, it is not with him, for 'no one felt anything but kindly' towards him (ch. 6). Really? Surely that remark once again indicates Mrs Gaskell's wish to impose a notion of re-conciliation on matters that can't be reconciled; it attempts to deflect attention from the crucial issue of how law comes into violent and inhuman conflict with individuals.

And yet of course one has immediately to add that it is also typical of Mrs Gaskell to raise the issue and to make it so dramatically central to her novel.

For it isn't only the argument between Daniel and Philip that counts, nor the killing of Darley. There is the riot itself and its aftermath. Wanting to press a good number of men the gang resorts to a particularly offensive trick.

One night the Monkshaven fire bell begins to ring. Acting from an entirely proper sense of conscience and duty the local men pour into the town square to volunteer to fight the fire. But the ringing of the bell has been the gang's doing and a large number of men are quickly rounded up and taken off to the only pub in the neighbourhood which has any sympathy with the press-gang's activities (it has been handsomely bribed).

Community feeling is outraged, and a body of men, Robson at
their head, decide to free their mates. In a scene very reminiscent of the sacking of the Maypole Inn in *Barnaby Rudge* the
men storm the Mariner's Arms, free the men and set the inn
alight. Throughout, Daniel behaves with typical decency. He
rescues animals from the blaze and, more important, gives
money to Bob Simpson, a decrepit wreck of a man, who has
been helping the press-gang, and whom the locals wouldn't
mind lynching.

> 'A had a three-crown piece, and a good pair o' breeches, and a shirt,
> and a dare say better nor two pairs o' stockings. A wish t'gang, and
> thee . . . and them mad folk up yonder, were a' down i' hell, a do.'
> 'Coom, lad,' said Daniel, noways offended at his companion's wish
> on his behalf. 'A'm noane flush mysel', but here's half-a-crown and
> tuppence; it's a' a've getten wi' me, but it'll keep thee and t'beast i'
> food and shelter to-neet, and get thee a glass of comfort, too. A had
> thought o' taken one mysel', but a shannot ha' a penny left, so a'll
> just toddle whoam to my missus' [ch. 23].

But Daniel's behaviour is more than merely decent: as the
riot develops he becomes genuinely heroic. He fearlessly leads
the men against the gang who have behaved so abominably,
yet he behaves with great restraint and does his best to restrain
others; and he is magnanimous to his enemies, Simpson included (Simpson will repay this by testifying for the prosecu-
tion at Daniel's trial, so ensuring his conviction and execution).
In other words Daniel now emerges as a man with whom we
can wholly sympathize. And this remains true even at the
agonizing and humiliating moment of his arrest, an episode
which is too long to quote – it takes up most of chapter 25 – but
which is utterly authentic in its establishing of Daniel's bravado
in the face of the arresting officers, and his tender concern for
his wife's terrible grief.

Yet in spite of all this Mrs Gaskell sees fit to apologize for
him. And she goes further. We are offered an explanation for
Robson's behaviour that goes clean counter to everything that
we know about him. So she says: '. . . probably the amount of
drink thus consumed weakened Robson's power over his mind,
and caused the concentration of thought on one subject. This
may be a physiological explanation of what afterwards was
spoken of as a supernatural kind of possession, leading him to

his doom' (ch. 22). *Probably . . . may be.* The havering makes clear how uneasy Mrs Gaskell is with her own limp explanation for Daniel's behaviour (here called Robson, we notice). And anyway who speaks of a 'supernatural kind of possession'? Nobody in the novel as we have it, that much is certain; and were anyone to do so, we could immediately place such a trivial, external judgement against what we actually see: the honourable and generous rage of a man which issues in a very real heroism – for which he is then condemned. This is what Mrs Gaskell actually says:

> The rescue of the sailors was a distinctly popular movement; the subsequent violence (which had, indeed, gone much further than has been described, after Daniel left it) was, in general, considered as only a kind of due punishment inflicted in wild justice on the press-gang and their abettors. The feeling of the Monkshaven people was, therefore, in decided opposition to the vigorous steps taken by the County magistrates, who, in consequence of an appeal from the naval officers in charge of the impressment service, had called out the militia . . . stationed within a few miles, and had thus summarily quenched the riots that were continuing on the Sunday morning after a somewhat languid fashion; the greater part of the destruction of property having been accomplished during the previous night. Still there was little doubt but that the violence would have been renewed as evening drew on, and the more desperate part of the population and the enraged sailors had had the Sabbath leisure to brood over their wrongs, and to encourage each other in a passionate attempt at redress, or revenge. So the authorities were quite right in the decided steps they had taken, both in their own estimation then, and now, in ours, looking back on the affair in cold blood. But at the time feeling ran strongly against them; and all means of expressing itself in action being prevented men brooded sullenly in their own houses [ch. 25].

I quote the passage at some length because it proves a notable example of Mrs Gaskell's attempt at fair-mindedness, and because it reveals just how inadequate the attempt is. For of course she cannot afford to investigate the rightness of that feeling which 'ran strongly against' the authorities. No wonder. After all, in writing about Daniel Robson as she did, Mrs Gaskell went a good deal further than she could possibly have intended. This passage is intended to correct the balance. It can hardly hope to do so. The authorities are on the side of the press-gang and of property. Yet there is no justice about the gang's methods, be it ever so wild; and as for property – the 'enraged

sailors' are not even allowed custodianship of their own bodies.
They become the gang's property. 'I'm a man, and yo're
another, but nation's nowheere.' The bitter irony of that remark shines clear through this central clash of *Sylvia's Lovers*.
'The authorities were quite right.' What then of the rights of
man?

Mrs Gaskell's balancing act is a failure because the anarchic
element in her imaginative make-up triumphs yet again. For
what counts is not what she can offer by way of authorial comment but what she shows us. It is her grasp on the actualities
of the situation, her sure sense of what the conflict of rights
means to individuals at a particular point in time, that makes
Sylvia's Lovers so fine a novel and lifts it quite clear of that
theoretic approach to history which damage *Adam Bede* and
Romola.

Robson's defeat inevitably brings with it a sense of loss,
though it is not a final one. We do not have to refer to Barton
and Higgins to remind ourselves that for Mrs Gaskell human
decencies perpetually renew the struggle against what is 'right'.
We do, however, need to note the consequences of Daniel's
defeat, which include the loss of Haytersbank Farm and
Sylvia's marriage to Philip. Philip is in no sense a villain. His
agonized conscientiousness is, indeed, brilliantly caught in his
efforts to help Daniel escape the law after the riots, even though
he is convinced that Daniel has behaved wrongly. And it is
impossible to dismiss as hypocrisy his mental torment about
whether he should tell Sylvia of Kinraid's impressment.

Yet after the freedom and activity of Haytersbank and the
dash of Charlie's courtship, Philip's way of life becomes a kind
of death for Sylvia. Her sense of loss is acute: 'She missed the
free open air, the great dome of sky above the fields; she
rebelled against the necessity of "dressing" [as she called it] to
go out, although she acknowledged that it was necessary where
the first step beyond the threshold must be into a populous
street' (ch. 30). Gloomily, she contrasts the 'stately party' at the
house of one of Philip's friends with the 'merry country parties
at the Corney's, and [the] bright haymaking romps in the open
air'. Her weekly church-going, 'which Philip seemed to expect
of her, became a tie and a small hardship, which connected
itself with her life of respectability and prosperity'; and although

she is allowed to take her baby for long walks over the country-side, 'she paid for these happy troubles . . . by the impression which awaited her on her re-entrance into the dark, confined house that was her home; its very fullness of comfort was an oppression' (ch. 13).

Impossible not to be impressed by Mrs Gaskell's handling of this, her success in registering Sylvia's progress towards respectability and away from an earlier, happier and fuller life. Yet Mrs Gaskell will not schematize. Her novel does not make abrupt distinctions between the one life and the other. Sylvia's mother had wanted respectability for her daughter. 'It's a fine thing, tho', as is learning. My mother and my grandmother had it: but th' family came down i' the world, and Philip's mother and me, we had none of it; but I ha' set my heart on thy having it, child' (ch. 8). Which means having Philip. And naturally Mrs Robson favours Philip's suit. Sylvia, however, instinctively shrinks from his respectability, his anxious and considerate manner and his townsman's ways. Early on in the novel, as she watches a whaling ship come in, Sylvia has her hand grasped by another girl, who is delighted to see the ship come over the bar.

> 'Sylvia, how came you to know that girl?' asked Philip, sternly. 'She's not one for you to be shaking hands with. She's known all down t' quay-side as "Newcastle Bess".'
> 'I can't help it,' said Sylvia, half inclined to cry at his manner even more than his words. 'When folk are glad I can't help being glad too, and I just put out my hand, and she put out hers' [ch. 3].

Sylvia's ready spontaneity and abundant vivacity naturally lead her to respond to Kinraid, who is identified with Daniel's indifference as to 'respectable' forms of behaviour. Philip protests at Daniel's habit of taking Sylvia into public houses. 'She were wi-him at t' Admiral's Head' upo' All Soul's Day that were all. There were many a one there beside, – it were statute fair; but such a one as our Sylvie ought not to be cheapened wi t' rest' (ch. 1). And Mrs Robson agrees with him. Their mutual feeling that Sylvia ought to become respectable is a tactfully alert way of making palpable an element in the social process, the striving for status and the losses and gains that accompany it.

But we need to note that the novel does not end as we might

expect – with the triumph of Philip over an 'older' way of life. For he is dead, destroyed by the integrity of his own conscience. No, it is Charlie who survives, and who accommodates himself to a way of life that had initially been the opposite of his own. He ends as a 'Commander in the Royal Navy', willingly fighting against 'Boney', and respectably married to a 'pretty, joyous, prosperous little bird of a woman', their house on the eminently respectable Clifton Downs, above Bristol. I used to think that this ending was a mistake, merely a way of tying up loose ends in order to let us know what happened to the novel's main characters. I realize now that it is necessary, for it is a final underlining of the way history actually works, and the more poignant in that although Charlie isn't himself dead – in a sense he's very much alive – what he had earlier been identified with is, tactfully, shown to be dying. And while the official side of Mrs Gaskell may approve of such accommodation as Charlie's and even the accommodation of Sylvia to Philip's world (for one can hardly imagine her *in propria persona* approving of the girl's being in pubs and her resistance to church-going), it is obvious how deeply she feels the loss of those energies which she had celebrated in Daniel, Sylvia and Charlie, and the life of Haytersbank Farm.

IV

But the finest of the works under present consideration is without doubt *Cousin Phillis*. Indeed, having read and reread it some half-dozen times I am fairly sure that it is the most perfect story in the language. And, as with *Sylvia's Lovers*, so here, one is struck by the astonishingly tactful and truthful way in which Mrs Gaskell deals with inevitabilities of social change. But there is no interposed view in this lovely story, no allowance made for that liberal, conciliatory, account of conflict which occasionally threatens the achievement of the full-length novel.

Conflict may seem a strident word to use of *Cousin Phillis*. Yet the fact is that the tale is about conflicting life-styles, personal and social, collisions which establish or hint at how change happens, the way things are and must become. It is true that at first glance Mrs Gaskell chooses names for her characters

which may seem to suggest an 'archetypal' fable that is somehow outside history. And there is no doubt that the names
subtly underpin the story's feeling of inevitability. But they do
not qualify its social resonance. Phillis is, of course, the classical
name for the innocent country girl – often enough the victim
of a false-hearted lover. Her father, Ebenezer Holman, is an
independent minister, and is presented in such a way that he
really does seem a whole man. When the narrator first sees
him: 'I thought I must be confusing the figures, or mistaken:
that man still looked like a very powerful labourer, and had
none of the precise demureness of appearance which I had
always supposed was the characteristic of a minister'; (that 'I
had always supposed' neatly enough demonstrates that a social
and temporal gap exists between the narrator and Holman
himself, so that we share the sense of a real 'discovery' of this
kind of a man, are made to feel both his worth and his vulnerability to change). And Holdsworth, the outsider, exercises a
powerful and understandable fascination over the family on
which he intrudes: 'Before the day was out, I saw the unconscious hold that my friend had got over all the family.' Unconscious because he is a man of genuine worth.

Very little actually happens in *Cousin Phillis*. Paul Manning,
the young clerk who narrates the story, is sent with his superior,
the engineer Holdsworth, to open up a railway branch line
somewhere in Cheshire. Paul's mother tells him of a cousin of
hers who has married an independent minister and who lives
near to the town from which Paul and Holdsworth are working.
The young man goes to visit the minister and wife and discovers
that they have a daughter, Phillis. He introduces Holdsworth
to the family, Holdsworth and Phillis fall in love, Holdsworth
is sent away to Canada to work on another engineering project,
and after some months a letter comes from him to say he has
married. Phillis falls ill, recovers. And that is all.

Except that *Cousin Phillis* is a masterpiece. Much of its per-
fection rests on Mrs Gaskell's wonderfully preserved neutrality,
her scrupulous regard for the inevitability of what she has to
record. There are no villains in this tale, nobody is to blame for
the sadness and feeling of defeat that provide its dominant tone.
Time, one might perhaps say, is the real villain. And yet we
have to note that nobody in this tale is merely the victim of

time. People exist in and through time, change and are changed.
From the very beginning our attention is drawn to the fact and
nature of change. The narrator explains that his father had
secured the clerkship for him: 'Which was in a position rather
above his own in life; or perhaps I should say, above the station
in which he was born and bred; for he was raising himself every
year in men's consideration and respect' (pt 1). And before the
tale has come to an end we learn that Paul's father has been
taken into partnership in his firm, and also that Holdsworth has
great respect for his inventive skills. The social process is continuous, subtle, not to be schematized in terms of past and
present, stasis versus flux, old against new. Holdsworth, the narrator tells us, 'was a young man of five-and-twenty or so, and
was in a station above mine, both by birth and education;
and he had travelled on the Continent, and wore mustachios
and whiskers of a somewhat foreign fashion' (pt 1). One could
be forgiven for thinking that Mrs Gaskell is once again about
to step forward in her role of reconciler: Holdsworth and the
older Manning, despite their differences, will be found to be
essentially alike. Not so. And though Holdsworth and Holman
delight in one another's company there can be no final reconciliation between them either. Yet Holman is passionately keen
to be up-to-date. We note the implications of a remark made
by Paul's landlord about Hope Farm, the Holman home: 'It's
an old place, though Holman keeps it in good order.' The
minister makes Holdsworth explain the premises of engineering
to him, on which he 'thought clearly and reasoned logically',
for as he explains to Phillis, 'now that the railroads are coming
so near us, it behoves us to know something about them'. And
later Paul comments on the fact that although

> . . . the minister had at more than one time spoken to me of [Holds-
> worth] with slight distrust, principally occasioned by the suspicion that
> his careless words were not always those of soberness and truth . . . it
> was more as a protest against the fascination which the younger man
> evidently exercised over the older one – more, as it were to strengthen
> himself against yielding to this fascination – that the minister spoke
> out to me about this failing of Holdsworth's, as it appeared to him. In
> return, Holdsworth was subdued by the minister's uprightness and
> goodness, and delighted with his clear intellect – his strong healthy
> craving after further knowledge. I never met two men who took a
> more thorough pleasure and relish in each other's society [pt 3].

That passage provides a good indication of the poised neutrality which is so crucial to the tale's achievement, as well as making subtly evident where, in spite of all accord, conflict must lie: 'The minister spoke . . . about this failing of Holdsworth's, as it appeared to him.' And it also testifies to Mrs Gaskell's wonderfully sure feeling for social change, her imaginative fineness in creating such representative characters. How near they are to one another, and yet how far apart. It is also worth noting with what deftness she touches on the regard that Paul's father and Holman and Holdsworth have for one another; and how such regard isn't allowed to degenerate into the pieties of reconciliation. Of his father's friendship with Holman, Paul remarks: 'It was odd and yet pleasant to me to perceive how these two men, each having led up to this point such totally dissimilar lives, seemed to come together by instinct, after one quite straight look into each other's faces' (pt 2). But the dissimilarities cannot be wished away. Paul's father returns to the city. He has more in common with Holdsworth than with Holman, is, if you like, accommodated to a process from which Holman stands apart.

And yet it is worth repeating that Holman is not outside history, provides no complacent or merely nostalgic image of natural simplicity (the temptation to draw a comparison between what might – wrongly – be made of him and what has – wrongly – been made of many of Hardy's characters is irresistible). Holman is himself part of a changing world. He is a landowner and an employer of men. And in his unremitting toil and feeling for living a useful life he feels very like the kind of person Cobbett revealed himself as having been.

> I did not lead an idle life; I had to work constantly for the means of my living; my occupation required unremitting attention; I always saw the possibility, and even the probability, of being totally ruined by the hand of power; but happen what would, I was resolved, as long as I could cause them to do it, my children should lead happy lives; and happy lives they did lead, if ever children did in this whole world.[3]

To be sure, Holman is free of the smugness that mars Cobbett's own account of his own life, but he belongs very much to that kind of sturdy, independent life-style, rooted in place.

We come here to the crucial difference between Holman and Holdsworth, like and respect one another as they may. For

Holdsworth is essentially rootless, cosmopolitan: 'he had
travelled on the Continent', he can speak foreign languages;
and he goes to Canada. Before he has met the Holman family,
Paul tells him of his own visits to Hope Farm, and we learn that
Holdsworth likes hearing of the visits, 'liked it, I mean, as much
as he liked anything that was merely narrative, without leading
to action'. It is an ominous sentence, because it implies that for
Holdsworth – if not for us – Hope Farm and all it stands for is
somehow unreal, at best an idyllic pastoral interlude in his
life. Just before he leaves for Canada he tells Paul: 'Activity
and readiness go a long way in our profession. Remember that,
my boy!' Activity is not what he values at the Farm, though it
is there right enough, in the toil of the minister and his family.
Holman asks Paul if he knows any

> '... simple book on dynamics that I could put in my pocket, and study
> a little at leisure times in the day?'
> 'Leisure times, father?' said Phillis, with a nearer approach to a
> smile than I had ever seen on her face [pt 1].

But Holman's activity is rooted in place, Holdsworth's is not.
And inevitably Holdsworth's view of the farm is a sentimental
one. Still, he exerts his fascination over Holman and over
Phillis. Paul takes him to the farm – he has been suffering from
a slight illness – and:

> 'This is Mr. Holdsworth, Phillis,' said I, as soon as I had shaken hands
> with her. She glanced up at him, and then looked down, more flushed
> than ever at his grand formality of taking his hat off and bowing; such
> manners had never been seen at Hope farm before [pt 2].

It is early summer, the weather is perfect, and Holdsworth is
content. He tells Paul:

> 'This week in the country has done wonders for me.'
> 'You have enjoyed yourself, then?'
> 'Oh! it has been perfect in its way. Such a thorough country-life!'
> [pt 2].

Holdsworth is on holiday from reality. He is therefore inevitably
ignorant of what is and isn't important at the farm. Mrs Gaskell
establishes this fact with extraordinary delicacy and without
ever qualifying her entirely sympathetic presentation of
Holdsworth. For example. On Paul's first visit to the farm the
minister quotes Virgil to him, adding, 'It's wonderful ... how

exactly Virgil has hit the enduring epithets . . . and yet how it
describes to a T what is now lying before us . . .' (pt 1). When
Holdsworth is at the farm he discovers Phillis trying to master
Italian, and tells Paul that he has lent her *I Promessi Sposi*, 'just
the thing for a beginner'.

> 'But I don't think the minister will like your having given her a novel
> to read?'
>   'Pooh! what can be more harmless? Why make a bugbear of a word!
> You don't suppose they take Virgil for gospel?' [pt 2].

And just after this Holman tells Paul that Holdsworth 'makes
Horace and Virgil living, instead of dead, by the stories he tells
me of his sojourn in the very countries where they lived, and
where to this day he says – But it is like dram-drinking. I listen
to him till I forget my duties and am carried off my feet' (pt 2).

It is Phillis, however, who is disastrously carried off her feet.
Paul comes on the girl, with her father and Holdsworth in the
fields, 'joined together in an eager group over Holdsworth's
theodolite'. Suddenly a thunderstorm breaks over them. The
symbolism is delicate and apt. For Phillis is perhaps not so
much in love with Holdsworth as radically upset and confused
by his ways: his badinage, his easy acquaintance with books
which are for her 'gospel', his sophistication. And so she is
totally altered by him. One notes the emblematic moment
when she gives Holdsworth some flowers she has picked (and
again the symbolism is delicate and apt): 'I saw their faces. I
saw for the first time an unmistakable look of love in his black
eyes; it was more than gratitude for the little attention; it was
tender and beseeching – passionate. She shrank from it in
confusion' (pt 3).

And immediately after this Holdsworth learns he is to go to
Canada. For him the idyllic interlude is over.

But for Phillis his departure is the beginning of a terrible
ordeal. She pines for him until Paul tells her that Holdsworth
loves her – Holdsworth had indeed told Paul as much before
leaving. Phillis begins to recover but then comes the letter
telling of Holdsworth's marriage in Canada, and Paul has to
communicate the news to his cousin, on an afternoon when 'the
heavy thunder clouds were over-spreading the sky'.

The news comes as an appalling shock to her and also to her

father. Holman rebukes Paul for repeating 'that man's words' to Phillis, and Phillis intervenes to tell him not to blame Paul.

> 'I don't understand,' said her father; but he was beginning to understand. Phillis did not answer till he asked her again. I could have struck him now for his cruelty; but then I knew all.
> 'I loved him, father!' she said at length, raising her eyes to the minister's face.
> 'Had he ever spoken of love to you? Paul says not!'
> 'Never.' She let fall her eyes, and drooped more than ever. I almost thought she would fall.
> 'I could not have believed it,' said he, in a hard voice, yet sighing the moment he had spoken. A dead silence for a moment.
> 'Paul! I was unjust to you. You deserved blame, but not all that I said.' Then again a silence. I thought I saw Phillis's white lips moving, but it might have been the flickering of the candlelight – a moth had flown in through the open casement, and was fluttering round the flame; I might have saved it, but I did not care to do so, my heart was too full of other things. At any rate, no sound was heard for long endless minutes. Then he said,
> 'Phillis! did we not make you happy here? Have we not loved you enough?'
> She did not seem to understand the drift of this question; she looked up as if bewildered, and her beautiful eyes dilated with a painful, tortured expression. He went on without noticing the look on her face; he did not see it, I am sure.
> 'And yet you would have left us, left your home, left your father and your mother, and gone away with this stranger, wandering over the world.'
> He suffered, too; there were tones of pain in the voice in which he uttered this reproach. Probably father and daughter were never so far apart in their lives, so unsympathetic. Yet some new terror came over her, and it was to him she turned for help. A shadow came over her face, and she tottered towards her father; falling down, her arms across his knees, and moaning out, –
> 'Father, my head! my head!' and then she slipped through his quick-enfolding arms, and lay on the ground at his feet.

Everything counts there, from Holman's cry of 'I don't understand' onwards. He doesn't because he can't yet grasp that his world isn't sufficient for Phillis, that in some sense she yearns away from him. When he does understand it is inevitable that he should be cruel, being in pain himself. And Phillis doesn't herself understand her father's cruelty, his questioning and cannot understand what is happening between the two of them – or perhaps cannot understand why he is making her suffer.

She is on the point of complete breakdown and cannot now speak. Her white lips move, but no sound comes until she collapses in and through her father's arms. And the breakdown signals her helpless division between the life at the farm ('Have we not loved you enough?') and her feelings for Holdsworth ('I loved him, father!'). It is this division which makes father and daughter 'so far apart' and which divides Phillis from herself, as it were. For her breakdown must be read in precisely the way that Pip's has to be in *Great Expectations*. His collapse signals a radical fracturing of his own sense of identity, of where and to what he belongs, and as such seems to me an authentically imaginative way of demonstrating the cost to a sure sense of self that goes with social change and the ways that individuals are inevitably caught up in the process. (Just as later Miriam Trocchi and Catharine Furze will break down because they can't anneal the two selves which force them in different directions).

In all these cases the strain, the breaking of self, is appalling, and registers just how seriously Mrs Gaskell, Dickens and Hale White took the effects of separation on and within the individual. For that is what it amounts to. Again and again in the novelists with whom I'm concerned in this book one sees how the social process forces choice on individuals, which in turn forces a crisis of identity on them. Phillis's crisis, the shattering of herself, is as agonizing as any. And, though she recovers, the end of the story acknowledges that she can never be returned to her earlier self. She asks if she may accompany Paul to Birmingham, 'where there was a niche already provided for me in my father's prosperous business'. 'I thought my father and mother would allow her to go and stay with them for a couple of months. She blushed a little, as she faltered out her wish for a change of thought and scene. "Only for a short time, Paul! Then – we will go back to the peace of the old days. I know we shall; I can, and I will!" ' It is like Pip's desire to go home again, and as with that so we know that this cannot be. The story ends with Phillis's hopeful, despairing words. Ends, as it must, on the note of sadness that sounds through her wish for a change of thought and scene, her tacit admission of the inevitability of change that Holdsworth and all he stands for has wrought in her.

2

Engels, Mrs Gaskell and Manchester

ENGELS arrived in Manchester at the end of November 1842. By one of history's great ironies he had been sent there by his father, a rich textile manufacturer of the Rhineland town of Barmen, to study its business and mercantile methods. He remained in Manchester for the best part of two years, and although he travelled to other cities during that time his base remained the city which seemed to him – and others – most bewilderingly and precisely to typify the facts and effects of industrialism. By the time he came to leave he had completed the manuscript of one of the classics of the modern world, *The Condition of the Working Class in England in 1844*.[1] 'England' is perhaps a misnomer. True, the text makes reference to cities other than Manchester: there are mentions of most of the major northern industrial towns and of Glasgow, and a study of the miners' strike in the Northumberland coalfields is thrown in for good measure. Yet in spite of all this it is obvious that Engels's real concern is Manchester. In particular, he wants to register and explain what he regards as an undeniable fact: 'The working-men are on a war-footing towards their employers' (p. 249).

Now Engels was by no means the first distinguished foreigner to visit Manchester, nor the first to declare that the relationship between worker and employer was one of direct antagonism. As Asa Briggs has pointed out, by the early 1830s it had become a commonplace to attribute 'basic social and political differences to economic divisions of interest between mill owners and workers, factory hands and handloom weavers'. It had also become commonplace to see the differences as absolute. 'Here there seems no sympathy between the upper and lower classes of society . . . there is no mutual confidence, no bond of attachment.' Those words come from a Manchester newspaper of 1819, and they may be set beside *The Times*'s reporting of the aftermath of Peterloo where, writing of 'the working-classes', the reporter claims: 'Their wretchedness seems to madden them against the rich, whom they dangerously imagine engross the fruits of their labour without having any sympathy for their wants.' In 1831 *A Reformer's Prayer* circulated in Manchester. It was a biting parody of the Litany: 'from all those damnable bishops, lords and peers, from all those bloody murdering Peterloo butchers, from all those idle drones that live on the earnings of the people, good Lord deliver us'.[2]

Eleven years later Love and Barton published a handbook to Manchester, called *Manchester As It Is* (it had first appeared in 1839, but the 1842 text is considerably revised). We know that Engels consulted it and it is reasonable to suppose that one chapter in particular was of interest to him. It is called 'Habits and Social Conditions of the Operatives in Manchester' and it makes frequent use of the observations of a Canon Parkinson, including the following:

> There is no town in the world where the distance between the rich and the poor is so great, or the barrier between them so difficult to be crossed. I once ventured to designate the town of Manchester the most *aristocratic* town in England; and, in the sense in which the term was used, the expression is not hyperbolical. The separation between the different classes, and the consequent ignorance of each others habits and conditions, are far more complete in this place than in any other country of the older nations of Europe, or the agricultural parts of our own kingdom.[3]

The fact of this separation could easily lead contemporaries to despair of Manchester and all it stood for. And indeed de Tocqueville famously used the word when he passed through the city in 1835. To be exact, he claimed that it was the respect paid to wealth that caused him to despair. Which serves to remind us of the famous anecdote where Engels records his meeting with a Manchester bourgeois, whom he allows to be a good husband and family man, to have other virtues beside, and to appear, in ordinary intercourse, a decent and respectable man. Yet ultimately it is money and self-interest which alone determine him. 'I spoke to him of the bad, unwholesome method of building, the frightful condition of the working-

36   *The Literature of Change*

people's quarters, and asserted that I had never seen so ill-built a city. The man listened quietly to the end, and said at the corner where we parted: "And yet there is a great deal of money made here; good morning sir." ' Engels concludes: 'It is utterly indifferent to the English bourgeois whether his working-men starve or not, if only he makes money' (pp. 301–2).

Yet unlike de Tocqueville and others, Engels does not despair at what he sees. On the contrary, he finds in the condition of the English working class what, though it is certainly no matter for rejoicing, is nevertheless the full and necessary cause of revolution. He maintains: 'Without the great cities and their forcing influence upon the popular intelligence, the working-class would be far less advanced than it is'; and he then goes on to provide a famous argument for revolutionary potential:

> Only when estranged from his employer, when convinced that the sole bond between employer and employee is the bond of pecuniary profit, when the sentimental bond between them, which stood not the slightest test, had wholly fallen away, then only did the worker begin to recognize his own interests and develop independently; then only did he cease to be the slave of the bourgeoisie in his thoughts, feelings, and the expression of his will [pp. 152–3].

The Condition of the Working Class is written out of two related convictions: one, that the new, industrialized, working class has been appallingly exploited; two, that out of such exploitation triumphant revolutionary energy must emerge. At the very end of his work Engels confidently prophesies that 'the people will not endure more than one more crisis'. By which he means that they can be expected to put up with another severe economic depression, which he calculates will occur in 1846–7, but that when the next one comes along – he estimates 1852 or 1853 – then 'the war of the poor against the rich will be the bloodiest ever waged. Even the union of a part of the bourgeoisie with the proletariat, even a general reform of the bourgeoisie, would not help matters' (p. 320). And he ringingly predicts:

> The war of the poor against the rich now carried on in detail and indirectly will become direct and universal. It is too late for a peaceful solution. The classes are divided more and more sharply, the spirit of resistance penetrates the workers, the bitterness intensifies, the guerilla skirmishes become concentrated in more important battles, and soon a

slight impulse will suffice to set the avalanche in motion. Then, indeed, will the war-cry resound through the land: 'War to the palaces, peace to the cottages!' – but then it will be too late for the rich to beware [p. 322].

One can find other writers of the 1840s similarly prophesying revolutionary confrontation between the poor and the rich, but Engels is alone in welcoming it. His is an optimistic vision, very unlike Carlyle's wrathful gloom. And it is bolstered by his attention to fact. *The Condition of the Working Class* is indeed remarkable for the amount of factual information that Engels has taken the trouble to ferret out and which he uses in order to give substance to his picture of a city balanced precariously over disaster. And in this he is very different from those other distinguished visitors to Manchester, who came to record their impressions, to shudder and to escape. De Tocqueville, Faucher, Emerson: each of them sets down an account of his personal revulsion from what he saw, but none of them is very specific; and indeed, granted the little time they spent in the place they could hardly hope to be so. Henry Colman is representative of their attitude. Colman was a Bostonian whose impressions of Manchester are to be found in his two-volume *European Life and Morals*,[4] and very revealing they are too. For Colman simply hasn't any adequate means of describing the city. He speaks, for example, of 'wretched, defrauded, oppressed, crushed human nature, lying in bleeding fragments all over the face of society'; and one inevitably notices how such hopelessly generalized, abstractive language fails either to describe or to define. Yet Colman had seen for himself some of the worst sites and sights of Manchester or, as he put it, 'exhibitions of the most disgusting and loathsome forms of destitution, and utter vice and profligacy'. But he told a friend that he feared to give details for 'the paper, I fear, would be absolutely offensive to the touch'.[5] In turning away from detail, and in having to rely on a language that couldn't confront the unique actuality of Manchester, Colman seems to me thoroughly representative of all those who came to Manchester during the 1830s and 1840s.

With the exception of Engels, that is. For his account of the city is determinedly specific. And as Steven Marcus has pointed out in his important, *Engels, Manchester and the Working Class*, one

of the greatest virtues of Engels's study is that it employs a
language adequate to its author's experience of the city. He
makes his readers face facts about Manchester and tries to be
exact about his own response, his engaged awareness of what
the city means to him.

Yet here we come to a crucial problem. Do facts amount to
the truth? Is Engels's picture of Manchester the full story? And
is his experience of it finally adequate? This is not merely a
question of an empiricist approach. I do not suggest that one
can gather more facts than Engels in order to correct his account (that could be done of course, but the arguments about
how to interpret the facts would only just be beginning). No,
the real problem facing us is whether we believe Engels is in a
position to know how to relate facts to experience, to make the
most sensitive interpretations and connections: in short,
whether we can trust him to know what he's talking about.

Engels himself had no doubts on this score. Manchester, he
says, 'is the classic type of a modern manufacturing town, and
because I know it as intimately as my own native town, more
intimately than most of its residents know it, we shall make a
longer stay here' (p. 75). Bold words, and ones that Marcus
fully endorses. Wrongly, so I think. For at the very least one
expects a man who claims to know a town intimately to have
some naturally shared and absorbed sense of place and time,
which in the nature of things Engels couldn't have. He was an
outsider, he spent rather less than two years in the town, and
he knew very little about the *kinds* of people who made up
Manchester. For those people hadn't just growed. As they came
in from the surrounding countryside they brought with them
various habits of life, of speech, of amusement, which formed
an intrinsic part of their consciousness (whereas for Engels consciousness really operated only in the factories and mills).
Change, growth of consciousness, development of class relationship and class antagonism: all these things are bound to be
more complicated than Engels, with the best will in the world,
could understand.

It is a point to return to, but before I do so it is only proper to
pay attention to the very real nature of Engels's achievement.
He does all that can be done by keen inquiry, unflinching
curiosity, intelligence and readiness to report facts. To take a

notable instance. Engels sets out to describe in detail the lives of the operatives. He wants us to become aware of the ways in which they live: their houses, their clothes, their food, their physical ailments and disabilities. Above all, perhaps, he concentrates on their housing. He draws maps, he illustrates how unscrupulous builders will make maximum use of the minimum number of bricks, he pries, pokes, wanders about; he won't go away. And always, and remorselessly, he gives us the details. He spends five or six pages on a section of the old town: 'In one of these courts there stands directly at the entrance, at the end of the covered passage, a privy without a door, so dirty that the inhabitants can pass into and out of the court only by passing through foul pools of stagnant urine and excrement' (p. 82). And that is only one such court. 'Everywhere heaps of *débris*, refuse, and offal; standing pools for gutters, and a stench which alone would make it impossible for a human being in any degree civilized to live in such a district' (p. 84). He turns his attention to the river Irk which runs past these courts:

> . . . full of *débris* and refuse. . . . In dry weather a long string of the most disgusting, blackish-green, slimy pools are left standing on the bank, from the depths of which bubbles of miasmatic gas constantly arise and give forth a stench unendurable even on the bridge forty or fifty feet above the surface of the stream. But besides this, the stream itself is checked every few paces by high weirs, behind which slime and refuse accumulate and rot in thick masses. Above the bridge are tanneries, bone mills, and gas works, from which all drains and refuse find their way into the Irk, which receives further the contents of all the neighbouring sewers and privies. It may easily be imagined, therefore, what sort of residue the stream deposits. Below the bridge you look upon the piles of *débris*, the refuse, filth and offal from the courts on the steep left bank . . . [p. 83].[6]

On and on it goes, this staggering account, with its terrible hammer-blow repetitions of *débris*, offal and excrement. And then Engels concludes:

> Such is the old town of Manchester, and on re-reading my description, I am forced to admit that instead of being exaggerated, it is far from black enough to convey a true impression of the filth, ruin and un-inhabitableness, the defiance of all considerations of cleanliness, ventilation and health which characterise the construction of this single district, containing at least twenty to thirty thousand inhabitants. And such a district exists in the heart of the second city of England, the first manufacturing city of the world. If any one wishes to see in how

little space a human being can move, how little air – and *such* air! –
he can breathe, how little of civilization he may share and yet live, it
is only necessary to travel hither [p. 86].

Engels may be right in saying that his description is far from
black enough, but in its remorseless cataloguing of the details,
of the horrifying actuality of life in Manchester, his account
stands alone.

Alone that is until 1848, when *Mary Barton* was published.
For in that remarkable first novel Mrs Gaskell provides a
description of a part of Manchester that comes very close to the
actualities which Engels had so pitilessly described. John
Barton and George Wilson, both of them out of work, go to
visit a sick acquaintance, Ben Davenport, who lives somewhere
in the old town. They find themselves in an especially dirty
street:

> It was unpaved: and down the middle a gutter forced its way, every
> now and then forming pools in the holes with which the street
> abounded. . . . As they passed, women from their doors tossed slops of
> *every* description into the gutter; they ran into the next pool, which
> overflowed and stagnated. Heaps of ashes were the stepping-stones, on
> which the passer-by, who cared in the least for cleanliness, took care
> not to put his foot. Our friends were not dainty but even they picked
> their way, till they had got to some steps leading down to a small
> area, where a person standing would have his head about one foot
> below the level of the street, and might at the same time, without the
> least motion of his body, touch the window of the cellar and the damp
> muddy wall opposite. You went down one step even from the foul area
> into the cellar in which a family of human beings lived. It was very
> dark inside. The window-panes many of them were broken and stuffed
> with rags, which was reason enough for the dusky light which pervaded
> the place even at mid-day . . . the smell was so foetid as almost to knock
> the two men down . . . they began to penetrate the thick darkness of
> the place, and to see three or four little children rolling on the damp,
> nay wet brick floor, through which the stagnant filthy moisture of the
> street oozed up; the fireplace was empty and black; the wife sat on
> her husband's lair and cried in the dark loneliness [Italics Mrs
> Gaskell's].

Wilson goes to open a door at the back of the cellar, hoping to
let in some fresh air, only to find that it 'led into a back cellar,
with a grating instead of a window, down which dropped the
moisture from pigsties, and worse abominations. It was not
paved; the floor was of bad-smelling blood' (ch. 6).

Now Engels remarks that in the old town:

... another feature most injurious to the cleanliness of the inhabitants is the multitude of pigs walking about in all the alleys, rooting into the offal heaps, or kept imprisoned in small pens. ... In almost every court one or even several such pens may be found, into which the inhabitants of the court throw all refuse and offal ... and the atmosphere, confined on all four sides, is utterly corrupted by putrefying animal and vegetable substances [p. 86].

He is describing the conditions in which the Davenports live.

Davenport is suffering from a low, putrid kind of 'typhoid'; an illness which literally plagued the old town and caused its periodic closure and compulsory cleansing. After which it would be reopened and in very little time returned to the conditions that both Engels and Mrs Gaskell so graphically describe. That this should be allowed is, for Engels, quite simply 'murder'. He uses the word in a particularly vigorous and eloquent passage, which comes in his section on 'Results':

> When society places hundreds of proletarians in such a position that they inevitably meet a too early and unnatural death, one which is quite as much a death by violence as that by the sword or bullet; when it deprives thousands of the necessaries of life, places them under conditions in which they *cannot* live – forces them through the strong arm of the law, to remain in such conditions until that death ensues which is the inevitable consequence – knows that these thousands of victims must perish, and yet permits these conditions to remain, its deed is murder just as surely as the deed of the single individual; disguised, malicious murder, which does not seem what it is, because no man sees the murderer, because the death of the victim seems a natural one, since the offence is one of omission rather than commission. But murder it remains [pp. 126–7].

As you read *Mary Barton* you quickly become aware of the high number of deaths that occur within its pages or are referred to in passing. Mrs Barton dies, so does Ben Davenport. So do the Wilson twins – 'helpless, gentle, silly children' they are called (ch. 7), and the phrase serves to indicate that they have been regularly dosed with Godfrey's cordial, a mixture which could be guaranteed to produce 'imbecility, caused by a suffusion of the brain, and an extensive train of mesenteric and glandular diseases. The child sinks into a low torpid state.'[7] Mr Wilson dies, we hear of the death of Barton's favourite son, Tom, and of his mother, 'from the absolute want of the necessaries of life'.

We know that *Mary Barton* was begun not long after the death of Mrs Gaskell's own son, but it is arrant nonsense to suggest, as some critics have done, that his death is sufficient to explain the number of deaths in her novel, and it is not much more sensible to suggest that they are there to offer the chance for Christian reflections on life's uncertainty and how we are all in God's hands. The sub-title of *Mary Barton* is 'A Tale of Manchester Life' and one of the inescapable facts about Manchester life was that it was soon over. The registrar of deaths for Manchester remarked in 1849 that over the previous seven years 13,362 children had died 'over and above the mortality natural to mankind';[8] and if we turn to the famous *Report on the Sanitary Condition of the Labouring Population of Great Britain* (1842), we discover that the average age of death for 'mechanics, labourers and their families' was seventeen. That is what Engels means by 'murder', and not all the huffings and puffings of the 'Manchester Masters' can obscure the plain justness of his word.

Mrs Gaskell's recording of death in *Mary Barton* puts her very much on Engels's side. No wonder, then, that the masters themselves, led by W. R. Greg, should have been so outraged by her novel, nor that they should have insisted that she is providing mere 'caricatures' of the employers.[9] And yet when one reads the novel one is bound to notice that Mrs Gaskell goes out of her way to sympathize with the employers and to adopt their point of view. So, for example, after the death of Mrs Barton, Mrs Gaskell speaks of the immense contrast between wealth and poverty in the city, even in times of acute depression.

> Carriages still roll along the streets, concerts are still crowded by subscribers, the shops for expensive luxuries still find daily customers, while the workman loiters away his unemployed time in watching these things, and thinking of the pale, uncomplaining wife at home, and the wailing children asking in vain for enough food – of the sinking health, of the dying life of those near and dear to him. The contrast is too great. Why should he alone suffer from bad times?
>
> I know that this is not really the case; and I know what is the truth in such matters: but what I wish to impress is what the workman thinks and feels [ch. 3].

It is an undeniably forlorn moment. 'I know what is the truth in such matters.' If so, one can only remark that Mrs Gaskell keeps it very much to herself. The only knowledge we are given access to is the fact of death (murder?). But as a consciously middle-class liberal Mrs Gaskell can hardly be expected to face up to that knowledge. And so she later insists that during the worst years of the depression, 1840–2, 'in a Christian land, it was not known even so feebly as words could tell it, or the more happy and fortunate would have thronged with their sympathy and aid' (ch. 8). The 'feeling of alienation between the different classes of society' is therefore put down to an unfortunate ignorance which it is of course the task of *Mary Barton* to dispel. It is worth contrasting that routine piety with Engels's insistence that 'society knows how injurious such conditions are to the health and life of its workers, and yet does nothing to improve these conditions. That it *knows* the consequences of its deeds; that its act is, therefore, not manslaughter, but murder' (p. 127). Mrs Gaskell would hardly want to accept *that* kind of knowledge, for her novel is a conscious attempt to promote the concept of brotherhood 'in a Christian land'. It therefore comes as no surprise when we are told at the end of the novel that Carson, the manufacturer, wants to work for

> . . . a perfect understanding, and complete confidence and love . . . between masters and men, that the truth might be recognised that the interests of one were the interests of all, and as such, required the consideration and deliberation of all; that hence it was most desirable to have educated workers, capable of judging, not mere machines of ignorant men, and to have them bound to their employers by the ties of respect and affection, not by mere money bargains alone; in short, to acknowledge the Spirit of Christ as the regulating law between both parties.

Mrs Gaskell is even prepared to go to the extent of blaming Barton for extravagance, on the occasion of the tea party which he and his wife give for the Wilsons. And in doing so she precisely anticipates the advice given to the Bartons of the world by the *Westminster Review*, which felt, however, that Mrs Gaskell hadn't gone far enough in driving home the lesson of thrift to the working man: 'In the commencement of the tale he is in full work, with high wages and possesses a comfortable home. But in possessing that comfortable home, like too many around him . . . the enjoyment of the present is alone attended to; while the provision for a continuation of even moderate enjoyment for the future, seems to be scarcely heeded.'[10] Compare Mrs Gaskell: 'with childlike improvidence, good times will often dissipate his grumbling, and make him forget all prudence and foresight' (ch. 3).

Yet she knows that such remarks are hopelessly inadequate. For although she may accuse Barton of extravagance and, in so doing, behave in a perfectly orthodox manner, she adds that he is one who 'endured wrongs without complaining'; and she knows that he *can't* save, not if he is to live at all decently. Which doesn't mean merely eating moderately well, but acting generously towards his friends. And in recognizing this much, Mrs Gaskell is again at one with Engels. There is a splendid moment in the *Condition of the Working Class* where Engels takes up the proffered advice of thrift to the working man, and contemptuously points out:

> To save is unavailing, for at the utmost he cannot save more than suffices to sustain life for a short time, while if he falls out of work, it is for no brief period. To accumulate lasting property for himself is impossible; and if it were not, he would only cease to be a working man and another would take his place. What better can he do, then, when he gets high wages, than live well upon them? The English bourgeoisie is violently scandalised at the extravagant living of the workers when wages are high; yet it is not only very natural but sensible of them to enjoy life when they can [p. 147].

And he is properly scornful of the dream of reconciliation that Mrs Gaskell intermittently entertains in her novel. He gives us a wonderful parody of the 'enlightened' bourgeois attitude:

> If [in the cities] the workers are not educated (i.e. to obedience to the bourgeoisie), they may view matters one-sidedly, from the stand-point of a sinister selfishness, and may readily permit themselves to be hoodwinked by sly demagogues; nay, they may even be capable of viewing their greatest benefactors, the frugal and enterprising capitalists, with a jealous and a hostile eye [pp. 151–2].

There are passages in *Mary Barton* which come uncomfortably close to the position Engels is here exposing; and when he repeatedly and bitterly points out that the only education given to the workers is in Sunday-schools or through nonconformity, which preach submission and forgiveness, we can hardly avoid thinking of the last pages of Mrs Gaskell's novel and of Carson's wish that 'a perfect understanding, and complete confidence and love, might exist between masters and men'.

Yet although Mrs Gaskell undoubtedly betrays an anxious

middle-class sense of wanting to defend the masters and the system from which they profit, I think that the real strengths of her novel show her to be decisively at one with much of Engels's account of Manchester. Death, exploitation, misery, suffering, injustice, and the sheer detail with which the novel abounds: these go clean counter to her recommendations. For what she recommends cannot cope with the state of affairs that *Mary Barton* reveals. At the end of the novel Job Legh tells Carson that Barton was 'a loving man before he grew mad with seeing such as he was slighted. . . . At one time, I've heard him say, he felt kindly towards every man, rich or poor, because he thought they were all men alike. But latterly he grew aggravated with the sorrows and sufferings that he saw, and which he thought the masters might help if they would' (ch. 37). But of course we have seen that Barton's grievance has very little to do with social recognition. He wants work and money, he knows he is entitled to them, but he also knows that he is in no position to guarantee them for himself. And for all that Carson may reply to Job that 'we suffer just as much as you can do', given what Mrs Gaskell shows of the man, we are bound to recall Engels's remark:

> I have never seen a class so deeply demoralised, so incurably debased by selfishness, so corroded within, so incapable of progress, as the English bourgeoisie. . . . True [they] are good husbands and family men, and have all sorts of other private virtues, and appear, in ordinary intercourse, as decent and respectable as all other bourgeois . . . but how does this help matters? Ultimately it is self-interest, and especially money-gain, which alone determines them [p. 301].

And then follows the famous anecdote about the amount of money made in Manchester. It might well have been spoken by Carson.

How remarkable it seems, that the young, ardent Rhinelander and the mild-mannered liberal lady should have so much in common. And what a tribute to her powers. Yet there are important distinctions. Mrs Gaskell doesn't in the end offer precisely the same account and diagnosis as Engels, even though Steven Marcus thinks that she does. 'What Mrs Gaskell does have to say in large measure and at almost every critical juncture confirms what Engels had said before her.'[11] It won't do, and not simply because she sees more. No, the fact is that she understands things that he didn't, knows about matters of which he's inevitably ignorant, and therefore implicitly challenges his position. We do not need to take seriously that when she is at her weakest she goes against Engels (and in doing so unintentionally reveals the rightness of his analysis of bourgeois attempts at self-justification). But we do need to take very seriously the fact that her account of the condition of the working class in Manchester can be at odds with him at precisely those moments where she is at her strongest.

By way of trying to pin down some important distinctions between the two, and of suggesting why Engels's account is insufficient, let me begin with him on London. He observes a London crowd, jostling and thronging footpaths, and he remarks:

> The brutal indifference, the unfeeling isolation of each in his private interest becomes the more repellant and offensive, the more these individuals are crowded together, within a limited space. And, however much one may be aware that this is the isolation of the individual, this narrow self-seeking is the fundamental principle of our society everywhere, it is nowhere so shamelessly barefaced, so self-conscious as just here in the crowding of the great city. The dissolution of mankind into monads of which each one has a separate principle and a separate purpose, the world of atoms, is here carried out to its utmost extreme [p. 58].

Marcus at least sees that this passage is strikingly inadequate. As he admits, the confusion is not so much in the object 'as in the observing eye and mind . . . it is an incapacity to differentiate, to discover articulated structures in – or impose them upon – the materials of existence'. And Marcus instances a parallel example in *Nicholas Nickleby*, where 'objects are contiguously related, but the contiguity is precisely the term of their disrelatedness as well'.[12] In short, Engels's atomistic view of the city is inadequate because external, too little aware of structures of relationship in the experience avowedly being studied or explored. In a word, he doesn't know enough.

Now when he gets to Manchester, he more or less repeats what he had said about London, though with a slight, and I think undeveloped (perhaps unperceived?), difference. 'The great towns are chiefly inhabited by working-people . . . these workers have no property whatsoever of their own and live

wholly upon wages, which usually go from hand to mouth.
Society, composed wholly of atoms, does not trouble itself about
them . . .' (p. 106). The important shift is of course that Engels
has now set up an opposition between workers and society,
whereas in the case of London society was the whole. Why the
change? The reason must be that Engels wants to insist that the
working class in Manchester has its own consciousness, which
by its very nature must be anti-atomistic, which is entirely new,
and which depends absolutely on these people being *workers in
the city*. It is out of the combination of worker and city that the
new consciousness springs, for it creates the energy of violent
hatred. Or so Engels insists. And Marcus agrees with him.
There are no other articulated structures of experience, or none
that can be regarded as relevant to the creation and growth of
working-class consciousness. Here is Marcus both paraphrasing
Engels and endorsing his view:

> [The workers' settlements] embody a division of labour on an un-
> precedented mass social scale, and are immense industrial barracks or
> encampments. They are at this moment in their history almost purely
> functional or skeletal communities and have not yet provided them-
> selves with such visible structures as make manifest these extra-
> economic institutions and activities through which communities of men
> are also ordinarily regarded as maintaining themselves, their ancestors
> and their children. They and their work represent a new, frightening
> and highly developed order of human existence. Yet what is most
> striking about this complexity is its inexpungeable, contradictory
> uniformity – uniformity of life, of style, even of colour. This uniformity
> is part of the experience of murderous, quasi-military discipline that
> generations of working men have had to undergo. . . .[13]

Reading that and the passages in Engels's work which it relates
to, and recognizing how near it is to the unsatisfactory externality of Dickens's presentation of Coketown – 'It contained
several large streets all very like one another, and many small
streets still more like one another, inhabited by people equally
like one another' – I return with a sense of unease and suspicion
to Engels's claim that he knows Manchester 'as intimately as
my own native town, more intimately than most of its residents
know it'.
    For at the very least one is forced to regard the claim as
extraordinarily daring when one thinks that Engels had no
naturally acquired knowledge of the place's history, and did not

even know where the majority of its inhabitants had come from, and what that might mean. In the new towns Engels remarks, 'The centralization of property has reached the highest point; here the morals and customs of the good old times are most completely obliterated; here it has gone so far that the name Merry Old England conveys no meaning, for Old England itself is unknown to memory and to the tales of our grandfathers' (p. 56). Not so. The people coming in off the land brought their customs with them, and they survive all right, in no matter how modified a form. Folk song blends into industrial ballad, field sports into street games, fairs continue in new surroundings and become important festive – and potentially revolutionary – occasions, family ties remain for all the terrific strains they have to undergo. Are these things trivial, of no account in the development of working-class consciousness? I do not think so. And there is nothing trivial in Engels's mistaken claim: 'The English working-man is no Englishman nowadays. . . . English nationality is annihilated in the working man' (p. 239). As the Irish poor who lived in little Ireland, one of the worst slum areas in Manchester, had every reason to know, nationality could assert itself in decidedly ugly if partly understandable ways (ways which are brought out in Mrs Gaskell's *North and South*). In 1851 Queen Victoria visited Manchester and was able to report:

> The streets were immensely full . . . and the cheering and enthusiasm most gratifying. The order and good behaviour of the people, who were not placed behind barriers, were the most complete we have seen in our many progressions through capitals and cities. . . . Everyone says that in no other town could one depend so entirely upon the quiet and orderly behaviour of the people as in Manchester. You had only to tell them what ought to be done, and it was sure to be carried out.

And this, it should be noted, although the Queen recognized that it was 'a painfully unhealthy-looking population'.[14]

National pride blends into regional pride, a matter that is of profound importance in *North and South*, but about which Engels seems quite unaware. I think, for example, of the moment where he says: 'It is not suprising that the working-class has gradually become a race wholly apart from the bourgeoisie. The bourgeoisie has more in common with every other nation of the earth than with the workers in whose midst it

lives. The workers speak other dialects, have other thoughts and
ideals, other customs and moral principles, a different religion
and other politics than those of the bourgeoisie' (p. 154). Yes,
but that isn't the whole truth, and although Engels is of course
quite right to stress the differences, he is surely wrong to over-
look the fact that workers and bourgeoisie have one thing at
least in common – Manchester itself. So Margaret Hale does
her best to dissuade Nicholas Higgins from seeking work as a
rural labourer: 'You would not bear the dullness of the life; you
don't know what it is; it would eat you away like rust. . . . You
could not stir them up into any companionship, which you get
in a town as plentiful as the air you breathe, whether it be good
or bad – and that I don't know; but I do know, that you of all
men are not the one to bear such a life among such labourers'
(*North and South*, ch. 37).

Now companionship is an important feature of both Mrs
Gaskell's Manchester novels and to some extent her recognition
of its possibility depends on her awareness of different kinds of
living conditions among working-class people, which she knows
to be important, yet which Engels doesn't see at all or, if he
does, takes to be of no account. The result is that Mrs Gaskell
can present evidence of structures of experience, ways of living,
adaptations and changes that are importantly present in the
creation of working-class consciousness, though they are set
quite apart from the shop floor. This is in no way to deny that
Mrs Gaskell shares Engels's perception of the energy of hatred
that has much to do with the creation of that consciousness. It
should cause no surprise, Engels insists, if the workers 'can
maintain their consciousness of manhood only by cherishing the
most glowing hatred, the most unbroken rebellion against the
bourgeoisie in power' (p. 144). When John Barton returns from
the forlorn presentation of the 1842 charter, he tells Job Legh:
'It's not to be forgotten, or forgiven either, by me or many
another. . . . As long as I live, our rejection that day will abide
in my heart; and as long as I live I shall curse them as so
cruelly refused to hear us . . .' (ch. 9). And we learn much
earlier that after the death of his son Barton builds 'hoards of
vengeance in his heart against the employers'.

Mrs Gaskell indeed presents Barton as very much a man of
hatred, and quite clearly feels nervous enough about the prob-

ability of our finding him both credible and sympathetic to
warn us that his heart is touched with 'sin'. Engels would
approve of John Barton, right enough; but there is more to the
man than hatred. For Mrs Gaskell doesn't think that hatred
and vengeance make the sum total of working-class consciousness. Engels does. It is only *there* that the working class is anti-
atomistic, becomes more than merely a congregation of
monads. Or rather, for all the few attempts he makes to go
beyond that – for example, quoting and agreeing with Canon
Parkinson that 'only the poor give to the poor' – he does not
seem to me to have succeeded in all that he avowedly set out to
do. 'I wanted', he says, 'to see into your own homes, to observe you in your every-day life, to chat with you on your conditions and grievances, to witness your struggles against the
social and political power of your oppressors. I have done so.'
He has done many of those things, yes; and done them magni-
ficently. Nevertheless some things remain undone or insufficiently done. Or perhaps it is rather that Engels simply
didn't understand all that he experienced – and as a result
assumed that he was experiencing something else. To be
specific. At the end of his long and harrowing account of
working-class living conditions, Engels sums up:

> We must admit that 350,000 working people of Manchester and its
> environs live, almost all of them, in wretched, damp filthy cottages,
> that the streets which surround them are usually in the most miserable
> and filthy conditions, laid out without the slightest reference to venti-
> lation, with reference solely to the profit secured by the contractor. In
> a word, we must confess that in the working-man's dwellings of
> Manchester, no cleanliness, no convenience, and consequently no
> comfortable family life is possible; that in such dwellings only a
> physically degenerate race, robbed of all humanity, degraded, reduced
> morally and physically to bestiality, could feel comfortable and at home
> [p. 96].

We may be impressed by the rhetoric, we can hardly fail to be
moved and appalled by the detail which Engels has so insistently
thrust at us. Yet at the same time we are bound to feel that
Engels's standards are those of the rich Rhinelander, and that
as such he is hardly likely to make important distinctions
between, shall we say, the Barton and Wilson households, or the
Davenport and Alice Wilson cellars.[15] Yet the distinctions are
important, and Mrs Gaskell knows how to make them. Alice

Wilson's cellar is called 'humble', but the word isn't a polite evasion. Its floor 'was bricked, and scrupulously clean, although so damp that it seemed as if the last washing would never dry up'. Mrs Gaskell isn't suggesting that Alice Wilson should have to live in such conditions. But the fact is that Alice does achieve some degree of cleanliness, convenience and hence comfortable family life. And of course one of her strengths is that she can still recall her earlier days in rural surroundings, has a sense of continuity in human assertiveness which Engels would want to deny her.

And what is true of Alice's achievement is truer still of the Bartons. I need to quote Mrs Gaskell's description of their house at some length:

> The party proceeded home, through many half-finished streets, all so like one another, that you might easily have been bewildered and lost your way. Not a step, however, did our friends lose; down this entry, cutting off that corner, until they turned out of one of those innumerable streets into a little paved court, having the backs of houses at the end opposite to the opening, and a gutter running through the middle to carry off household slops, washing suds, &c. The women who lived in the court were busy taking in strings of caps, frocks, and various articles of linen, which hung from side to side, dangling so low, that if our friends had been a few minutes sooner, they would have had to stoop very much, or else the half-wet clothes would have flapped in their faces: but although the evening seemed yet early when they were in the open fields – among the pent-up houses, night, with its mists and darkness, had already begun to fall.
>
> Many greetings were given and exchanged between the Wilsons and these women, for not long ago they had also dwelt in this court. Two rude lads, standing at a disorderly looking house-door, exclaimed as Mary Barton . . . passed, 'Eh, look! Polly Barton's getten a sweetheart.'
>
> Of course this referred to young Wilson, who stole a look to see how Mary took the idea. He saw her assume the air of a young fury, and to his next speech she answered not a word.
>
> Mrs. Barton produced the key of the door from her pocket; and on entering the house-place it seemed as if they were in total darkness, except one bright spot, which might be a cat's eye, or might be, what it was, a red-hot fire, smouldering under a large piece of coal, which John Barton immediately applied himself to break up, and the effect instantly produced was warm and glowing light in every corner of the room. To add to this (although the coarse yellow glare seemed lost in the ruddy glow from the fire), Mrs. Barton lighted a dip by sticking it in the fire, and having placed it satisfactorily in a tin candlestick, began to look further about her, on hospitable thoughts intent. The room was tolerably large, and possessed many conveniences. On the right of

the door, as you entered, was a longish window, with a broad ledge. On each side of this, hung blue-and-white check curtains, which were now drawn, to shut in the friends met to enjoy themselves. Two geraniums, unpruned and leafy, which stood on the sill, formed a further defence from out-door pryers. In the corner between the window and the fire-side was a cupboard, apparently full of plates and dishes, cups and saucers, and some more nondescript articles, for which one would have fancied their possessors could find no use—such as triangular pieces of glass to save carving knives and forks from dirtying table-cloths. However, it was evident Mrs. Barton was proud of her crockery and glass, for she left her cupboard door open, with a glance round of satisfaction and pleasure. On the opposite side to the door and window was the stair-case, and two doors; one of which (the nearest to the fire) led into a sort of little back kitchen, where dirty work such as washing up dishes, might be done, and whose shelves served as larder, and pantry, and storeroom, and all. The other door, which was considerably lower, opened into the coal-hole – the slanting closet under the stairs; from which, to the fire-place, there was a gay-coloured piece of oil-cloth laid. The place seemed almost crammed with furniture (sure sign of good times among the mills). Beneath the window was a dresser, with three deep drawers. Opposite the fire-place was a table, which I should call a Pembroke, only that it was made of deal, and I cannot tell how far such a name may be applied to such humble material. On it, resting against the wall, was a bright green japanned tea-tray, having a couple of scarlet lovers embracing in the middle. The fire-light danced merrily on this and really (setting all taste but that of a child's aside) it gave a richness of colouring to that side of the room. It was in some measure propped up by a crimson tea-caddy, also of japan ware. A round table on one branching leg, really for use, stood in the corresponding corner to the cupboard; and, if you can picture all this, with a washy, but clean stencilled pattern on the walls, you can form some idea of John Barton's home [ch. 2].

Most of those details have very obviously been observed rather than invented. As to the house itself, it is worth noting that it clearly exists at the newer end of the town ('many half-finished streets'), and that the reference to 'backs of houses' shows that it fronts on to the street, which made for better ventilation (this was a regulation that applied to all house-building in the later 1840s). And to say this, of course, is to suggest that for all that the novel opens in the late 1830s, Mrs Gaskell is probably thinking of houses that were being built some time later, closer to the time of actual writing. I don't think this much matters. What does matter is whether the Barton house is a spectacular exception to the rule which Engels lays down about working-class living conditions.

As it happens, we can check Mrs Gaskell's account against another, written a year later. In October and November 1849 the *Morning Chronicle* carried a series of reports on Manchester and the surrounding textile districts. Their author, Angus Bethune Reach, had been sent to Manchester by the paper following the severe outbreak of cholera there in the summer of 1849. Reach's articles are impressive pieces of investigative journalism, and he offers well-researched accounts of many aspects of working-class life in Manchester, including the matter of housing. He compares the houses and house interiors of Hulme (a newish part) with those of Ancoats (an older part). He reports of the furniture that 'a fair proportion of what was deal in Ancoats was mahogany in Hulme. Yet the people of Hulme get no higher wages than the people of Ancoats. The secret is that they live in better built houses, and consequently take more pleasure and pride in their dwellings.'[16]

We are told that the Wilsons live in Ancoats, and it seems very likely that the Bartons live in Hulme. Certainly, Reach's description of Hulme accords very well with Mrs Gaskell's account of the Barton house and area. 'Between every street', Reach tells us, 'were two rows of the best class of operatives' houses, each with four rooms and a cellar a-piece; and between each of the rows, running the whole length, was a paved courtway, with a gutter in the centre. . . .' And he describes in some detail the parlour of one of these houses:

> The room was about ten feet by eight, and hung with paper of cheap quality and ordinary pattern. In at least two of the corners were cupboards of hard wood, painted mahogany fashion, and containing plates, teacups, saucers, &c. Upon the chimney-piece was ranged a set of old-fashioned glass and china ornaments. There was one framed print hanging from the wall – a steel engraving of small size, reduced from the well known plate of the 'Covenanter's Marriage'. Beside this symbol of art was a token of allegiance to science, in the shape of one of the old-fashioned tube barometers, not apparently in the most perfect state of order. There were two tables in the apartment – a round centre one of ordinary material, and a rather handsome mahogany Pembroke. Opposite the fireplace was one of those nondescript pieces of furniture which play a double part in domestic economy – 'a bed by night, a wardrobe all the day'. The chairs were of the comfortable old-fashioned Windsor breed; and on the window-ledge were two or three flower-pots, feebly nourishing as many musty geraniums.[17]

As that passage makes clear Reach's attitude is pretty well that

C

of the superior outsider. Had he known more of Manchester
life he might not have referred so glibly to the 'token of allegiance to science'. (Mrs Gaskell's Job Legh is a convincing
study of the kind of autodidact regularly to be found in working-
class life during the nineteenth century, as we know from any
number of Autobiographies and Memoirs).[18] Yet whatever
Reach's shortcomings it is obvious that his description of life in
Hulme is much closer to Mrs Gaskell's description of life at the
Bartons than to anything that we can find in Engels. But what
then can survive of Marcus's claim that Engels has done full
justice to the 'inexpungeable, uniformity of life, style, even of
colour' in Manchester working-class life? Not as much as either
he or Engels would have us believe. 'I have observed you in your
everyday life,' Engels claims. Yet there are things he hasn't
at all observed, and not simply because they hadn't been there
to observe in 1844. True, between that year and 1849 all sorts
of improvements had taken place, for example the introduction
of the ten-hour act, the enforcing of certain sanitation laws and
new building regulations. And at the end of *Mary Barton* Mrs
Gaskell is able to speak of 'many of the improvements now in
practice in the system of employment in Manchester'. But I
am not particularly concerned to advance an empiricist argument: I don't want simply to tot up the facts and see who comes
out on the right side. Facts, in the end, are not what matter. Or
rather, they are a disadvantage to the sort of survey that Engels
is conducting because they mean that he is incapable of seeing
significant differences between the Barton and Davenport
households: differences of values, customs, ways of experiencing. For him it is all one unending horror.[19]

Now in many ways this is so decent and humane a response
that it would be offensively wrong to rebuke him for not fully
understanding what it was that he imagined he was experiencing. But the truth is that just because he insists that in
Manchester there can be 'no comfortable family life' for the
working class, he leaves out something crucial to the development of working-class consciousness: which is precisely the
determination to create a comfortable family life, and structures
of experience related to and dependent on it. To put it bluntly:
Engels takes the creation of working-class consciousness to occur
essentially on the factory floor and to be fostered in a spirit of

hate, of enmity. *Mary Barton* testifies to the fact that although the hold on comfort is terribly precarious and can be exploited, degraded and destroyed by the corruptions of the system, it none the less keeps reasserting itself. And accompanying it are patterns of living about which Engels was profoundly and inevitably ignorant yet which, in various forms and modifications, belong with the growth of working-class consciousness. Alice Wilson brings from her childhood knowledge of country medicines, herbal foods, ways of speaking, which imply something about continuity and adaptation, about the ways in which consciousness changes patterns and is changed by them.

But it is not merely in the comparatively exceptional figures of Alice and Job Legh that we discover something that is missing from Engels's account of the growth of working-class consciousness. How odd, for example, that he should say nothing about the grimness, acidity, sadness and sometimes consoling wit and warmth of work songs. How odd that he should think every pub is a gin palace. How odd that he has nothing to say about entertainment: about cheap 'blood-tub' theatres, musical events, clubs, halls even; or about the possibilities of railway excursions. Reach has a fascinating section on Manchester pub and club entertainments, and he mentions the social function of the railway. By the end of *Mary Barton* Margaret Legh, Job's blind granddaughter, has started on a career of club singing and the novel as a whole takes in the experiences of work songs,[20] of family teas, visits, marriages, exchanges of hospitality, kinship. And Mrs Gaskell's story, *Libbie Marsh's Three Eras* (1847), mentions railway excursions, boat trips on the canals, picnics. None of which has any part to play in Engels's account of Manchester.

To say this is not to decry the importance of the *Condition of the Working Class*. It remains a masterpiece of observation and fierce anger; and its account of how Manchester developed, of the strategies implicit in the creation of high streets, shops, suburbs etc., is formidably intelligent and thoroughly convincing. And as I have shown, in many ways Mrs Gaskell endorses Engels's study of working-class life in the town. But her understanding of the growth of working-class consciousness inevitably goes wider and deeper than his. (Not that she would put her understanding in the terms I have used). Of course he was right to emphasize the terrible degradation of many working-class lives, the squalor, misery, and human insufficiency that often typified life in Manchester and which made hundreds of thousands of human beings helpless victims of a system which they could do very little about. But not to recognize that some discriminations are necessary, not to see that there are structures of experience which are positive and not merely created out of negativeness or enmity – however excusable such failures of vision may be, they finally limit Engels's 'intimate' knowledge of Manchester. That is why we need *Mary Barton*.

3

William Hale White and the Problems of Deliverance

I

WRITING to his friend, Sophia Partridge, in 1897, Hale White told her: 'I belong to the Tennyson–Carlyle–Ruskin epoch. When I was a boy, these men were the appointed channels through which the new life was poured into me. . . .' A year later he wrote to her that he was glad to find that his feeling for George Eliot 'has lost none of its intensity, and that, as a whole, what I thought of her five-and-thirty years ago is what I think of her now'.[1] And he pays eloquent tribute to her in a late essay, protesting at Leslie Stephen's daring to call her 'eminently respectable'. She was nothing of the sort, Hale White retorts, because she was quite incapable of mental compromise: 'She never terminated inquiry till she had gone as far as her powerful intellect permitted her to go, and she never refused to act upon her investigation. If she did not outrage the world by indecency, it was not because she was "respectable", but because she had not deduced indecency as the final outcome of thinking or the highest achievement of art.'[2]

Put these remarks together and they fairly enough suggest Hale White's heritage: high-Victorian seriousness, a mind exercised over questions of religious faith, evolution, the natural sciences (he is included in Basil Willey's group of honest doubters); concerned with democracy and 'the people'; deeply impressed with the need to free women from the trivializing of their lives. It is a heritage which is unmistakably present in all of his writing.

Yet it does not tell the whole story. After all Hale White died in 1913, and the bulk of his writing belongs to the last two de-

cades of the nineteenth century. For all his heritage Hale White
is very much a late Victorian. His hard-earned stoicism seems
to me qualitatively different from George Eliot's because it is
deeply impressed with a sad awareness that her great consola-
tions are not available to him. One of the characters of *The
Revolution in Tanner's Lane* speaks with what I take to be the
author's approval when she says that 'the highest form of
martyrdom, though, is not even living for the sake of a cause,
but living without one, merely because it is your duty to live'
(ch. xxiv). Hale White lacks George Eliot's moral fervency because he knows only too well that it has failed to answer to the
problematic reality of his times. In the face of that reality he has
to work hard to convert a deep ennui, an enervate melancholy,
into a disciplined stoicism. In *Deliverance* Mark Rutherford
remarks: 'The characteristic of much that is said and written
now is melancholy; and it is melancholy, not because of any
deeper acquaintance with the secrets of man than that which
was possessed by our forefathers, but because it is easy to be
melancholy, and the time lacks strength' (ch. viii). *Deliverance* is
set in the 1840s, but Mark's words apply much more accurately
to the 1880s (*Deliverance* was published in 1884).[3] Of course,
Mark Rutherford is not Hale White. Indeed there is an obvious
preacher-like complacency about his brisk-up attitude that
could never be mistaken for his creator's. The point is rather
that Mark's words reveal an uneasy awareness of problems,
issues, complexities which he can hope to cope with only by
evasion, by turning them into the opportunity for rhetoric ('it is
easy to be melancholy, and the time lacks strength'). But
rhetoric won't reach to where the problems lie. They lie
partly, of course, in Mark's own consciousness: anyone who
puts the matter as he does plainly can't acknowledge his own
sense that language is betraying him.

When Clara Hopgood goes to work for a bookseller in Holborn, 'everything she touched was foul with grime . . . a loathsome composition of everything disgusting which could be
produced by millions of human beings and animals packed
together in soot' (*Clara Hopgood*, ch. xviii). Later her friend
Baruch Cohen tells her: 'I do not like crowds; I dislike even the
word, and dislike "the masses" still more. I do not want to think
of human beings as if they were a cloud of dust, and as if each

atom had no separate importance. London is often horrible to
me for that reason' (ch. xxiv). Sentences such as those do not
belong to the high-Victorian novel: they inevitably occur at a
time when the best kind of bourgeois liberal consciousness sees
the city – London above all – as a place of dreadful night, a
heart of darkness; in short, when a baffled and baffling pessimism has finally overwhelmed the determined faith in Comte's
reading of history that had sustained George Eliot. At such a
moment melancholy can establish itself as the only available
response to what the bourgeois consciousness confronts.

And it is not merely London which creates a sense of human
beings as atoms of 'no separate importance'. 'Crowhursts had
been buried at Cross Lanes ever since it existed, but the present
Crowhursts knew nothing of their ancestors beyond the genera-
tion immediately preceding. What was there to remember, or
if there was anything worth remembering, why should they
remember it? Life was blank, blind, dull as the brown clay
in the sodden fields in November . . .' (*Catherine Furze*, ch.
xviii).

Given his understanding of the economic realities underlying
production and their disposal of the myth of a natural world and
natural relationships belonging to it, it is not surprising that
there should be no saints of humanity in Hale White's fiction,
though there are people who behave well, simply because it is
their duty to live. And in *Clara Hopgood* we are offered Baruch
Cohen as an antidote to melancholy. For Cohen accepts 'the
inevitable order of nature, and he tried to acquire, although
often he failed, that blessed art of taking up lightly and even
with a smile whatever he was compelled to handle' (ch. xix).
As the name suggests, Baruch is a Spinozistic man, and that
serves to remind us that Hale White was a sensitive and per-
ceptive admirer of the great Jewish philosopher. He was not of
course the first Victorian to discover Spinoza's importance
(Matthew Arnold's 'Spinoza and the Bible' was probably the
first influential essay on him), but I think that he needs Spinoza
more than most. In the essay that was originally the revised
preface to the second edition of his translation of Spinoza's
Ethic, and which he later reprinted in *Pages from a Journal*, Hale
White notes that 'the sorrow of life is the rigidity of the material
universe in which we are placed. . . . Spinoza's chief aim is to

free us from this sorrow, and to free us from it by *thinking*.' And
he ends by declaring that he has found Spinoza's works 'pro-
ductive beyond those of any man I know of that *acquiescentia
mentis* which enables us to live'.[4]

Baruch Cohen repeatedly utters or meditates on Spinozistic
concepts, as for example, when he turns over in his mind 'that
the will and power of God are co-extensive: that there is nothing which might be and is not. It was familiar to Baruch, but
like all ideas of that quality and magnitude – and there are not
many of them – it was always new and affected him like a starry
night, seen hundreds of times, yet for ever infinite and original'
(ch. XXIV).[5] The simile is not a casual one. Hale White was an
enthusiastic amateur astronomer; and in his fiction those who
fix their attention on the natural universe are offered a bene-
diction, a kind of resolution, an ability to live (where that
means more than to endure) which releases them from the
torments of doubt or grieving speculation or from the possible
awareness that

> The world rolls round for ever like a mill;
> It grinds out death and life and good and ill;
> It has no purpose, heart or mind or will.[6]

I quote from Thomson's poem because the lines plainly
chime with the condition in which Hale White's leading
characters so often find themselves and from which they find
release only as they can be rapt from the isolate self: which is
what attention to the natural universe means. Paraphrasing
Spinoza's argument about genuine freedom, Hale White says:
'In other words, being part of the whole, the grandeur and
office of the whole are ours. We are anxious about what we call
"personality", but in truth there is nothing in it of any worth,
and the less we care for it the more "blessed" we are.' With such
a remark in mind, one can see why the Wordsworths were so
important to Hale White.[7] I do not know of anyone who has
written better about Dorothy Wordsworth, especially in the
essay on her Scottish Journal, where he remarks that, 'Dorothy,
always awake, continually turned the attention of her intro-
spective brother to the significance of external objects, and
saved his poetic gifts by the provision of reality', and where he
goes on to remark: 'It is in her peculiar ability to get so much

out of the common world that Dorothy is remarkable. The reason why she can get so much from it is that she can look long and steadily, and is free from any conscious desire to do more than look.'[8]

That may seem faint praise. It is anything but that. The key to Hale White's deeply sympathetic understanding of Dorothy Wordsworth lies at the end of the passage quoted above. He is not indulging in any kind of Victorian nature worship, still less recommending what it now seems usual to call a positivistic account of the universe, and which is little more than an extension of the eighteenth-century acceptance of nature as matter for observation. No, what he recognizes and responds to is Dorothy's ability to travel beyond self or 'personality': she is free from *any conscious desire* to do more than look. The journals provide ample evidence of Hale White's readiness to look at the natural world: small note-like entries, observations of 'July', 'A Sunday Morning in November', 'Romney Marsh', 'Early Morning in January', 'The End of October', 'The Break Up of a Great Drought' – and many more. None of these seems to me very remarkable (they certainly don't compare with Dorothy Wordsworth's *Journals*); but taken together they clearly indicate his Spinozistic determination to find 'genuine freedom' in recognizing that 'there is nothing which might be and is not'. And this entails neither a boringly empiricist position nor an escapist pastoralism. His concern is to achieve freedom from the constrictions of the isolate self as merely perceiver – tortured by the essentially aesthetic pains of observation (*The City of Dreadful Night* is an anti-picturesque) and of self-perceived solitariness (those 'separate atoms'). Such a concern is stoic, but grandly so.

And it occupies an important place in the fiction. I think, for example, of the emblematic figure of the butterfly-collector in the *Autobiography*. He is a man with a tragic personal history, which has led him to breakdown and near madness (we learn later that the cause of this was his wife's death in childbirth and the fact that his son grew up to be a hideously unnatural satyr, who died young in a lunatic asylum). He tells Mark: 'I went on gazing into dark emptiness, till all life became nothing for me. I did not care to live, because there was no assurance of existence beyond. By the strangest of processes, I neglected the world, because I had so short a time to be in it. It is with absolute horror now that I look back upon those days, when I lay as if alive in a coffin of lead. All passions and pursuits were nullified by the ever-abiding sense of mortality.' Then he travels abroad and discovers an interest in tropical butterflies. And gradually, absorption in this interest wins him back to an interest in life. 'A good deal of my satisfaction, perhaps, was unaccountable, and no rational explanation can be given of it. But men should not be too curious in analysing and condemning any means which nature devises to save them from themselves . . .' (ch. VIII). Though the phrasing of that last sentence could belong to mid-Victorian literature, the underlying idea seems to me peculiarly Hale White's and an inevitable element in the late-nineteenth-century ethos. For there is no forceful suggestion in it of a wisdom and spirit of the universe, no far-off divine attempt to which the whole creation moves. Simply, a man finds that contemplation of the natural universe saves him from himself: from 'introspection' and from 'melancholy', those kinds of consciousness which Hale White knew as contemporary inevitabilities, and which he had so frequently to struggle against in his own life.

In *The Revolution in Tanner's Lane* George Allen's silly but loved wife, Priscilla, dies and, 'He thought of her lying in her grave – she whom he had caressed – of what was going on down there, under the turf, and he feared he should go mad.' His religion cannot help him. 'He was helped by no priest and by no philosophy; but Nature helped him, the beneficent Power which heals the burn or scar and covers it with a new skin' (ch. XXVI). Agreed that this may mean simply that time heals all. But the capitalizations suggest more; and although I think the passage to be not entirely successful – the deifying of nature is too readily available as a way of intensifying the emotional throb[9] – one is again confronted with that stoic idea which is much more beautifully articulated in *Clara Hopgood*, in the meditation of Baruch's which I have already quoted, and in the truly marvellous moment when Clara realizes the rightness of her agonizingly painful decision to turn away from his love and allow Madge to claim him. They have gone for the weekend into the Surrey countryside, and Clara walks alone to a stone bridge overlooking a river:

The water on the upper side of the bridge was dammed up and fell over the little sluice gates under the arches into a clear and deep basin about forty or fifty feet in diameter. The river, for some reason of its own, had bitten into the western bank, and had scooped out a great piece of it into an island. The main current went round the island with a shallow, swift ripple, instead of going through the pool, as it might have done, for there was a clear channel for it. The centre and the region under the island were deep and still, but at the farther end, where the river in passing called to the pool, it broke into waves as it answered the appeal, and added its own contribution to the stream, which went away down to the mill and onwards to the big Thames. On the island were aspens and alders. The floods had loosened the roots of the largest tree, and it hung over heavily in the direction in which it had yielded to the rush of the torrent, but it still held its grip, and the sap had not forsaken a single branch. Every one was as dense with foliage as if there had been no struggle for life, and the leaves sang their sweet song, just perceptible for a moment every now and then in the variations of the louder music below them. It is curious that the sound of a weir is never uniform, but is perpetually changing in the ear even of a person who stands close by. One of the arches of the bridge was dry, and Clara went down into it, stood at the edge and watched that wonderful sight – the plunge of a smooth, pure stream into the great cup which it has hollowed out for itself. Down it went, with a dancing, foamy fringe playing round it just where it met the surface; a dozen yards away it rose again, bubbling and exultant.

She came up from the arch and went home as the sun was setting. She found Mrs. Caffyn alone.

'I have news to tell you,' she said. 'Baruch Cohen is in love with my sister, and she is in love with him' [ch. xxix].

This is the kind of writing that Hale White manages uniquely well. Its qualities are elusive, difficult to characterize adequately. For it is not symbolic in any obvious way (though as I shall show later, Hale White is a minor master in the discreet use of symbols). This is after all a Surrey chalk stream and not the river of life. Yet neither is the rapt, absorbed description there for its own sake. Clara's almost tranced awareness of the life of the stream, her sense of its variousness and irresistible forceful motion, are clearly conditioning factors in her ability to accept what is, and to travel beyond self. Hale White keeps his distance here: he does not intrude to tell us what is happening to Clara. That is why the simplicity of her utterance to Mrs Caffyn is so dramatically right, and moving. There is in it what amounts to an extinction of self. Or rather an extinction of self as personality.

One might try to put it rather differently and say that at this juncture Clara finally renounces egoism for altruism. (She goes to offer her services to Mazzini and we hear at the end of the novel that she has died in the effort to 'free the poor people of Italy who were slaves'.) But no, it won't do. Or rather, though she may think in those terms, Hale White doesn't endorse them. For he consciously belongs to that later moment in time, when George Eliot's kinds of formulation are unavailing. To repeat, he had no saints of humanity. Writing in 1896, the year in which *Clara Hopgood* was published, Joseph Jacobs remarks:

> It is difficult for those who have not lived through it to understand the influence that George Eliot had upon those of us who came to our intellectual 'majority' in the 'seventies'. Darwinism was in the air, and promised, in the suave accents of Professor Huxley and in the more strident voice of Professor Clifford, to solve all the problems of humanity. George Eliot's novels were regarded by us not so much as novels, but rather as applications of Darwinism to life and art.[10]

Unfair to George Eliot, no doubt, but one sees what he means. Hale White's novels pretend to solve none of the 'problems of humanity'. Their reading of life is more muted, the politics more pessimistic. For now an application of Darwinism to life is likely to bring to awareness those separate atoms of existence, purposeless human lives which the best liberal bourgeois consciousness registers so intensely as to find release only in the achievement of selflessness – and that is perilous, intermittent. A comparison of the last sentences of *Middlemarch* and *Clara Hopgood* will make that much plain. The achieved stoicism can lead to a disciplined withdrawal from life or to commitment, but either way the possibilities are strictly limited. Perfectibility, progress, the age of positivism: they play no part in Hale White's fiction. To see why this should be I need to look at how he deals with social change.

II

Coming away from the six novels we can surely be in no doubt that their author is a well-disposed liberal: his voice, his conscience, his kind of awareness testify to his concern over the multiplying horrors of industrialized society, fearful of what they may portend, dubious as to whether any good can come out of mass democracy. The people must be looked after; whether they can look after themselves is not at all clear. In *Deliverance* Mark Rutherford reflects: 'Our civilization seemed nothing but a thin film or crust lying over a volcanic pit, and I often wondered whether the pit would not break up through it and destroy us all' (ch. v). *Deliverance* was published in 1884. Two years later Henry James published the *Princess Cassimassima*, in which he hoped to give some account of the forces gathering under the 'vast smug surface' of society, which might at any moment erupt with terrible destructive power.[11]

James and our author are at one in their appalled recognition of their ignorance of what those forces are. And this brings us to a quite crucial point. For who *is* the author of *Deliverance*, of *The Revolution in Tanner's Lane*, and the rest of them? Well, Hale White, obviously enough. Yes, but the title page of each of the novels insists that the author is Mark Rutherford, and that the manuscript has been 'edited by his friend REUBEN SHAPCOTT'. What are we to make of this? Is it merely a bagatelle, or a piece of elaborate deception for obscure reasons that have never been brought to light? Neither, I think. Hale White has to be distinguished from Mark Rutherford, because in the novels the narrator is clearly part of the novel: that is to say, his voice, conscience and kind of awareness are what, in part at least, the novels are about. Nor is this evasiveness. To be sure, Hale White shares many habits of thought with Mark Rutherford. Even so, he often uses Mark in order to expose the inevitable limitations of Mark's view of the events he narrates and though this is not of great importance in the last three novels it is very important in the earlier ones.

To take one example. In a little essay called 'An Apology', Hale White writes: 'I feel that Milton and Shakespeare are luxuries, and that I really belong to the class which builds palaces for its pleasure, although men and women may be starving on the roads.'[12] In *The Revolution in Tanner's Lane* Mark Rutherford writes: 'Talk about the atrocities of the Revolution! All the atrocities of the democracy heaped together ever since the world began would not equal, if we had any gauge by which to measure them, the atrocities perpetrated in a week upon the poor, simply because they are poor; and the marvel

is, not that there is every now and then a September massacre
at which all the world shrieks, but that such horrors are so
infrequent' (ch. IX). One can find the equivalent of this passage
in *Catherine Furze* and *Clara Hopgood*: bitterly ironic protests at
the plight of the agricultural poor, for example. Yet Rutherford
himself emerges as basically anti-democratic. Shortly after he
has made his remarks about the atrocities of the Revolution, he
notes: 'Nothing is more saddening than the spectacle of a huge
mass of humanity goaded, writhing, starving, and yet so
ignorant that it cannot choose capable leaders, cannot obey
them if perchance it gets them, and does not even know how
to name its wrongs' (ch. XI).

The voice of middle-class liberalism is there unmistakable.
Rutherford is at this point specifically thinking of the march of
the Blanketeers, which occupies an important place in the first
half of *The Revolution in Tanner's Lane*, and about which there
will be more to say. But it is worth noting that he would find
at least one thing more saddening than an unsuccessful movement by a 'huge mass of humanity', and that is a successful one.
In short, Rutherford exhibits the classical dilemma of the liberal
conscience; and the fact that he does so, and the way in which
he does, is surely part of what Hale White's novel is about?
'The Blanketeers shivering on Ardwick Green, the weavers who
afterwards drilled on the Lancashire moors, and were hung
according to law, or killed at Peterloo, are less ridiculous than
those who hung or sabred them, less ridiculous than the
Crimean war and numberless dignified events in human
history, the united achievements of the sovereigns and mini-
stries of Europe' (ch. XIII). Well, yes and no. One wants to
agree with the sentiments, and yet the word 'ridiculous' won't
quite allow that. There is too much vicarious anger in the
rhetoric, too little awareness of how those Blanketeers have
earlier been made nearly ridiculous by Rutherford himself –
'goaded, writhing, starving' – and too much a sense that they
can now safely be made objects of pity because they are dead,
because their protest has so completely failed. For one can
hardly avoid Rutherford's sense of superiority, condescension
even, which heavily qualifies though it doesn't make absurd his
response to popular movements. Such movements are to be
pitied when they fail, anathematized when they succeed

(though of course they never do: at best they create a local and regrettable disturbance, and become examples of the folly of doing as one likes and of not choosing 'capable leaders').

It is worth noting here the riot in Cowfold that follows on the Tory candidate's victory. The issue on which the election has been fought is the repeal of the corn laws, which is about property versus other human rights. The supporters of the defeated candidate break into the taproom of The Angel, one of Cowfold's two pubs, and, 'The spirit-casks were broached, and men turned the gin and brandy taps into their mouths without waiting for glasses. Many of them, especially those who first entered, were at once overcome and dropped, lying about the room and in the gutter perfectly insensible. The remainder, who could only drink what was left, became more and more riotous, and a general sack of all purple property was imminent.' It is of course reminiscent of the great scene of the storming of the Maypole in *Barnaby Rudge*, and even more of the attack on the press-gang in *Sylvia's Lovers*. But Dickens would never be guilty of thinking that if you drink spirits you will be 'at once overcome'. And after all, his great anarchic genius – and just possibly the moment at which he is writing – allows him to see the takeover more in terms of a holiday than is possible in Rutherford's account, or in Mrs Gaskell's. For both of them seem to me classically liberal in their desire to excuse the riot in terms of drink, and excuse the rioters in terms of their thick-headedness. George Allen helps to quell the Cowfold riot, and is aided by one or two magistrates and many property owners. 'Panic and scattering flight at once followed, not, however, before some dozen or other of the fugitives had recovered what little sense they ever had by virtue of sundry hard knocks on their skulls, and a dozen or more had been captured' (ch. xxv).

One could write a very long essay on middle-class Victorian assumptions that all radical behaviour is mixed up with drink, and on the connections between the temperance movement and liberal notions of social melioration (we will be your leaders, and we urge you to keep away from the bottle). For drink is intimately connected with the public-house atmosphere of working-class politics, and therefore of movements which seem to threaten middle-class hopes of melioration; and of course radical political groups nearly always made the public house their place of resort. Mark Rutherford's immediate equation of riot with drunkenness and men of little sense clearly owes a great deal more to a fictional tradition than it does to fact, and sufficiently indicates how he himself can be studied as a subject of great interest: as one kind of well-meaning middle-class man.

The Revolution in Tanner's Lane was published in 1887, and I think of it as a novel very much of the 1880s. It has to be linked with such novels as *Demos*, *The Old Order Changes* and *The Princess Cassimassima* because like them it broods over the possibilities of social upheaval and its consequences. Unlike them, however, it is in part a provincial novel and is set back in time. The *Autobiography* opens with Mark Rutherford remarking that he believes his manuscript to have some historical value, 'for I feel increasingly that the race to which I belong is fast passing away, and that the Dissenting minister of the present day is a different being altogether from the Dissenting minister of forty years ago'. *The Revolution in Tanner's Lane* takes us even further back, to 1814, and moves forward to the 1840s – the time at which all the other novels are set. Why 1814? The answer is that Hale White wants to set before us the political conscience of Dissenters in the early years of the nineteenth century, and then show how that conscience had largely dissolved by the middle of the century.

The novel opens with Zachariah Coleman, London printer, dissenter and radical republican, watching the procession of Louis XVIII through London, on his way home to France. Zachariah has his hat knocked off by a drunken drayman, and is himself saved from severe battering by a Major Maitland, who appears from nowhere and displays a skill in boxing which is altogether too much for the drayman. The Major then accompanies Zachariah home, and enlists him in his Friends of the People Club, a radical-revolutionary organization that meets to debate the people's cause and to make plans for upholding and furthering it.

The Major is an interesting creation. He is no doubt partly based on Major Cartwright, whose portrait hangs in Zachariah's quarters, and on Byron, to whose poetry the Major introduces Zachariah. And Zachariah is equally interesting. Yet in a sense what is most interesting about him is a certain evasiveness in the way he is presented. In the first place, Zachariah appears to have no political contacts until the Major takes him to his club, which is decidedly odd in a man who is surely meant to be representative of intransigent and committed radicalism? As E. P. Thompson has pointed out, it was the artisans – including printers – who were most deeply committed to the radical cause, at least in the large towns, and 'the vast area of Radical London between 1815 and 1850 drew its strength from no major heavy industries . . . but from the host of smaller trades and occupations'.[13] It is astute of Hale White to make Zachariah a printer, odd that he should stress his isolation. Yet one can see why it is done. For Rutherford's implication is that Zachariah's isolation is somehow typical, that there is no powerful popular movement to which he can attach himself. And this is very much an attitude of the 1880s. It belongs to a moment of middle-class panic when the need to play down the possibilities of social upheaval led to the denigration of any popular movement, and even to scepticism about its very popularity. Rutherford remarks that Zachariah 'did not know what the masses really were; for although he worked with his hands, printers were rather a superior set of fellows, and his was an old-established shop which took the best of its class. When brought actually into contact with swearers and drunkards as patriots and performers he was more than a little shocked' (ch. II). The tone of this perfectly captures Rutherford's condescension towards Zachariah, his determination to pinpoint the almost comic unreality of Zachariah's devotion to the cause of radicalism, even though Rutherford wants to honour such devotion. (It is another instance of the split in his conscience.) Certainly the Friends of the People Club is pathetically isolated. Here is Zachariah's introduction to it.[14]

> Entering a low passage at the side of a small public-house, they went up some stairs, and found themselves opposite a door, which was locked. The Major gave three taps and then paused. A moment afterwards he tapped again twice; the lock was turned, and he was admitted. Zachariah found himself in a spacious kind of loft. There was a table running down the middle, and round it were seated about a dozen men, most of whom were smoking and drinking beer. . . . The men and women of that time, although there were scarcely any newspapers, were not fools, and there was not a Nottingham weaver who put a morsel of bread in his hungry belly who did not know that two morsels

might have gone there if there were no impost on foreign corn to maintain rents, and if there were no interest to pay on money borrowed to keep those sacred kings and lords safe in their palaces and parks. Opinion at the Red Lion Friends of the People Club was much divided. Some were for demonstrations and agitations, whilst others were for physical force. The discussion went on irregularly amidst much tumult. . . .

The discussion continued irregularly, and Zachariah noticed that about half-a-dozen of those present took no part in it. At about ten o'clock the chairman declared the meeting at an end; and it was quite time he did so, for the smoke and the drink had done their work [ch. II].

It is a revealing passage. For one thing, Hale White has clearly done his homework with remarkable thoroughness, so that his author can be in a position to know something of those secret meetings that were such a marked feature of radical politics from the 1790s onwards. For another, it is equally clear that Mark cannot find it in himself to be other than condescending towards the kind of meeting he here records.[15] He knows *why* such movements should exist, but he chooses to regard them as faintly comic. For after all, what possible activity can a dozen men commit themselves to? The Red Lion Friends of the People Club is neither ideologically serious nor in any sense representative of a popular movement (how can twelve men be representative of anything?). That is, perhaps, why Zachariah is permitted to belong to it, for 'Zachariah, it will be borne in mind, although he was a Democrat, had never really seen the world. He belonged to a religious sect. He believed in the people, it is true, but it was a people of Cromwellian Independents.' How's that for playing games with the word 'people'?

Zachariah and the Club and his friends, the Major and Caillaud, are thus made somehow peripheral or exotic. Yet at the same time they become representative. That is, what they represent is seen as far more threatening than Rutherford has any right to assume, granted his initial presentation of them. Consider this moment at the Club:

Differences of opinion had arisen as to future procedure, many of the members, the Secretary included. [We know that by now he is in the pay of the government] advocating action; but what they understood by it is very difficult to say. A special call was made for that night,

> and Zachariah was in a difficulty. His native sternness and detestation
> of Kings and their ministers would have led him almost to any length;
> but he had a sober head on his shoulders. So had the Major, and so
> had Caillaud. Consequently they held back, and insisted, before
> stirring a step to actual revolution, that there should be a fair chance
> of support and success [ch. vɪɪɪ].

Now this seems to me very much of the 1880s. For like all novelists of that decade who write about revolution, Mark Rutherford is evading his own subject. Why '*is* it very difficult to say'
what action the many members wanted? Why use the present
tense? Who is Mark talking to? How many is many? On the
previous occasion it had been a dozen, now it feels as though the
many must run into hundreds. It would certainly have to be a
massive number for 'actual revolution' even to be contem-
plated. In short the muddle, coupled with the odd externality
of treatment, makes plain that Mark Rutherford is responding
in no neutral way to what he is apparently merely recording as
fact or history (and of course the novel makes a great deal of
use of historical fact). We are bound to notice that Zachariah,
the Major and Caillaud have become Mark's spokesmen at this
point. (What one might make of the reference to Zachariah's
'sober head') They hold back from revolution, indeed don't
know what the revolution is supposed to be about, even though
they are leading members of the Club!

And then we note that Mark is properly alarmed by his own
evasiveness and tries to make amends by suggesting that after
all his favoured trio were real revolutionaries and knew precisely what they were up to. So immediately after the passage
quoted above, we have this:

> To work hard for those who will thank us, to head a majority against
> oppressors, is a brave thing; but far more honour is due to the Mait-
> lands, Caillauds, Colemans, and others of that stamp who strove for
> thirty years from the outbreak of the French revolution onwards not
> merely to rend the chains of the prisoners, but had to achieve the more
> difficult task of convincing them that they would be happier if they were
> free [ch. vɪɪɪ].

I imagine that there is no need to spell out the confusion in this
passage: how being in the minority against a call for actual
revolution has passed into being a minority who *want* revolution
('to rend the chains of the prisoners'). It is a perfect example of
a typical contradiction in the liberal consciousness: we are to

identify with the trio because they hold back from revolution
and to identify with them because it's not their fault if there
isn't one. Put it another way. Zachariah, the Major and Caillaud are the 'demagogues' so brilliantly defined by E. P. Thompson. And it is worth noting his remark about Major Cartwright:

> It was not Cartwright's intention to form a 'working-class' Radical
> movement. Indeed, he thought it his duty to oppose – 'any attempt to
> excite the poor to invade the property of the rich. It is not by invasion
> of such property that the condition of the poor is to be amended, but
> by . . . EQUAL LAWS . . .'
>   Pressure for reform might best be obtained 'for the most part by
> means of the middle-classes'. He wished to divert insurrectionary
> discontent into constitutional forms, and to lay the basis for a nation-
> wide movement continually petitioning Parliament.[16]

Yes, we want revolution, but no, we don't want it: not unless
we can lead it, and thus make sure that it does not harm our
interests. Sensible enough, no doubt, from Mark's point of view,
but requiring some 'fixing' of history before it can hope to
emerge as fictionally plausible. And as I hope I have shown,
the fixing is inadequate, the fiction *deliberately* implausible
(Hale White's doing).

Only late in the novel does Zachariah announce that 'I believe in insurrection', (whatever happened to his sober head?),
and at this moment his 'republican and revolutionary ardour'
are said to return to him. Yet as we have seen that ardour had
never been so truly revolutionary as to include a belief in insurrection. If he announces a belief in it now (i.e. in the 1840s)
it is only because it is safe for Mark to let him do so, since there
is no chance of it being realized. By which I mean that Mark's
initial audience knew that the 1840s weren't different from the
period between 1814–20, if only because there were *no* insurrec-
tions during the later period. Yes, yes, there should have been:
but thank goodness there weren't. Something like that is behind
the reason for Mark allowing Zachariah the words I have
quoted. And one should note how very much of the 1880s the
novel is when Pauline tells him: 'Father, that is all over now.
We must settle our quarrels in the appointed way.' To which
Zachariah replies: 'All past now, is it? You will see one of these
days' (ch. XXIV, entitled 'I Came Not to Send Peace, But a
Sword'). Those words clearly apply to the 1880s – they rise up

from under the vast smug surface – rather than to the 1840s. As does the fact that after a post-election riot in Cowfold (in the 1840s latter half of the novel), 'Men unknown and never before seen seemed suddenly to spring out of the earth, and as suddenly to disappear. Who were they? Respectable Cowfold, which thought it knew everybody in the place, could not tell. There was no sign of their existence the next day' (ch. xxv).

Now the brilliance of *The Revolution in Tanner's Lane* greatly depends on the fact that Mark's narrative keeps being shown up as contradictory or plain inadequate. For of course in spite of his air of bland confidence he doesn't really know what is going on (are the 'many' six or six hundred, it is difficult to say what the insurrectionaries want?). And so although no direct action results from the wishes of the Friends Club, things *nearly* happen: the secretary is mysteriously killed (his death is never cleared up); and the Major, Caillaud and Zachariah just as mysteriously are warned to make their get away. This section of the novel is altogether mysterious: matters are concealed from us because they are concealed from Mark. In a very proper sense he doesn't know what he's talking about. But what he tacitly admits is that the impetus to and contexts of popular movements are a good deal more complicated than he cares to think probable. Events, and their consequences, are inexplicable to him: they happen but he doesn't really know why.

This is why *The Revolution in Tanner's Lane* begins in 1814. For it is an exploration of the problematic roots of radicalism and working-class protest that was bound to be of immediate interest to an audience of the 1880s. And it is also bound to create interesting – and no doubt, conflicting – tensions of response. Indeed, they are present in Mark. The malign absurdity of the Prince Regent, the suspension of *habeas corpus*, the corrupt system of government spies, the terrible poverty of the newly emergent working class: he responds to these matters with appropriate shock, anger and distress. He also wants to understand the historical moment of which he is writing. There are therefore clumsy moments when he provides a summary of general conditions of the day. As here, for example: 'In 1816 the situation of the working classes had become almost intolerable. Towards the end of the year wheat rose to 103s. a quarter, and incendiarism was common all over England. A

sense of insecurity and terror took possession of everybody'
(ch. x). The clumsiness is the point. For it suggests a painfully
awkward determination to tell the truth, to be as objective as
possible. Yet, as I have shown, such objectivity is impossible,
because Mark's bourgeois consciousness requires that he 'interpret' events in a way that challenges and in the end prohibits
the hoped-for objectivity. We can see how this is so if we look
at the handling of the march of the Blanketeers.

After the discovery of the Friends' 'plot' (I may say that we
are never told what the plot actually involved and Zachariah
doesn't seem to know either), Caillaud and the Major flee the
country and Zachariah and his wife escape to Manchester.
Here, Zachariah meets William Ogden, who recognizes him
because 'he had been sent by the Hampden Club in Manchester
some six months before as a delegate to the Friends of the
People in London' (ch. IX).

The introduction of Ogden is astute for it implies something
of the undoubted mobility of radical leaders during this period
and of their efforts to combine and strengthen radical movements, and also, of course, because it provides further suggestion
of the authenticity of the story. The novel even makes mention
of Ogden's arrest, which happened in March 1817. Thompson
quotes Ogden from Cobbett's *Political Register* as saying that 'the
notorious J. Nadin . . . had for six weeks before declared to me,
from time to time, that if I did not discontinue my attendance
at public meetings he would apprehend me'.[17] Mark refers to
Nadin as the 'notorious chief constable' (ch. XIII), whereas he
was permanent deputy constable, but the error is trivial, and
in no sense affects the sense of actuality which the novel is at
this point striving for. What we have in this section is an
extremely well-managed suggestion of a gathering storm: law
versus radical protest.

The storm breaks with the march of the Blanketeers. But here
matters are far from simple. Caillaud and the Major manage to
get back to Manchester from exile and reluctantly agree to lead
the march. Both of them are killed: the Major sabred by a
soldier, Caillaud hung for shooting the soldier dead. They are
martyrs of the people. Well, there is no disputing the fact that
the march was a disaster. But why make such use of it? As soon
as we ask that question we are bound to realize that there are

subtle and perhaps betraying complexities in the choice and handling of the entire episode. Let me note that in the first place the march cannot be held representative of working-class protest. As Halévy points out, it was not only hopelessly ineffective, it was exploited by the government 'to stimulate public alarm and justify their policy of coercion'. A rumour was put about: 'It was not a mere handful of Lancashire mill hands who were prepared for the march, but the entire proletariat of Lancashire and Yorkshire. Twenty-five thousand firearms, it was reported, were stored at Birmingham ready to be delivered to the marchers as they passed through.'[18] The facts were very different, as Hale White knew from his reading of Bamford. Indeed, Bamford's account of his disapproval of the marchers' plans makes him sound very like the progenitor of Caillaud and the Major.

> 'Suppose,' I said, 'you got to Manchester in the manner recommended, it is ten to one against you, that the authorities of that town will not suffer you to depart in a body; besides, the idea is so monstrously absurd, that no person of common sense would entertain it one moment upon reflection. You tell me, that you suppose there will be many thousands going; how in the name of goodness can such a body be subsisted. If a cold wet night should happen, it would kill a number of you, who perhaps have not had anything like a belly full of meat these many weeks; you would be frozen stiff directly. . . . You should not give way to the notion that you will be everywhere welcome; you perhaps may be under the necessity of passing through some of the rotten Boroughs, against which you have so loudly and so justly complained in your Petition; how do you think the Burgesses of such places would receive you? They would bolt their doors against you and leave you to starve. . . .[19]

We may note that the Major warns the marchers of their inevitable fate, even when they are 'determined, in spite of all argument, to proceed. He pointed out that if they could be so easily scattered when they were thousands strong, every one of them would be cut down or captured before they were twenty miles on the road' (ch. XIII). And Mark is of course in the right of it when he says of the marchers that they were 'ragged many of them; ignorant all; fanatical, penniless', and when he notes 'the absence of all preparations on the part of these Blanketeers' (though whether he is entitled to find this 'in truth, very touching', is not so certain). The majority who set off on the march were country weavers; and Thompson points out that, 'The "rural patriots" were the backbone of the reform movements of these years.'[20] Mark has got that right, too. But what of his response to the march? My own view is that it can be fully appreciated only when we remind ourselves that we are dealing with an 1880s novel. For surely his attitude is contradictory: on the one hand, the marchers are to be taken seriously for they represent a threatening force; on the other, they can be virtually dismissed with a scarcely concealed condescending compassion (they are 'very touching'). 'Respectable Manchester was frightened when the Blanketeers met, and laughed them to scorn when they were dispersed. No wonder, at the laughter! What could be more absurd? . . . Of a truth, not only is the wisdom of this world foolishness, as it ever was, but that to which this world is foolishness is judged wisdom by the Eternal Arbiter.' The tone there subtly blends righteous indignation with a decent – but evasive – sympathy. And it tends to dissolve the real complexities of the situation, at the same time as being perhaps the most generous interpretation of events that we can reasonably expect. For I do not wish to give the impression that Hale White is in any sense unsympathetic to Mark, or that we are entitled to be so. It is simply that Mark's consciousness filters the historic actualities in a way that allows him to 'understand' them in terms of his liberalism, and that such understanding releases contradictions which he can hope to bring under control only by a tone of voice – a response – that is wise, sorrowing, indignant. For what Mark does is to fall back on his own dissenting faith as explanation and consolation. So, after the dispersal of the Marchers, he comments: 'The test of faith is its power under defeat, and these silly God-fearing souls argued to themselves that their Master's time was not their time; that perhaps they were being punished for their sins, and that when it pleased Him they would triumph.' Now that is perfectly just: Mark here pins down the chiliastic element in non-conformist religions, and also reveals the non-conformist habit of interpreting political reversals in irrelevant doctrinal terms. But then he goes on:

> Essentially right they were, right in every particular, excepting perhaps, that it was not for their own sins that this visitation came upon them. Visitation for sin it was certainly, but a visitation for the sins of

others – such is the way of Providence, and has been ever since the
world began, much to the amazement of many reflective persons. . . .
It was not yet God's time in 1817, but God's time was helped forward,
as it generally is, by this anticipation of it [ch. xiii].

So those 'silly' souls are essentially right. Yet again we note the
contradictions in what Mark says and recognize his conflicting
desires not to take the marchers seriously and, at the same time,
to do them full justice. And that is why Hale White chooses to
make much of the march: it is a historical moment that can't be
made convenient sense of from a liberal point of view. Indeed
it is important because, as a moment of real crisis, it produces
crisis and contradiction in any liberal attempt to account for it.

III

After the episode of the Blanketeers and the deaths of the Major
and Caillaud the novel jumps forward in time. Part Two, which
is about the revolution in Tanner's Lane, is set in a small south
Midlands town in the early 1840s. This half of the novel is at
least partly about the decay of dissent.[21] It no longer attracts or
moulds men of principle. Instead, dissenters are typically corrupted by their desire for respectability. The interests of trade
and of class – no dissenter is sure he will not need to climb –
conspire to erode the structures of a once-potent intellectual,
moral and political movement.

Anyone reading the novel is bound to notice how odd, jagged
and abrupt the break between the two parts feels. But of course
this is Hale White's point. It is not evidence of faulty construction, but a proper means of dramatizing his own sense of a
crumbling tradition: there are very few links or continuities
between Zachariah's kind of dissenting conscience and that of
the community in Tanner's Lane. Indeed, the plotting of the
novel emphasizes discontinuity. When Zachariah's first wife
dies, he marries Caillaud's daughter, Pauline. She dies in
childbirth, leaving an only daughter who is also called Pauline,
and who is as fierce a radical as her mother and grandfather had
been. Near the end of the novel, George Allen's silly but loved
wife dies and since George is friendly with Zachariah and of an
age with Pauline and a radical, all is set for their marriage. But

it does not happen. Instead, George sails with the rest of his family for America. Pauline is lost to sight. She disappears into history, carrying with her the disappearance of one phase of radical thought. The novel ends with these words: 'What became of Zachariah and Pauline? At present I do not know.'

There are continuities, of course. The fact that Zachariah proves to be a friend of the Allens, who are the only real radicals of the Tanner's Lane community, is evidence of that. Nor is it merely playing with words to say that the tradition to which Zachariah belongs is shown to be continuously in decline. Indeed, he himself is part of it. He finds he cannot bear witness to his faith before the Major, Caillaud and the elder Pauline. 'He was at least a century and a half too late. He struggled, wrestled, self against self, and failed, not through want of courage, but because he wanted a deeper conviction' (ch. VI). And when he sees Caillaud's daughter Pauline dance 'he would liked to have got up and denounced Jean and Pauline, but somehow he could not. His great great grandfather would have done it, beyond a doubt, but Zachariah sat still' (ch. v).

Yet Zachariah is a man who struggles hard to abide by his conscience; and who, as we have seen, is a radical. Mark admires him, and makes him admirable to us. Zachariah is, indeed, one of those touching and entirely authentic studies of the dissenting conscience at which Hale White excels, as he does with another type to which Zachariah belongs: that of the intelligent, inquiring man or woman who, without any conventional social advantages, take for granted their right to exercise their intelligence as fully as they can. Hale White knew such people well enough, and he knew their opposite: the smug, hypocritical, intellectually vacuous kind represented by the aptly named Mr Snale of the *Autobiography* and by the Reverend John Broad in *The Revolution in Tanner's Lane*. He had met them in the Bedford of his boyhood, on which Cowfold is based. In the *Autobiography* the dissenting community is shown as a good deal more stifling and joyless than it is in *The Revolution in Tanner's Lane*. This is not surprising, for in the later novel Mark is writing as an outsider, whereas in the first two novels he is his own chief subject. And his deliverance is from the kind of suffocating emphasis on self (and especially self-unworthiness) that non-conformism occasions. There is a particularly powerful episode when Mark, already beginning to experience doubts because of his association with the free-thinking journalist, Edward Mardon, is taken on by a Unitarian community. Its method, he says,

> . . . was as strict as that of the most rigid Calvinist. They plumed themselves, however, greatly on their intellectual superiority over the Wesleyans and Baptists round them; and so far as I could make out, the only topics they delighted in, were demonstrations of the unity of God from texts in the Bible, and polemics against tri-theism. Sympathy with the great problems then beginning to agitate men, they had none. Socially they were cold, and the entertainment at their houses was pale and penurious [ch. vii].

The *Autobiography* can be linked to such works as *Robert Elsmere* and *Father and Son,* all of them accounts of loss of faith, of the aching gaps that open up between an individual and that community which claims his allegiance. But Hale White emerges as clearly superior to Mrs Humphry Ward and Gosse, not simply in the fact that he writes very much better than either, but because of his ability to give the *feel* of such a community (a gift he shares with the Arnold Bennett of *Anna of the Five Towns*): its piety, earnestness, at its best, caring, at its frequent worst, small-minded nastiness.

Of course Hale White is a master of the provincial novel, a fact which yet again reminds us of his admiration for George Eliot. But one important difference between them is that the characteristic movement of a Hale White novel is carried through the individual's growing sense of separation from his community; and in this sense he is more like Hardy than George Eliot. His awareness of the constant series of ruptures between an individual and his sense of community, and his recognition that this is a continuous and ceaseless process is very like Hardy, as is his understanding that there is no such thing as a 'settled' past. No phase of these movements and ruptures is offered as isolated or exotic. Where he is like both George Eliot and Hardy is in recognizing the tensions that are bound to be set up between an individual's sense of belonging and his equally strong sense of wanting to be free from commitment to community; and of the agonies that such tensions can cause. In the *Autobiography* and *Deliverance* Mark seeks escape from these

tensions by moving to London and eventually by marrying; and
this is a pattern which tends to be repeated in all the novels. I
shall return to this point, because it is crucially important. But
before I do so I need to say a little more about the treatment of
dissent in the novels, and especially in *The Revolution in Tanner's
Lane*.

We are told that John Broad's predecessor in Tanner's Lane
had been a man called Harden. The Bunyan-like names make
their point. Whereas Harden had been a man of uncompromis-
ing principle, Broad is a man of no principle whatsoever. He
believes in keeping clear of politics. Indeed, he counsels his son,
Thomas, not to have anything to do with Zachariah and
Pauline, when Thomas goes to London (in fact Thomas tries to
seduce Pauline, but she is more than a match for him).
Zachariah, he tells his son, is reputed to be 'inclined towards
infidelity', and also is 'not considered respectable' (ch. xix).
The double irony is obvious enough, but it is important to
register its significance. For it is the desire for respectability
which above all else spells death for dissent, simply because it
destroys the principles of which dissent depends. In the *Autobiography* Mark notes:

> Salvation is the spectacle of a victory by another over foes like our own.
> The story of Jesus is the story of the poor and forgotten. He is not the
> Saviour for the rich and prosperous, for they want no saviour. The
> healthy, active and well-to-do need Him not, and require nothing
> more than is given by their own health and prosperity. But every one
> who has walked in sadness because his destiny has not fitted his
> aspirations; everyone who, having no opportunity to lift himself out
> of his little narrow town or village circle of acquaintances, has thirsted
> for something beyond what they could give him; everybody who, with
> nothing but a dull, daily round of a mechanical routine before him,
> would welcome death, if it were martyrdom for a cause; every humblest
> creature, in the obscurity of great cities or remote hamlets, who
> silently does his or her duty without recognition – all these turn to
> Jesus, and find themselves in Him [ch. iv].

That is the true voice of dissent, I think, and it explains why
Hale White should see the decay of dissenting movements as
intimately bound up with class considerations, with the whole
complicated movements up and down the social scale which in
a very real sense is what English society in the nineteenth century is all about. John Broad desires respectability (we are told

that that was why he went to Dissenting College in the first place). He will not give support to anything smacking of radical politics for that will lose him some of his 'better' congregations (in the *Autobiography* Mr Snale, who is in trade, writes a letter against Mark's interest in a drainage scheme, protesting his surprise that 'a minister of religion should interfere in politics'). The long-smouldering row between the Broads and the Allens, which is very well observed, finally breaks out because in the local election Broad seems to be giving his support to the Tory cause rather than the Whig (which is identified with the repeal of the corn laws).

Broad's son doesn't go to the day school because his mother objects to the 'mixture'. And like his father, he is sent to Dissenting College not because he has any sense of a calling for the ministry but because it will be an eminently respectable profession. It is significant that when Thomas goes to see the Colemans he fails to recognize the portrait of Major Cartwright. The clear-cut virtues of this part of the novel require no comment.

In the next two novels the decadence of dissent is taken for granted. *Miriam's Schooling* is also set in Cowfold in the 1840s. Hale White neatly establishes the town's somnolent, incurious way of life and in doing so establishes the fact that Mark as narrator is now utterly remote from a world that the *Autobiography* had shown him to be originally a part of. The remoteness comes out in such passages as the following: 'In those days in Cowfold the church people, and for that matter the Dissenters too, did not read their Bible; but among the Dissenters there was here and there a remnant of the ancient type to whom the Bible was everything. Among the church people there were none' (p. 65).[22] *Catherine Furze* is set in a Midlands town called Eastthorpe, yet again in the 1840s; and is much concerned with Mrs Furze's desire to 'rise'. This means that among other matters she wants the family to abandon their present home, above Mr Furze's ironmongery shop, and move to the Terrace, which will be, she tells her husband, 'a good opportunity for us to exchange the chapel for the church. We have attended the chapel regularly, but I have always felt a kind of prejudice there against us, or at least against myself, and there is no denying that the people who go to church are vastly more

---

genteel, and so are the service and everything about it – the vespers – the bells – somehow there is a respectability in it' (ch. II). There is some fine fun in the novel at the expense of Mrs Furze's social ambitions, in particular a richly comic scene where she is endlessly embarrassed by her housemaid while trying to impress the brewer's wife, Mrs Colson. But what she represents is serious enough, and is taken seriously. For as with *The Revolution in Tanner's Lane* so *Catherine Furze* is about discontinuities.

'Mrs. Furze's separation from her former friends was now complete' (ch. IX). The words indicate surely enough one of the main concerns of this novel. And they have an interest which goes beyond what they tell us of Mrs Furze. We are invited to respond to her with contempt, as we are the Reverend John Broad. Yet their sense of separateness from their community, and their desire to belong to another 'higher' one is shared by Miriam, by Catherine and by Madge and Clara Hopgood. And by Mark himself: 'The society amongst the students was very poor. Not a single friendship formed then has remained with me. They were mostly young men of no education, who had been taken from the counter, and their spiritual life was not very deep.' That comes from chapter two of the *Autobiography*, and its tone is one characteristic of the novel as a whole. Mark feels an aloof distaste for the various communities he is supposed to serve, and his deliverance is from them just as much as it is from the dissenting religions which help define the communities. Throughout the *Autobiography* we are kept aware of Mark's feeling of distaste, boredom and often plain revulsion for the society he encounters; and increasingly he retreats into himself – or into what he calls his 'monomania'. He uses the word after he has been rejected by Mardon's daughter, Mary. 'For weeks I was prostrate, with no power of resistance; the evil being intensified by my solitude' (ch. VII). For the alternative to identification with the community is identification with one or two others, in friendship and love. And to put the matter that way is again to see how important an invention Mark Rutherford is, and how his mode of consciousness is essentially that liberal one which comes increasingly into prominence towards the end of the nineteenth century and is so crucial a feature of much Edwardian fiction.

In *Catherine Furze* we are presented with two worlds: the one Mrs Furze wishes to inhabit and the one that appeals to her daughter, the world of the Bellamy's farm. Yet there is no escapist pastoral about this latter world, no suggestion of the kind of ahistoric paradise one associates with Hayslope farm, for example. Indeed, we are forced to recognize that this is a world of acute and terrible suffering. I think in particular of the long passage which is taken up with the death from consumption of Mrs Furze's maid, Phoebe. Catherine goes to sit with her:

Her father was an agricultural labourer, and lived in a little four-roomed, whitewashed cottage about a mile and a half out of the village. The living-room faced north-east, the door opening direct on the little patch of garden, so that in winter, when the wind howled across the level fields, it was scarcely warmer indoors than outside, and rags and dish-clouts had to be laid on the door-sill to prevent the entrance of the snow and rain. At the back was a place, half outhouse, half kitchen, which had once a brick floor, but the bricks had disappeared. Upstairs, over the living-room, was a bedroom, with no fireplace, and a very small casement window, where the mother and three children slept, the oldest a girl of about fourteen, the second a boy of twelve, and the third a girl of three or four, for the back bedroom over the out-house had been given up to Phoebe since she was ill. The father slept below on the floor. Phoebe's room also had no fireplace, and great patches of plaster had been brought down by the rain on the south-west side. Just underneath the window was the pigstye. Outside nothing had been done to the house for years. It was not brick built, and here and there the laths and timbers were bare, and the thatch had almost gone. Houses were very scarce on the farms in that part, and landlords would not build. The labourers consequently were driven into Ab-church, and had to walk, many of them, a couple of miles each way daily. Miss Diana Eaton, eldest daughter of the Honourable Mr. Eaton, had made a little sketch in water-colour of the cottage. It hung in the great drawing-room, and was considered most picturesque.

'Lovely! What a dear old place!' said the guests.

'It makes one quite enamoured of the country,' exclaimed Lady Fanshawe, one of the most determined diners-out in Mayfair. 'I never look at a scene like that without wishing I could give up London altogether. I am sure I could be content. It would be so charming to get rid of conventionality and be perfectly natural. You really ought to send that drawing to the Academy, Miss Eaton.'

That we should take pleasure in pictures of filthy, ruined hovels, in which health and even virtue are impossible, is a strange sign of the times. It is more than strange; it is an omen and a prophecy that people will go into sham ecstasies over one of these pigstyes so long as it is a gilt frame; that they will give a thousand guineas for its light and shade – light, forsooth! – or for its Prout-like quality, or for its quality of this, that, and the other, while inside the real stye, at the very moment when the auctioneer knocks down the drawing amidst applause, lies the mother dying from dirt fever; the mother of six children starving and sleeping there – starving, save for the parish allowance, for the snow is on the ground and the father is out of work [ch. xviii].

I should like to go on quoting from this, but perhaps I have offered enough for it to be clear how impressive a piece of de-mystifying it represents. Mark's consciousness is too acutely sensitive to permit him any suggestion that the rural world composes an idyll into which Catherine can escape from the pressures of the real world. Which is not to say that the Bel-lamy's farm isn't attractive, but that we – and she – have to recognize the existence of the real styes that make its attractive-ness possible. It is not 'perfectly natural' at all, but dependent on economic forces every bit as conditioning as those of the city.

Yet Catherine is offered a kind of escape – or so it may seem. Mrs Furze thinks that the girl should be sent away from home for a while. 'Her education is very imperfect, and there are establishments where young ladies are taken at her age and finished. It would do her a world of good' (ch. vi). We are reminded that Miriam had left Cowfold for London and that we have been shown the dullness of Cowfold life as sufficient cause for her pleasurable anticipation of the change (though what she actually finds in London is very different from her dream); and we may note that the Hopgood girls don't at all like Fenmarket. Their father has come from London and has made sure that his daughters 'received an education much above that which was usual amongst people in their position, and each of them – an unheard of wonder in Fenmarket – had spent some time in a school in Weimar' (ch. i).

We are certainly not meant to approve of Mrs Furze's snob-bishly conceived plans for Catherine, yet we are bound to recognize that elsewhere in the novels the yearning for freedom from the narrow bounds of provincial life is treated with under-standing and approval. It is so in the *Autobiography*, for example. Moreover, if we think of the fictions as a whole, which I think we are entitled to do since it is the one man who narrates them all, we can see that Mark's shifting attitudes to education form an essential part of his consciousness: they register a tussle that goes on within him, between the side that yearns for community and the other side which acknowledges its limitations and the frustrations they bring.

IV

From the *Autobiography* on, the central characters of all the novels are seeking marriages which will act as consolation against or refuge from the limitations of community. As we have seen, the young Mark Rutherford is oppressed by his sense of the petty-spirited people among whom he works; he feels himself to be remote from them, and he falls hopelessly in love with Mary Mardon. But before that he has been unofficially engaged to a girl called Ellen. Ellen is an ardent, incurious believer in the faith that he comes increasingly to doubt. Eventually he feels himself compelled to break off their engagement, because he recognizes that there is no intellectual compatibility between them. But he agonizes over his decision and makes up his mind to go through with it only when one of his very few friends, a Miss Arbour, tells him of her unhappy marriage to a Mr Hexton. She had disregarded her own impulse to reject him, she tells Mark: 'I thought him mean, and . . . felt he lacked sympathy with me', had married and soon found that 'he was entirely insensible to everything for which I most cared. Before our marriage he had affected a sort of interest in my pursuits, but in reality he was indifferent to them. He was cold, hard, and impenetrable' (ch. v). Fired by Miss Arbour's passionate plea that he should save himself and Ellen 'from something worse than death', Mark breaks off his engagement.[23] Mark's love for Mary is very different from his love for Ellen: 'I thought I chose Mary, but there was no choice. The feeblest steel filing which is drawn to a magnet would think, if it had consciousness, that it went to the magnet of its own free will. My soul rushed to her as if dragged by the force of a loadstone' (ch. vii). I quote that because the imagery reveals something about a *kind* of love which Mark experiences for Mary. It may almost be called an elective affinity, it is intensely romantic and, as we shall see, it is explored with great subtlety in *Catherine Furze* and *Clara Hopgood*.

D

Being denied Mary's love is a terrific shock to Mark, almost a denial of himself, a threat to his identity; which is of course what that kind of love is about ('Nellie, I *am* Heathcliffe'). For such a relationship provides a creation of self that can stand as a radical alternative to self defined in terms of relation to community. (It is no accident that Mary, the free-thinker, is a social outcast.) Now that Mark is cut off from any sense of relationship he is bound to feel appallingly insecure. The lowest point is reached when he agrees to teach at a school in Stoke Newington. He arrives one evening, before the beginning of the school term, and is given a meal.

> The tray was set down on the master's raised desk, and sitting there I ate my supper in silence, looking down upon the dimly-lighted forms, and forward into the almost absolute gloom. . . . I went to the window and looked out. There were scattered lights here and there marking roads, but as they crossed one another, and now and then stopped where buildings had ceased, the effect they produced was that of bewilderment with no clue to it. Further off was the great light of London, like some unnatural dawn, or the illumination from a fire which could not itself be seen. I was overcome with the most dreadful sense of loneliness [ch. vIII].

There is a most delicate blend of the outer and inner worlds in this remarkable passage, typified by the carefully placed phrase 'the almost absolute gloom' (the word has here the kind of resonance that one associates with Hardy's use of it). The gloom is both projected by the mind and received by it. The outer world cannot be made sense of, both because this man has lost all his bearings – religion, community, fiancée, love – and because it is terrifyingly unknowable. There is no clue to it. The lights which should illuminate fail to do so. Even the apparent cliché of 'the great light' of London is properly in place. Mark has been drawn to London to escape the miseries and restrictions he associates with his provincial world, but he has not entered a new world: the dawn is unnatural: he is still an outsider. Yet London may offer warmth and consolation – to others, if not to him. 'A fire which could not itself be seen', may suggest a hellishness, but it just as surely releases the notion of companionship, of human stir, from which he is excluded. The last sentence of the passage thus leads perfectly out of what has preceded it, and is in no sense abrupt or unprepared for.

The terrible turning-in on the self is underpinned when Mark, recalling that time, says: 'I remember the thought of all the happy homes which lay around me, in which there dwelt men who had found a position, an occupation, and, above all, affection' (ch. vIII). It is the nub of the matter. Denied love and companionship, Mark feels himself to be hardly human.

His situation worsens. The day after his arrival, he goes for a walk with some of the boys. 'My companions were dejected, and so was I.' He determines to escape and when he is clear of the school gates, 'I literally cried tears of joy.' Deliverance has begun. And one notes the Wordsworthian words by means of which it is signalled: the movement from dejection to joy is one which that great poet charted often enough. An inner assertion, a sudden spring of action, has brought Mark back to life.

I put it like that because it helps to explain what happens next, what 'deliverance' actually is. Mark moves from self-absorption to absorption in others. The crucial catalyst in aiding this movement is a girl called Theresa, whom he meets at the house of the publisher, Wollaston, for whom he now works and with whom he lodges. Wollaston and Theresa are, of course, based on Chapman and George Eliot, though it must be noted that they are properly present as fictional characters in the *Autobiography*, and that Hale White calls the girl Theresa not as a way of making a sly nod in the direction of *Middlemarch* but because it helps us to focus on the kind of intensity and significance that she has in his novel. The most important moment comes when Wollaston and Mark speak of a book 'which everybody was reading then, and I happened to say that I wished people who wrote novels would not write as if love were the very centre and sum of human existence. A man's life was made up of so much besides love.' Theresa bursts out at him.

'I do not agree with you,' said Theresa. 'I disagree with you utterly. I dislike foolish inane sentiment – it makes me sick; but I do believe, in the first place, that no man was ever good for anything, who has not been devoured, I was going to say, by great devotion to a woman. . . . A Man, worthy to be named a man, will find the fact of love perpetually confronting him till he reaches old age, and if he be not ruined by worldliness or dissipation, will be troubled by it when he is fifty as much as when he was twenty-five. It is the subject of all subjects. People abuse love, and think it is the cause of half the mischief in the

88 *The Literature of Change*

world. It is the one thing that keeps the world straight, and if it were
not for the overpowering instinct, human nature would fall asunder;
would be the prey of inconceivable selfishness and vices, and finally,
there would be universal suicide' [ch. ıx].

As the last part of the passage makes plain, Theresa is not
merely talking about the romantic love that Mark had felt for
Mary. Indeed, that kind of love has little relevance to her
words. Far more important is the notion of selfless love, of
altruism perhaps one should call it. And Mark's ultimate deliverance into something that we may call absorption in others,
is a kind of commitment that does service as best it can for the
sense of community which it largely replaces.

Putting the matter this way may make it seem heavily dependent on George Eliot's moral philosophy. And to be sure,
elements are akin. You must accept your fellow mortals, George
Eliot famously wrote in chapter xvıı of *Adam Bede*: 'you can
neither straighten their noses, nor brighten their wit, nor
rectify their dispositions; and it is these people – amongst whom
your life is passed – that it is needful you should tolerate, pity,
and love: it is these more or less ugly, stupid, inconsistent
people, whose movements of goodness you should be able to
admire – for whom you should cherish all possible hopes, all
possible patience.' Now in all of Hale White's fiction we find
examples of what it seems fair to call uninstructed goodness:
that is, more or less ugly, stupid, inconsistent people, who
behave selflessly, who demonstrate love for their fellow-men,
and who, in doing so, reveal a kind of decency, a way of living,
that has much to do with the prescription for moral magnani-
mity which George Eliot sets out in *Adam Bede*, and nothing to
do with what in *Deliverance* is called 'this poor petty self'.

'The very centre of existence of the ordinary chapel-goer and
church-goer needs to be shifted from self to what is outside self'
(*Deliverance*, ch. vı). Mark's words bring him very close to Hale
White's admiration for Spinoza's rejection of 'personality'. 'We
are anxious about what we call "personality" but in truth there
is nothing in it of any worth, and the less we care for it the more
"blessed" we are.'

The 'blessed' of Hale White's fictions include Mrs Carter,
who looks after both Zachariah and his wife when they are ill:
'Critics said she ruled her husband; but what husband would

not rejoice in being so ruled? . . . He wanted to be directed, and he gladly saw the reins in the hands of his "missus", of whom he was justly proud' (*The Revolution in Tanner's Lane*, ch. XIII). There is Miss Tippit, the despised spinster of *Miriam's Schooling*, who nurses Miriam through her fever although Miriam had been impatient of the older woman's earlier illness; there is Mrs Bellamy, whom Catherine Furze adores, and who does unerringly right by others, though a frustrated woman herself: 'Mrs. Bellamy's mind, unoccupied with parental cares, with politics, or with literature, lets itself loose upon her house, her dairy, and her fowls. . . . She brooded much, and the moment she had nothing to do she became low-spirited and unwell' (ch. IV). And there is Mrs Caffyn, who helps Madge Hopgood when the girl is heavy with her illegitimate baby, and of whom it is said that 'the stamp on Mrs. Caffyn's countenance was indubitable; it was evidently no forgery, but of royal vintage' (*Clara Hopgood*, ch. XI). It is worth noting that all these selfless people are women, that all are 'uninstructed' in that they are either illiterate or incurious about ideas and basically anti-intellectual, and that all are spoken of in terms that inevitably recall Mrs Poyser or Dolly Winthrop or Mary Garth.

Yet having said this much it is necessary once again to point to the difference between George Eliot and Hale White, one that again shows just how much of a late-nineteenth-century novelist he is. For running through his fiction is a dark awareness of the pitiful frailty of the actions of his good people. Without love 'human nature would fall asunder'. Theresa's words help to occasion Mark's deliverance; but the long look at the worst of contemporary life which is then forced on him decisively undermines the kind of resilience to be found in George Eliot's fiction, and which she can maintain because of her careful control over historical setting. History is a mess to Mark, and it offers no comfort to Hale White.

Deliverance opens with Mark in the appallingly hostile and miserable world of London, where 'hope, faith and God seemed impossible amidst the smoke of the streets' (ch. I). He becomes friendly with a fellow journalist, M'Kay, whose pathetic but unsatirically treated hope is 'nothing less than gradually to attract Drury Lane to come and be saved'.

> The first Sunday I went with him to the room. As we walked over the Drury Lane gratings of the cellars a most foul stench came up, and one in particular I remember to this day. A man half dressed pushed open a broken window beneath us, just as we passed by, and there issued such a blast of corruption, made up by gases bred by filth, air breathed and rebreathed a hundred times, charged with odours of unnameable personal uncleanness and disease, that I staggered to the gutter with a qualm which I could scarce conquer. At the doors of the houses stood grimy girls with their arms folded and their hair disordered. Grimier boys and girls had tied a rope to broken railings, and were swinging on it. . . . There was no break in the uniformity of the squalor; nor was it even possible for any single family to emerge amidst such altogether suppressive surroundings. All self-respect all effort to do anything more than to satisfy somehow the grossest wants, had departed [ch. II].

This is the London of Gissing's *Nether World*, although obviously not explored as Gissing explores it, for Hale White's concern is to register the shock of the city on Mark's sensitive mind (his response to it, as voyager through its hell, is in its attempted precision of statement sharply reminiscent of Engels's on Manchester, or of Andrew Mearns's in *The Bitter Cry of Outcast London*, as is his tendency towards generalization: 'All self-respect, all effort' etc.). What counts for most is the exposure of the frail absurdity of Mark's Christian hopes. For he registers this world as one of utter spiritual death and degradation. 'The desire to decorate existence in some way or other with more or less care is nearly universal. . . . It is the commentary on the text that man shall not live by bread alone. It is evidence of an acknowledged compulsion – of which art is the highest manifestation – to *escape*. In the alleys behind Drury Lane this instinct, the very salt of life, was dead, crushed out utterly, a symptom which seemed to me ominous, and even awful to the last degree' (ch. II). And there we have the liberal consciousness at its most melioristic and therefore vulnerable, brought to final awareness of its pathetic inadequacy. Its implicitly generous account of Jesus would have been powerless here; in fact, no known stimulus, nothing ever held up before men to stir the soul to activity, can do anything in the back streets of cities so long as they are the cesspools which they are now.' There is some deliverance from despair in the rhetorical anger of the last part of that sentence. And yet the rhetoric is hardly more than a kind of escapism, and is itself rebuked by

the actuality of human suffering which Mark is made to confront as he and M'Kay work at their hopeless plans for the
Drury Laners. For the fact is that *no* individual response, no
matter how generously intentioned, can cope with the realities
that confront it and with which it tries to deal.

> To stand face to face with the insoluble is not pleasant. A man will do
> anything rather than confess it is beyond him. He will create pleasant
> fictions, and fancy a possible escape here and there, but this problem
> of Drury Lane was round and hard like a ball of adamant. The only
> thing I could do was faintly, and I was about to say, stupidly hope –
> for I had no rational, tangible grounds for hoping – that some force
> of which we are now not aware might some day develop itself which
> will be able to resist and remove the pressure which sweeps and
> crushes into hell, sealed from the upper air, millions of human souls
> every year in one quarter of the globe alone [ch. v].

That passage is one of the most remarkable evocations of the
liberal conscience that I know, and once again demonstrates
the rightness of Hale White's invention of Mark. It doesn't
satirize him, nor does it invite us to distance him from our
sympathies. But it does troublingly lay bare the hopelessness of
his hoped-for solutions (toleration, pity, love?), reveal them, as
he confesses, as no more than 'pleasant fictions'. And by that I
take him to mean that one or two atypical individuals will of
course struggle free from their hell, will achieve a thoroughly
unrepresentative deliverance from it (as we read on, deliverance and escape seem, ominously, to become almost interchangeable words).

It is not surprising, and again is no cause for satire, that
Mark should seek to evade the full implications of his look at the
worst. So we have this meditation from him:

> No theory of the world is possible. The storm, the rain slowly rotting
> the harvest, children sickening in cellars are obvious; but equally
> obvious are an evening in June, the delight men and women take in
> one another, in music, and in the exercise of thought. There can
> surely be no question that the sum of satisfaction is increasing, not
> merely in the gross but for each human being, as the earth from which
> we sprang is being worked out of the race, and a higher type is being
> developed [ch. VI].

The optimistic Darwinism of that makes Mark sound not unlike
Frederic Harrison (or George Eliot at her most unguarded),
and is irreconcilably at odds with his perception of London as

hell – as, indeed, an exemplar of a thoroughly pessimistic
reading of Darwin. Everything tends down, not up; the fittest
alone survive, and they are comparatively few. Walking along
the Edgware Road one night in the 1890s, Arthur Symons
wondered at the people he passed, wondered:

> Why these people exist, why they take the trouble to go on existing. . . .
> As I passed through the Saturday night crowd lately, between two
> opposing currents of evil smells, I overheard a man who was lurching
> along the pavement say in a contemptuous comment: – 'Twelve o'clock:
> we may all be dead by twelve o'clock.' He seemed to sum up the
> philosophy of that crowd, its listlessness, its hard unconcern, its failure
> to be interested. Nothing matters, he seemed to say for them; let us
> drag out our time until the time is over, and the sooner it is over the
> better.[24]

That kind of appalled pessimism strikes a note almost identical
with one to be found in *Miriam's Schooling*, where Miriam,
adrift in London, finds herself in

> A dismal, most depressing region, one on which the sun never shone,
> gloomy on the brightest day. It was impossible to enter it without
> feeling an instantaneous check to all lightness of the heart. . . . Thither
> went Miriam that night; and when she reached the dock, the tempta-
> tion presented itself to her with fearful force to throw herself in it and
> be at rest. . . . Miriam did not know that her misery was partly a
> London misery, due to the change from fresh air and wholesome living
> to foul air and unnatural living [pp. 112–13].

It is a crucially important passage because it draws our attention to Mark's intervening voice, offering to explain and as-
suage the horror of Miriam's experience. Once again, he
attempts to deflect attention from a full look at the worst to a
comforting notion of fresh air and wholesome living (he later
suggests that 'the peculiar sourness of modern democracy is due
perhaps to deficiency of oxygen and sunlight', p. 124), and
once again we notice how deliverance and escape can look like
interchangeable words.

But London, its horrors and what they portend, is inescapably
present. In *Deliverance* we are introduced to four of the Drury
Laners for whom escape is an impossibility. There is Taylor, a
broken-spirited messenger, who can have no possible way out
of the humiliations to which he is constantly subjected. There
is Cardinal, a travelling salesman, constantly at the mercy of a
crazed, jealous wife. There is Clark, who has a great love of

books, and whose passion for 'culture' makes him increasingly and hopelessly depressed with his own life. Clark, I may note, is infinitely more convincingly written about than is Leonard Bast, but he is like him and, for that matter, also like the failed literary characters of Gissing's *New Grub Street* and Bennett's *A Man from the North*, because in every case their presence is intend to imply a world of inevitable failure in the presentation of which there can be no possibility of irony, satire or moral rebuke. Simply, this is how it is.[25] 'Everything which he saw which was good and seemed only to sharpen the contrast between himself and his lot, and his reading was a curse to him rather than a blessing. I sometimes wished that he had never inherited any love whatever for what is usually considered to be the Best . . .' (ch. v). Impossible to avoid the implied reference there to be the liberal dreams of spreading sweetness and light through the Best that has been Thought and Said, and impossible to avoid recognizing the wanness of the dream.

The fourth man is John, a waiter of sixty, who has 'no particular character left in him. He may once have been this or that, but every angle was now knocked off, as it is knocked off from the rounded pebbles which for ages have been dragged up and down the beach by the waves' (ch. v). The image is significant. It reinforces the notion of those lives which are subject to a natural law indifferent to or even alien from human needs and purpose. This is the pessimistic Darwinism that acts as a final overthrow of any hope for meliorism or progress, and leaves only the hopeless hope for some 'force of which we are now not aware'. The dilemmas and contradictions which Mark's experience open him to are, of course, everywhere in Hale White's fiction, but perhaps never so relentlessly pursued as in *Deliverance*.

What then is 'Deliverance'? Deliverance from London itself, perhaps, for deliverance into absorption with others in terms of London can become so appallingly bleak a matter as to be no true deliverance at all (except in so far as it delivers Mark into an intermittent awareness of the illusions of his liberal beliefs). But deliverance from London means either escape into 'oxygen and sunlight' – and we have already seen how in the fiction that possibility is denied or turns out to be another middle-class dream – or it means deliverance from total isolation into marriage. Yet even this form of deliverance proves ambiguous. Certainly, it is presented as no rosy dream world of achieved withdrawal. Throughout *Deliverance* our attention is drawn to fractured or destroyed marriages. M'Kay is openly contemptuous of his wife's limited mind, John's marriage is ruined by his wife's drunkenness, Cardinal's by his wife's jealousy. Yet for each of them marriage is all that can be put against the final sense of loneliness in a world that is anti-purposive; and before her death M'Kay learns to defer to his wife so that 'she grew under the soft rain of his loving care, and opened out, not, indeed, into an oriental flower, rich in profound mystery of scent and colour, but into a blossom of the chalk-down' (ch. II). There is considerable tact in that image: it hints at M'Kay's wife's half-hidden attractiveness, her frailty, the brevity of her life; and of course it tries to establish their belatedly achieved love as natural, even purposive.

Towards the end of *Deliverance* Mark marries his first love, Ellen, and we learn something of her story. After the young Mark's rejection of her she had married a go-ahead man, Clement Butts, who virtually deserts her for the Squire's wife, and who is sent packing when the Squire comes across the pair in compromising circumstances. Butts takes his wife and daughter to Australia, dies, and the two women return to England. Mark learns of this, decides to seek them out, offers Ellen marriage and she accepts. He is now delivered from the alien world of London into the warmth and security of marriage.

Except that it isn't quite like that. For we are bound to remember that Mark had originally parted from Ellen because of his recognition of their intellectual incompatibility, and when he now says that he 'cared less for argument, and it even gave me pleasure to talk in her dialect' (ch. VIII), we become aware of the compromise required of him for his marriage to exist at all.

Perhaps that isn't very important. But the need for money is. Mark has to accept a clerical position that means he is 'away from home for eleven hours of every day, excepting on Sundays'. And he suffers very much the same kinds of indignities as Taylor and Clark. Like Wemmick, therefore, 'I cut off my office life from my life at home so completely that I was two selves, and my true self was not stained by contact with my other self' (ch. VIII). Dickens, of course, doesn't allow us to suppose that Wemmick's Walworth life represents his 'true self' any more than his life with Jaggers; but for Mark to put it that way makes clear that he does regard marriage as deliverance. He has now joined the world on which he had gazed from the despairing isolation of Stoke Newington. The novel ends with his wife catching typhoid fever and narrowly missing death. He remarks: 'We determined to celebrate our deliverance by one more holiday before the cold weather came.' The word is deliberately placed. And so perhaps is the reference to cold weather. Mark concluded by saying that 'the death of the summer brought no sadness. Rather did summer dying in such fashion fill our hearts with repose, and even more than repose – actual joy.' Under these words a line is drawn, and then we read this postscript:

> Here ends the autobiography. A month after this last holiday my friend was dead and buried. He had unsuspected disease of the heart, and one day his master, of whom we have heard something, was more than usually violent. Mark, as his custom was, was silent, but evidently greatly excited. His tyrant left the room; and in a few minutes afterwards Mark was seen to turn white and fall forward in his chair. It was all over! His body was taken to a hospital and thence sent home. The next morning his salary up to the day of his death came in an envelope to his widow, without a single word from his employers save a request for acknowledgment. Towards midday, his office coat, and a book found in his drawer, arrived in a brown paper parcel, carriage unpaid.

The passage serves to remind us, if reminder is needed, that we have been reading a novel and not Hale White's account of his own life. More important, it provides a final troubling and perhaps sardonic touch to the idea of marriage as deliverance. For we realize that the 'true self' cannot be separated from the man who dies in his office and is sent home like a parcel.

I do not mean to suggest that Reuben Shapcott's postscript cancels the value of Mark's words. For the value of love is real enough (Dickens and Hale White are at one in agreeing on that). It is rather that deliverance into love and marriage is seen as dreadfully frail and vulnerable. The world of 'a position, an occupation, and, above all things, affection' can be obliterated very easily.

Yet the possibility of marriage as deliverance is one that all

the subsequent novels take up, though it is never seen as more
than a possibility. Indeed, in *The Revolution in Tanner's Lane*, it is
hardly even that. In the first part of the novel we are witness to
Zachariah's unhappy marriage. Mrs Coleman is not a very
intelligent woman, and she lacks warmth. 'It was, [Zachariah]
feared, true he did not love her, nor she him; but why could
not they have found that out before?' (ch. i). The question
suggests that we may be confronted with a study of misalliance,
and of the right grounds for love and marriage. It is the kind of
study which looms large in late-Victorian fiction,[26] and without doubt Hale White was keenly aware of its potentialities.
But in fact *The Revolution in Tanner's Lane* touches on the subject
rather than exploring it. This is partly because Zachariah is
convincingly presented as a man who, after being 'only three
months a husband . . . had already learned renunciation.
There was no joy in life? Then he would be satisfied if it were
tolerable, and he strove to dismiss all his dreams and do his best
with what lay before him' (ch. i). Mrs Coleman – we never
learn her first name – is too silly a woman to be other than
pathetic. She isn't the stuff out of which anything of great
interest can be made. Which is not to say that she can be dismissed. Mark is good on her intellectual shallowness, her wan
readiness to be attracted by and attractive to Major Maitland
without degenerating into mere flirtatiousness; and he neatly
establishes her sexual reserve. After Zachariah has seen Pauline
dance and has found himself 'outlining every one of her limbs'
he hurries home, only to discover that his wife has been to a
weekly prayer meeting, 'and was not in a very pleasant temper.
She was not spiteful, but unusually frigid' (ch. v). It is typically
acute of the narrator to note that the cause for her coldness
should lie in Zachariah's desertion of her for people he finds
more attractive. For though she is silly she is also aware of the
fact that she has little part to play in Zachariah's life. She is a
very lonely person. And there is one touching and delicately
handled scene where she follows her husband to the Caillaud's
lodgings in Manchester – in her understandable jealousy
masked by religious propriety she has forbidden the 'infidels'
entrance to her house – and from the dark, empty street looks
up at the lighted window and sees that 'her husband and
Pauline were talking earnestly across the table. Apparently

both of them were very much interested, and his face was lighted up as she never saw it when he was with her' (ch. xii). The sudden switch of point of view – for we customarily see her through Zachariah's eyes – allows us to understand a good deal about Mrs Coleman's sense of exclusion from her husband's life. The pair are locked into silent incommunicableness.

> He felt suddenly as if he would have liked to throw himself on his knees before her, and to have it all out with her; to say to her all he had said to himself; to expose all his misery to her; to try to find out whether she still loved him; to break or thaw the shell of ice which seemed to have frozen round her. But he could not do it. He was on the point of doing it, when he looked at her face, and there was something in it which stopped him. No such confidence was possible, and he went back into himself again.
> 'Shall I read to you?'
> 'Yes, if you like.'
> 'What shall I read?'
> 'I don't care; anything you please.'
> 'Shall it be Cook's Voyages?'
> 'I have just said I really do not care' [ch. xiv].

And then a smouldering, suppressed row breaks out between them. For the Major is now dead and Mrs Coleman half-accuses Zachariah of cowardice in allowing his death to happen and of identifying with the irreligious Caillaud. Of course she doesn't mean what she says. Underlying her actual words is a hurt and hurtful suggestion that the Major was the only one of the three men who meant much to her and one senses her jealousy at Zachariah's relationship with Pauline, in which there is an undoubted sexual element (he will marry her after his first wife's death).

Now all this is done well and is quite clearly the work of a serious novelist. But the effect is necessarily weakened because Mrs Coleman is often made so silly that the presentation of the marriage simply becomes a matter of asking our sympathy for Zachariah. And this also seems to me true of the treatment of George Allen's marriage to Priscilla Broad. We are told that Priscilla 'had a very difficult part to play in Cowfold, for she was obliged to visit freely all Tanner's Lane, but at the same time to hold herself above it and not to form any exclusive friendships' (ch. xviii). Her parents intend her to marry well, and are not altogether pleased at her choice, even though

George's education 'had been that of the middle-classes of those days' (ch. xviii). There is some nicely observed comedy in the ways in which Mrs Broad and Mrs Allen try to outdo one another in condescension (shades of the Hon. Mrs Gowan being reminded that it never does); and Hale White is good on the young couple's infatuation with one another. (I see no point here in separating Mark out from the novelist, because there is nothing to suggest a gap between them.)

But as soon as they are married we are given a Priscilla of such vapid stupidity that she becomes almost ridiculous, and the marriage a farce. Priscilla's inability to cope with household crises, her total failure to grasp anything at all about political questions (George gets nowhere when he tries to explain to her about free trade and the need to repeal the corn laws): these and other matters are treated in a way that seriously threatens the study of their marriage. And this is important because Hale White clearly wants us to see that Zachariah and George have not been helped as they should have been. Neither Mrs Coleman nor Priscilla is of use in their husbands' political activities, they play no part in the struggle. The two Paulines represent the possibility of marriage as true deliverance, but it is one that *The Revolution in Tanner's Lane* turns away from when George decides to emigrate.

By contrast, Miriam Trocchi does eventually find deliverance in marriage. Miriam is the clearest example of Hale White's debt to George Eliot. She is a girl of frustrated energies and intelligence, smouldering with an intense desire to live. Cowfold denies her any possibility of realizing her desire. The town is shown at its sleepiest in the opening pages of *Miriam's Schooling*. It is said of Miriam's brother, Andrew, that 'it seemed as if he would one day in the fulness of time do what Cowfold for centuries had done before him – that is to say, succeed his father in his business, marry some average Cowfold girl, beget more average Cowfold children, lead a life unvexed by any speculation or dreams, unenlightened by any revelation, and finally sleep in Cowfold churchyard with thousands of his predecessors, remembered for perhaps a year, and then forgotten for ever' (p. 51). Mark is obviously with Miriam in her desire to escape from this stultifying world. And deliverance of an obviously attractive form soon presents itself. Miriam and her brother are to go to London, he to work for an uncle who has a butcher's shop, she to keep house for him. At a low level this is a realistic dream of great expectations, and represents a common enough fortune of Victorian life (and fiction).

As does the ironic aftermath. Andrew quickly tires of the tedium of work in the shop, takes to drink and his uncle dismisses him. He falls ill and nearly dies. Miriam meanwhile has become attracted to an acquaintance of her brother's, Montgomery, for whom London has also failed to produce the deliverance expected of it. An actor *manqué*, he makes his living by singing sentimental and dubious songs in music halls. Montgomery tries to seduce Miriam, she fights him off and later sees him going into his lodgings with a prostitute. Our last view of him is in a hospital, where he has been brought to die, following an accident in which he has fallen under a cart and been horribly crushed.

London is a monster and reduces Miriam to near despair from which she has painfully to struggle free. Is this her schooling? Yes and no. Certainly she is brought to realize that the big city doesn't offer the freedom to develop potentialities, but equally she has to learn the need to extinguish her egoism.

From the beginning, Miriam has an impulse to do good. She pleads for a Cowfold man accused of setting fire to his premises in order to claim the insurance money. But her impulsiveness is not backed by any rational self-knowledge or knowledge of others. Or of the ways of the world. And here we need to take note of the epigraph from Euripides which prefaces the tale: 'That man amongst mortals who has acquiesced in Necessity is wise and is acquainted with divine things.' *Miriam's Schooling* is really a fable built on Euripides' statement. At first Miriam's egoism inclines her to see the world as answering to her purpose. She is therefore bitterly enraged and frustrated when events persist in not going her way. She is furious at having to look after her ill landlady, Miss Tippit, when she had planned a visit to the music hall, and she is full of hatred for her weakling brother: 'the prospect of his death disturbed her only as far as it interfered with herself. . . . Andrew was still very weak – he could hardly speak; and as he lay there impassive, Miriam's hatred of his silent white face increased' (pp. 108 and 111).

Shortly after this Miriam herself becomes ill and her physical collapse heralds the change in her attitude (Hale White is one of many Victorian novelists who use breakdown as a very proper means of symbolizing a crisis in consciousness). Her landlady comes to nurse her through the worst of her illness. 'What claim have I on you?' Miriam asks her, wonderingly. And with her recovery comes the burden of two thoughts. 'She was oppressed with a sense of her own nothingness and the nothingness of man. . . . Suddenly, and without any apparent connection with what had gone before, and indeed in contrast with it, came into Miriam's mind that she must do something for her fellow-creatures' (pp. 116–17). The ideas are of course connected. Miriam can be rescued from a sense of nothingness by a striving for service. From egoism to altruism. The debt to George Eliot could hardly be clearer.

And it continues with the ironic handling of her desire to train as a nurse. She throws herself into the scheme with all her energy but after a while 'she was obliged to confess to herself that the light of three months ago, which had then shone round her great design, had faded'. And shortly afterwards she is dismissed. 'She sought her friend Miss Tippit. To Miss Tippit the experience was not new. She had herself in her humble way imagined schemes of usefulness, which were broken through personal unfitness; she knew as how at last the man who thinks he will conquer a continent had to be content with the conquest of his kitchen-garden, fifty feet by twenty.'[27] Miss Tippit advises Miriam to return to Cowfold. Mark describes this as 'the best of all advice', and comments: 'Perhaps the worst effect of great cities, at any rate of English cities, is not the poverty they create and the misery which it brings, but the mental mischief which is wrought, often unconsciously, by their dreariness and darkness' (p. 124). And then follows the remark about the sourness of modern democracy being perhaps due to the deficiency of oxygen and sunlight. Inevitably the question of Mark's own attitude becomes of importance. For it does look as though he is characterizing the city in a manner which would be thought pretty odd by most city dwellers. 'Dreariness and darkness.' Surely the words apply to Cowfold just as much as to London? After all it was not London which was earlier said to be 'unenlightened by any speculation'; and London didn't begin Miriam's mental mischief. Now, however, London is routinely identified with hell, Cowfold with light and grace.

Miriam returns to Cowfold and marries a basketmaker called Didymus Farrow. He is a good man, but dull:

> He never opened a book, and during the winter, when the garden was closed, amused himself with an accordion, or in practising his part in a catch, or in cutting with a penknife curious little wooden chairs and tables. This mode of passing the time was entertaining enough to him, but not so to Miriam, who was fatally deficient, as so many of her countrymen and countrywomen are, in that lightness which distinguishes the French or the Italians, and would have enabled her, had she been so fortunately endowed with it, to sit by the fire and prattle innocently to her husband, whatever he might be doing [pp. 127–8].

I do not think that Mark is being ironic here, but I do think that Hale White is being ironic about Mark. For the dream of a pastoral idyl can be kept alive only if Miriam chooses to renounce any of the energy and intelligence that had distinguished her in the first place and had inevitably made her discontented with Cowfold life. It looks suspiciously as though acquiescing in Necessity is true deliverance in that it means no more nor less than accepting marriage and accommodating yourself to its limitations. For deliverance read prattle.

Unfair, yes, but after all Miriam does learn to accept her marriage when she discovers her husband's enthusiasm for astronomy and his ability to construct an orrery. The tale ends with them in an achieved harmony of mood and mind. Miriam has finally freed herself from egoism, has accepted marriage and her husband, and accepted Cowfold.

It is not very satisfactory. And the fault lies partly with Hale White. For though I think he is to be distinguished from Mark, the distinction isn't a controlled one. The fable seems somehow muddled. It is right enough for it to be ironic (what happens to Miriam is not what she had hoped for) but wrong that she should be brought so completely to accept a kind of life which she had instinctively rejected – and with Mark's approval. Mark tells the tale and the contradictions are therefore obviously his. But it seems to me that Hale White may be standing too close to him. Acquiescing in Necessity ought to have more irony to it than that: ought to be stronger, ought to tell of the cost of frustrated strengths: ought not to be so glib.

Catherine Furze comes next (1893), and is in some ways a re-working of *Miriam's Schooling*. It is worth noting that the last three novels have women as their centres of interest, a matter which is of obvious importance in the fiction of the 1890s. For *Catherine Furze* is partly about the nature of female sexuality and about how that cannot really be considered apart from the social context in which it has to declare, or not declare, itself. There is a moment of oddly heavy irony when Mark says:

> Had Catherine been born later it would have been better. She would perhaps have been able to distract herself with the thousand and one subjects which are now got up for examinations, or she would perhaps have seriously studied some science, which might at least have been effectual as an opiate in oppressing sensibility. She was, however, in Eastthorpe before the new education, as it is called, had been invented. There was no elaborate system of needle points, Roman and Greek history, plain and spherical trigonometry, political economy, ethics, literature, chemistry, conic sections, music, English history, and mental philosophy, to draw off the electricity within her, nor did she possess the invaluable privilege of being able, after studying a half-crown handbook, to unbosom herself to women of her own age upon the position of Langland as an English poet [ch. x].[28]

The facing-all-ways position of that belongs to Mark, but the uneasily jokey tone is as much a part of the 1890s as his attitudes to popular movements in *The Revolution in Tanner's Lane* had been a part of the 1880s.

Catherine Furze, like its successor *Clara Hopgood*, belongs with those novels of the end of the nineteenth century which in very different ways explore man–woman relationships from the point of view of the woman in order to reappraise the current notions of woman's identity. I think of Gissing's *Odd Woman*, of Meredith's *Amazing Marriage*, of Grant Allen's *Woman Who Did*, of Bennett's *Anna of the Five Towns*, of Hardy's *Tess of the d'Urbervilles*.[29] It is also worthwhile thinking of the *Woodlanders*, when considering *Catherine Furze*. For there is a close parallel between the frustrated relationships of the two novels. In Hardy's great novel Marty South loves Giles Winterbourne who aspires to Grace who aspires to Fitzpiers. In *Catherine Furze* Phoebe loves Tom Catchpole, who aspires to Catherine who aspires to Cardew. In both cases love is seen as conditioned by social status (Mrs Furze's desire to rise and have Catherine 'finished' has fairly obvious parallels with Melbury's rise and his dreams for Grace).

Yet it would be wrong to make a great deal of considerations of class and status when trying to characterize the novel's achievement. For though these things matter and are shown to be integral to Catherine's experience of herself and of others, it is nevertheless true that, as the novel's title implies, the focus is on the girl herself. Catherine is very close indeed to Miriam.

> Miss Catherine generally, even at that early age, carried all before her, much to her own detriment. Her parents unfortunately were perpetually making a brief show of resistance and afterwards yielding. Frequently they had no pretext for resistance, for Catherine was right and they were wrong. Consequently the child grew up accustomed to see everything bend to her own will, and accustomed to believe that what she willed was in accordance with the will of the universe – not a healthy education, for the time is sure to come when a destiny which will not bend stands in the path before us, and we are convinced by the roughest processes that what we purpose is to a very small extent the purpose of Nature [ch. III].

There looks to be an echo of a famous sentence in *Emma* about that passage. 'The real evils indeed of Emma's disposition to think a little too well of herself; these were the disadvantages which threatened alloy to her many enjoyments.' But the differences are far more significant. Jane Austen's sentence is a good deal better written than anything in the passage from *Catherine Furze*; it has about it an air of practised ease and confidence wholly lacking in Mark's prose. Of course. For Jane Austen can content herself with noting the 'alloy' that threatens Emma's enjoyments; there is no attempt to enlarge the remark, give it a quasi-metaphysical status. Mark, on the other hand, plays with the words 'will' and 'purpose' in order to try to see Catherine as subject to universal laws (a phrase which Jane Austen uses with comic, deflating, intent, as at the beginning of *Pride and Prejudice*). The attempt is hardly successful, because the phrases 'the will of the universe' and 'the purpose of Nature' mark a forlorn effort to discover a general pattern or meaningfulness by means of gestures towards Schopenhauer and Darwinian/Spencerian science which are, perhaps, obligatory and which certainly give a hectoring note to the passage as a whole. 'A destiny which will not bend stands in the path before us.' Yes, it reminds us of George Eliot, reminds us too that destiny is the hallmark of a certain kind of plotting (enter Raffles) which is occasioned by real uncertainty, no matter how strongly certainty and inevitability may be appealed to as justification for such plotting.

Faced with the passage I have quoted, we may well expect *Catherine Furze* to be a study of a chastened egoism. But in fact the novel has precious little to do with that, and what little there is of it is either irrelevant to, or contradicts, what is most important about it. True, Catherine falls in love with the unattainable Mr Cardew, vicar of a nearby parish and married to a woman he doesn't much love; and true, the novel ends with Catherine's death that can be made to look like a final act of atonement. And Mark offers us some intrusive moral comment, but in fact the conventionality of plot and narrative intrusion are matters against which something very unconventional is being played off.

Not with Cardew. He is mostly seen from the outside and whenever he is described there is a customary tartness in the narrative which, if it reminds us of Meredith's way with self-satisfied men, also reminds us that at his best Meredith can do this sort of thing uniquely well. Cardew is a university man (and there are precious few of *those* in Hale White's novels). We are told that he 'fell in love with himself, married himself, and soon after discovered that he did not know who his wife was' (ch. x). When he finds out he discovers he doesn't much care for her. In particular, he is scornful of her intellect. 'He did not take into account that . . . if his wife was defective at one point, there were in her whole regions of unexplored excellence, of faculties never encouraged, and an affection to which he offered no response.' It reminds us of M'Kay and his wife. And for her part Mrs Cardew thinks: 'Perhaps, as they grew older, matters might become worse, and they might have to travel together down the long, weary road to death' (ch. vii). I take it that the echo of *Epipsychidion* is intended, and it serves to remind us of the fact that in the 1890s novelists were much exercised over the 'marriage tie and its permanence':[30] by the end of the novel the Cardews have come together. This is partly due to Catherine's act of renouncing the possibility of Cardew's love, which frees him from the spell of her enchantment. At the very end of the novel, he visits her when she is on her death bed.

'Mr. Cardew, I want to say something.'
'Wait a moment, let me tell you – *you have saved me*.'

She smiled, her lips moved, and she whispered – '*You* have saved *me*.'

By their love for each other they were both saved. The disguises are manifold which the Immortal Son assumes in the work of our redemption.

Now this has got to be absurd. The understandable sentimentalities of Catherine and Cardew are reinforced by Mark's conventional pieties, even though the plain fact is that Catherine's love for Cardew destroys her. The destiny which will not bend and which stands in her path is, however, less the fact that Cardew is married than the nature of her love. Which is as much as to say that she cannot cope with her own nature. Yet even to put it that way smacks of the moralizing that would lead us to accept Mark as a trustworthy narrator. And we cannot really want to take *Catherine Furze* as a moral fable about what happens if you rashly fall in love with a man who is basically unworthy of you. That is merely the outer casing. Inside it is something far more subtle, far richer, more questioning, hesitant. (It may of course seem odd for me to keep dividing Mark from Hale White, but I think that in both *Miriam's Schooling* and here there are certain evasions, muddles and inconsistencies and that it's as well to consider them either intended or allow that Hale White's pseudonym gave him a certain freedom to explore doubts and hesitancies in his own mind that probably couldn't otherwise have been given a place in the fictions.)

The outer casing is utterly conventional. Catherine loves Cardew and is aware of his love for her, though they never speak of it. She falls into a mood of dreadful depression from which she is partially released by Dr Turnbull, the humane physician, who speaks one of the novel's available wisdoms when he encourages her to nurse the dying Phoebe (from self to selflessness) and later advises her: 'Strive to consider yourself, not as Catherine Furze, a young woman apart, but as a piece of common humanity and bound by its laws. It is infinitely healthier for you. Never, under any pretext whatever, allow yourself to do what is exceptional. If you have any originality, it will better come out in an improved performance of what everybody ought to do, than in the indulgence of singularity.' And he speaks with open contempt of Cardew, comparing him with his wife whose 'care of the poor in his parish makes her almost a divinity to them. While he is luxuriating amongst the cowslips, in what he calls thinking, she is teaching the sick people patience and nursing them. She is a saint, and he does not know half her worth' (ch. xx).

After this there is a good deal of plot, dealing with the disgrace of Tom Catchpole, who is 'framed' by Mrs Furze because she mistakenly thinks that he and Catherine are in love and she won't have *him* as a son-in-law, and whose innocence is eventually proved. The plotting is there, I think, to make us forget the sheer ineffectualness of Turnbull's words to Catherine. For the plain fact is that Catherine wants to die. 'The bliss of life passed over into contentment with death, and her delight was so great that she could happily have lain down amid the hum of insects to die on the grass' (ch. xxi). Denied her sexual identity she simply gives up on life. For she is most herself when fully aware of her love for Cardew. At the very least, she is as much herself when in love with him as when she is behaving well by Phoebe. Mark admits the fact. And this is where we come to what is truly important about the novel.

After Tom's disclosure of his love for her and his subsequent dismissal from her father's business, Catherine enters into a condition of black melancholy. She knows that she is regarded by her parents as marriageable property, knows, too, that conventional wisdom denies her the man she loves: she must be bound by the laws of humanity and not allow herself to do what is exceptional. 'It was a crisis, for the pattern of her existence was henceforth settled, and she was to live not only without that which is sweetest for woman, but with no definite object before her. The force in woman is so great that something with which it can grapple, on which it can expand itself, is a necessity, and Catherine felt that her strength would have to expand itself on twisting straws' (ch. xvii).

Take the outer plot and you may think of *Catherine Furze* as a source for *A Room With A View* or *Ann Veronica*, social comedies which deal with a young girl's right to choose her partner and not be bound by conventionalities. But consider such a passage as this and at once you see the difference. It is there in the phrase 'the force in woman'. The kind of language has nothing to do with the kinds of fiction that Forster and Wells produce. If it anticipates any later novelist it must be Lawrence; and I think it almost certain that Lawrence learnt from Hale White. Dr Turnbull's words are hopelessly inadequate to Catherine's case not because of their mere moral conventionality but because they have nothing to do with, and cannot take account of, the 'force' which *is* Catherine. She must think of herself as a piece of common humanity, he says, and as bound by its laws. But which laws? The law of force? To obey that is to go against the laws of moral certainty. Unless that is, obeying the law of force is the final morality (it is for Lawrence, of course). I am not going to suggest that Hale White is a kind of nineties Nietzschean, but I think it important to stress how deeply he is committed to undermining Mark's (and Turnbull's) conventionalities in the interest of presenting as sensitively as he can the nature of Catherine's sexual identity. I can perhaps best show how he does this by quoting from one long, wonderfully imagined and well-written scene, where Catherine and Cardew first become powerfully aware of one another.

> One afternoon, late in August, Catherine had gone with the dog down to the riverside, her favourite haunt. Clouds, massive, white, sharply outlined, betokening thunder, lay on the horizon in a long line; the fish were active; great chubb rose, and every now and then a scurrying dimple on the pool showed that the jack and the perch were busy. It was a day full of heat, a day of exultation, for it proclaimed that the sun was alive; it was a day on which to forget winter with its doubts, its despairs, and its indistinguishable grey; it was a day on which to believe in immortality. Catherine was at that happy age when summer has power to warm the brain; it passed into her blood and created in her simple, uncontaminated bliss. She sat down close to an alder which overhung the bank. It was curious, but so it was, that her thoughts suddenly turned from the water and the thunderclouds and the blazing heat to Mr. Cardew, and it is still more strange that at that moment she saw him coming along the towing-path. In a minute he was at her side, but before reaching her she had risen.
>
> 'Good morning, Miss Furze.'
>
> 'Mr. Cardew! What brings you here?'
>
> 'I have been here several times; I often go out for the day; it is a favourite walk.'
>
> He was silent, and did not move. He seemed prepossessed and anxious, taking no note of the beauty of the scene around him.
>
> 'How is Mrs. Cardew?'
>
> 'She is well, I believe.'
>
> 'You have not left home this morning, then?'
>
> 'No; I was not at home last night.'
>
> 'I think I must be going.'

'I will walk a little way with you.'

'My way is over the bridge to the farmhouse, where I am staying.'

'I will go as far as you go.'

Catherine turned towards the bridge.

'Is it the house beyond the meadows?'

'Yes.'

It is curious how indifferent conversation often is just at the moment when the two who are talking may be trembling with passion.

'You should have brought Mrs. Cardew with you,' said Catherine, tearing to pieces a water lily, and letting the beautiful white petals fall bit by bit into the river.

Mr. Cardew looked at her steadfastly, scrutinisingly, but her eyes were on the thunderclouds, and the lily fell faster and faster. The face of this girl had hovered before him for weeks, day and night. He never for a moment proposed to himself deliberate love for her – he could not do it, and yet he had come there, not, perhaps, consciously in order to find her, but dreaming of her all the time. He was literally possessed. . . . Catherine felt his gaze, although her eyes were not towards him. At last the lily came to an end, and she tossed the naked stalk after the flower. She loved this man; it was a perilous moment: one touch, a hair's breadth of oscillation, and the two would have been one. At such a crisis the least external disturbance is often decisive. The first note of the thunder was heard, and suddenly the image of Mrs. Cardew presented itself before Catherine's eyes, appealing to her piteously, tragically. She faced Mr. Cardew.

'I am sorry Mrs. Cardew is not here. I wish I had seen more of her. Oh, Mr. Cardew! how I envy her! how I wish I had her brains for scientific subjects! She is wonderful. But I *must* be going; the thunder is distant: you will be in Eastthorpe, I hope, before the storm comes. Good-bye,' and she had gone.

She did not go straight to the house, however, but went into the garden and again cursed herself that she had dismissed him. Who had dismissed him? Not she. How had it been done? She could not tell. She crept out of the garden and went to the corner of the meadow where she could see the bridge. He was still there. She tried to make up an excuse for returning; she tried to go back without one, but it was impossible. Something, whatever it was, stopped her; she struggled and wrestled, but it was of no avail, and she saw Mr. Cardew slowly retrace his steps to the town. Then she leaned upon the wall and found some relief in a great fit of sobbing. Consolation she had none; not even the poor reward of conscience and duty. She had lost him, and she felt that, if she had been left to herself, she would have kept him. She went out again late in the evening. The clouds had passed away to the south and east, but the lightning still fired the distant horizon far beyond Eastthorpe and towards Abchurch. The sky was clearing in the west, and suddenly in a rift Arcturus, about to set, broke through and looked at her, and in a moment was again eclipsed. What strange confusion! What inexplicable contrasts! Terror and divinest beauty;

the calm of the infinite stellar space and her own anguish; each an undoubted fact, but each to be taken by itself as it stood: the star was there, the dark blue depth was there, but they were no answer to the storm of her sorrow [ch. ix].

The symbolism of this scene is crucial to its meaning and success. The thunderclouds build with the turbulence of her emotions, the stripping of the lily tells of her desire to give herself to Cardew. The control over syntax and punctuation is delicate and exact. 'At last the lily came to an end, and she tossed the naked stalk after the flower. She loved this man; it was a perilous moment: one touch, a hair's breadth of oscillation, and the two would have been one.' The throwing away of the lily stalk points her readiness to abandon herself to Cardew (I use this worn phrase because after all Catherine does want to lose one side of herself: 'Who had dismissed him? Not she'). The readiness springs to consciousness after the full stop, with her candid admission: 'She loved this man.' That it is her thoughts we are given directly there is evident from the phrase 'this man'. But then Mark intrudes. The semi-colon indicates the break between her consciousness and his. His voice brings with it a moral warning – 'perilous moment' – which is an interpretation of her predicament that chimes with her own sense of social responsibility. And no matter how conventional the sense is, it is important to her, convincing her of the need to accept its dictates. The dismissal of Cardew follows.

And is itself followed by that sense of lost or divided identity which counts for so much in the passage's total achievement. 'Who had dismissed him? Not she. How had it been done? She could not tell.' No room for moralizing there. And none in her appalled awareness of her utter isolation – divided from herself and from others – as she sees in the calm wonder of the natural universe 'no answer' to her grievous sorrow. In other words there is no way in which Catherine's nature can be accommodated to the world she inhabits. Only by denying or conventionalizing her nature can she become accommodated. And this is precisely what Dr Turnbull counsels. He is the wise voice of his society, and the course of the narrative seems to identify with him. Certainly he is not satirized, is not a prototype for Ann Veronica's father. What the narrator makes happen to Catherine can look like a justification for Turnbull's views. Yet the novel as a whole also presents us with a Catherine who *resists* such narrative manipulation. There is no confident schematizing in *Catherine Furze* of the kind we can discover in *A Room With A View*, which in many ways can look like a rebuke to Hale White's fiction. Yet it is the earlier novel which is the more impressive. Catherine's experience is bewildering and grievous to her, and bewildering to us in its tentative, exploratory, almost uneasy manner. Once ignore the way in which the girl's experience is offered and you end up with a crushingly heavy-handed tale. But that is not Hale White's way at all.

V

'An inchoate mass of good material', was how the *Athenaeum* saw *Clara Hopgood*.[31] But to me Hale White's last novel seems his finest. It is a novel of ideas, but wonderfully fleshed out; and it hardly ever lends itself to the kind of schematizing analysis that mars Linda Hughes's otherwise interesting study of 'William Hale White's Spinozan Sisters'. Mrs Hughes argues that the novel is named for Clara, because she is always ahead of her sister, 'pointing to a higher order of existence',[32] and that this higher order is at one with Hale White's eager identification with the Spinozistic values. I agree that Clara does speak for these values, while doubting whether she is to be seen as the clear embodiment of the novel's most important truths. But to see why this should be requires us to look at the novel in a little detail.

Madge and Clara Hopgood live some ten miles east of Eastthorpe, in a town called Fenmarket. It is too provincial for them. 'The reason lay partly in their nature and partly in their history.' Mr Hopgood has provided his daughters with an education 'much above that which was usual amongst people in their position' (ch. 1), and it is their nature to be independently minded, curious and fearless.

There are also important differences between them, superbly dramatized in a game of chess they play one afternoon. Clara always beats Madge and on this occasion has her in check. Madge complains of her inability to do better and Clara replies:

'The reason is that you do not look two moves ahead. You never say to yourself, "Suppose I move there, what is she likely to do, and what can I do afterwards?" '

'That is just what is impossible to me. I cannot hold myself down; the moment I go beyond the next move my thoughts fly away, and I am in a muddle, and my head turns round. I was not born for it. I can do what is under my nose well enough, but nothing more. . . .'

'Then what makes the difference between the good and the bad player?'

'It is a gift, an instinct, I suppose.'

'Which is as much to say that you give it up. You are very fond of that word instinct; I wish you would not use it.'

'I have heard you use it, and say that you instinctively like this person or that.'

'Certainly; I do not deny that sometimes I am drawn to a person or repelled from him before I can say why; but I always force myself to discover afterwards the cause of my attraction or repulsion, and I believe it is a duty to do so. If we neglect it we are little better than the brutes and may grossly deceive ourselves.'

Now at this moment the sound of coach wheels is heard outside and Madge goes to the window, and as she does so 'a gentleman on the box-seat looked at her intently as he passed'. Madge goes back to her seat, looks anew at the chessboard and by a lucky move manages to beat her sister. 'Have you lost your faith in schemes?', she asks, and Clara replies: 'You are very much mistaken if you suppose that, because of one failure, or of twenty failures, I would give up a principle.' The talk then turns to love and Madge asks Clara whether she wouldn't rather obey her first impression and 'if you felt you loved him, would you not say "Yes"?' But Clara won't have it. 'Precisely because the question would be so important, would it be necessary to employ every faculty I have in order to decide it' (ch. iii).

It looks like a split between sense and sensibility, and it is worth noting that *Clara Hopgood* is one of the several distinguished novels which make use of two sisters in order to dramatize the exploration of polarities and contrasts. I am certain that Forster must have had *Clara Hopgood* at the back of his mind when he came to write *Howards End*, and in view of Lawrence's known admiration for Hale White it is more than possible *Women in Love* also owes something to it.

The chess scene gleams with ironies. Clara, after all, doesn't win. Madge's lucky move comes after she has seen the young

man gazing at her, and we sense from the turn she gives to the
conversation that she has already felt an attraction to him (it
will turn out to be both lucky, because it gives her a new
animation and unlucky, because she will bear his illegitimate
child). And from now on much of the novel is taken up with
Madge's relationship with the young man and its consequences.

Frank Palmer is his name. He is an attractive person. 'He
was not particularly reflective, but he was generous and
courageous, perfectly straightforward, a fair specimen of
thousands of English public-school boys' (ch. IV). A fairer
specimen, it may be, than Charles Wilcox. Certainly he acts
well, quickly and decisively, when he and the two girls are
menaced by a wild bull (ch. V). But for all that, he is conventional; and the conventionality decisively endangers his relationship with Madge.

Madge's impulsiveness is profound, not at all superficial. A
'dazzler', the narrator calls her, and in his mock-rueful way he
admits that 'it must be confessed that sometimes her spontaneity was truer than the limitations of speech more carefully
weighed' (ch. IV). (I should say that *Clara Hopgood* is the one
novel where Mark is a fully reliable narrator, i.e. *is* Hale White.)
Madge seems to me to be a good deal more credible than Helen
Schlegel, her intensities more authentic, her living for and
through the moment more dramatically realized. There is a
wonderful episode where she and Frank, as Miranda and
Ferdinand, act the cave scene of the *Tempest* in an evening of
amateur theatricals, at the end of which a wreath of flowers is
thrown to her and Frank puts it on her head. Later, going home,
Clara voices her annoyance that Shakespeare should have been
followed by 'something light' and Frank says that their
hostess 'had to suit all tastes'.

> There was something in this remark most irritating to Clara; the word
> 'tastes', for example, as if the difference between Miranda and the
> chambermaid were a matter of 'taste'. She was annoyed too with
> Frank's easy, cheery tones for she felt deeply what she said, and his
> mitigation and smiling latitudinarianism were more exasperating than
> direct opposition.
>
> 'I am sure,' continued Frank, 'that if we were to take the votes of
> the audience, Miranda would be the queen of the evening;' and he put
> the crown which he had brought away with him on her head again.
>
> Clara was silent. In a few moments they were at the door of their

> house. It had begun to rain, and Madge, stepping out of the carriage
> in a hurry, threw a shawl over her head, forgetting the wreath. It fell
> into the gutter and was splashed with mud. Frank picked it up, wiped
> it as well as he could with his pocket-handkerchief, took it into the
> parlour and laid it on a chair [ch. vi].

No one is mocked or sold short in that. One can understand the
sad loneliness – and silence – of Clara, the way in which her
integrity, her capacity for deep feeling and thought make her
an isolated person; one can understand and sympathize with
Frank's normality, his decency; and one registers the deft
symbolism of Madge's knocking the wreath into the gutter (the
following morning she throws it on the fire). For her the intensities of the moment have spent themselves in the acting; for
Frank it is only play-acting, and at the same time an opportunity for conventional sentiment; for Clara the whole thing is
a mockery of love. The book is named after her, not because
she points to a higher order of existence, but because she is
alone, intense, acting out of convictions that will trouble the
living stream but not, finally, compel it to alter course.

And so round her swirl Madge and Frank engaged with
different intensities in their love affair. Their great moment has,
indeed, already passed (the burning of the wreath tells us that
much). When Frank kisses her he is 'swept into self-forgetful-
ness' (rather as Paul Wilcox is); when she is with him she falls
into a 'delicious trance'. Their love is sensual and she knows
that it will not really do. She is aware of his shallowness, of the
fact that sensuality isn't enough.

> Madge had a desire to say something, but she did not know what to
> say, a burden lay upon her chest. It was that weight which presses there
> when we are alone with those with whom we are not strangers, but
> with whom we are not completely at home, and she actually found
> herself impatient and half-desirous of solitude. This must be criminal
> or disease, she thought to herself, and she forcibly recalled Frank's
> virtues. She was so far successful that when they parted and he kissed
> her, she was more than usually caressing, and her ardent embrace, at
> least for the moment, relieved that unpleasant sensation in the region
> of the heart [ch. viii].

But sensuality keeps coming back. 'She had read something of
passion, but she never knew till now what the white intensity of
its flame in a man could be.' It is something of a reworking of
material in *Catherine Furze*, and it is worth noting how well Hale

White succeeds in showing that Madge is aware of the contrary
tugs in her personality: towards sensual involvement with
Frank, an acceptance of her sexuality, and yet away from him,
and towards acceptance of her identity as a person beyond him.
What she wants, of course, is mutuality – in sexual as well as
other matters – and it is this which is denied her. Frank finds
himself 'the possessor of a beautiful creature', but it is she who
has to initiate the sexual act; and she does it by deliberately
putting aside her recognition of his triviality, of how in so many
ways he displeases her. It is she who takes his hand, who bends
her head towards him before they take refuge from a thunderstorm in a barn. Afterwards, his decent, pitiable conventionality comes out in a manner that recalls Bevis of the *Odd
Women*.

> 'I cannot, cannot go to-morrow,' he suddenly cried, as they neared the
> town.
> 'You *shall* go,' she replied calmly.
> 'But, Madge, think of me in Germany, think what my dreams and
> thoughts will be – you here – hundreds of miles between us.'
> She had never seen him so shaken with terror.
> 'You *shall* go; not another word.'
> 'I must say something – what can I say? My God, my God, have
> mercy on me.'
> 'Mercy! Mercy!' she repeated, half unconsciously, and then rousing
> herself exclaimed, 'You shall not say it; I will not hear; now, good-bye'
> [ch. IX].

The pathos of Frank's nature is finely sketched in there. He
should not have 'possessed' Madge; he sees himself as the one
who has offended by 'taking' her. And as her calmness indicates,
she is still the possessor of herself and now fully conscious of his
inadequacy (which, we can reasonably suppose, will include
sexual inadequacy). Being self-possessed, she dismisses him,
chooses to have their child alone and when he returns from
Germany will not let him make reparations. Which is fortunate
for him, since he's about to make an advantageous marriage.
But Hale White doesn't at all satirize him or cheapen his study
of the man. Indeed he provides a moving insight into Frank's
nature, says as much as can be said for him.

> He was in anguish because he found that in order to feel as he ought to
> feel some effort was necessary; that treason to her was possible. . . .
> He saw himself as something separate from himself, and although he

knew what he saw to be flimsy and shallow, he could do nothing to
deepen it, absolutely nothing! It was not the betrayal of that thunderstorm which now tormented him. He could have represented that as a
failure to be surmounted; he could have repented it. It was his own
inner being from which he revolted, from limitations which are worse
than crimes, for who, by taking thought, can add one cubit to his
stature? [ch. xv].

That note of bleak, considerate truthfulness is typical of Hale
White, and although one could point to other moments in the
novel that equally well demonstrate the author's way with
Frank, that one can stand for them all (though a full study
would take up the final meeting between the young man and
Madge, and the dialogue which bears comparison with 'Two
in the Campagna' and *Modern Love* in its rendering of half-
truths, evasions, attempted sincerities: two people trying to do
their best by themselves and to one another).

Madge refuses to marry Frank. 'It would be a crime,' she
tells him, and although he cannot understand what she means,
we can. The sisters move to London and there Clara meets
Baruch Cohen. I have no space to detail the sureness with
which Hale White writes of Cohen, but it is necessary to note
that he is convincingly presented as an intellectual, slightly
absurd – and aware of the fact – serious, fatalistic/stoic ('he
accepted . . . as well as he could, without complaint, the inevitable order of nature'), and ready to be in love with Clara,
with whom he has so much in common. But in fact she evades
his offer of marriage and he marries Madge. Clara goes off to
fight for Mazzini and the novel ends with these words.

> 'Father,' said a younger Clara to Baruch some ten years later as she
> sat on his knee, 'I had an Aunt Clara once, hadn't I?'
>   'Yes, my child.'
>   'Didn't she go to Italy and die there?'
>   'Yes.'
>   'Why did she go?'
>   'Because she wanted to free the poor people of Italy who were slaves.'

More than one commentator has been puzzled by this ending,
seeing in it something evasive or unsatisfactory. And indeed it
may well seem perverse of Clara to give up the man she loves
and who plainly loves her, and to let her sister take him. I don't
think that one can simply say that she chooses to sacrifice herself for a greater cause, because that would schematize in a way

that's clearly hostile to the complexities of the novel. And indeed it seems to me that Clara's behaviour is bound to be problematic, not easily accounted for. After all, Baruch's very last words are intendedly open-ended. How could one woman free the poor people of Italy? Have they been freed? Isn't it vainglory to want to be such a heroine? History looks back ambiguously, perhaps ironically, at the woman whose choice caused her double suffering: the loss of the man she loved, the loss of her own life, probably pointlessly.[33]

Why, then, end with this? I think because Hale White sees Clara in a sort of double perspective: she is a kind of George Eliot heroine, exchanging egotism for altruism; and at the same time an individual whose wished-for certainties may well be mocked by history. Her heroism, sacrifice, idealism, are, in an almost Meredithian way, highly problematic. She is the centre of the book, it is named for her, because she symbolizes Hale White's own ironic, dark, uneasy sense that the humanist position of those high Victorians, whom he so deeply admired and with whom he wanted to identify, might have been built on sand. It is difficult to pin the tone of the novel down because it *is* so problematic, agonized perhaps, open. Which is why a schematized account of *Clara Hopgood* is bound to be wrong, since it cannot take the measure of Hale White's hesitancies. I think, for example, of an important conversation between Clara and Baruch, which I shall have to quote at length (and which shows, among other things, that Baruch himself isn't to be taken as Spinozistic man in any other than a troubling way: his fatalism doesn't exclude the possibility of his own absurdity, and yet of course his realizing as much is part of his intelligence and candour). Baruch comes to see Clara in the bookshop where she works, and asks about a volume of essays written by a long-dead friend of his youth. The essays had made no impact, indeed most were sold as waste-paper. Baruch remarks that he had told his friend it was useless to publish, and Clara replies:

> 'I should have thought that some notice would have been taken of him; he is so evidently worth it.'
> 'Yes, but although he was original and reflective, he had no particular talent. His excellence lay in criticism and observation, often profound, on what came to him every day, and he was valueless in the

literary market. . . . So he died utterly unrecognised, save by one or two personal friends who loved him dearly. . . .'

'Do you believe that the good does not necessarily survive?'

'Yes and no; I believe that power every moment, so far as our eyes can follow it, is utterly lost. I have had one or two friends whom the world has never known and never will know, who have more in them than is to be found in an English classic. I could take you to a little dissenting chapel not very far from Holborn where you would hear a young Welshman, with no education beyond that provided by a Welsh denominational college, who is a perfect orator and whose depth of insight is hardly to be matched, save by Thomas À Kempis, whom he much resembles. When he dies he will be forgotten in a dozen years. Besides, it is surely plain to everybody that there are thousands of men and women within a mile of us, apathetic and obscure, who, if an object worthy of them had been presented to them, would have shown themselves capable of enthusiasm and heroism. Huge volumes of human energy are apparently annihilated.'

'It is very shocking, worse to me than the thought of the earthquake or the pestilence.'

'I said "yes and no" and there is another side. The universe is so wonderful, so intricate, that it is impossible to trace the transformation of its forces, and when they seem to disappear the disappearance may be an illusion. Moreover, "waste" is a word which is applicable only to finite resources. If the resources are infinite it has no meaning' [ch. xxii].

It is clearly this conversation which lodges in Clara's mind, working there until it helps her decide to leave Baruch for Mazzini. Not that Hale White spells the matter out, but it is implicit in how she responds to his near-declaration of marriage.

A husband was to be had for a look, for a touch, a husband whom she could love, a husband who could give her all her intellect demanded. A little house rose before her eyes as if by Arabian enchantment; there was a bright fire on the hearth, and there were children round it; without the look, the touch, there would be solitude, silence and a childless old age, so much more to be feared by a woman than by a man. Baruch, paused, waiting for her answer, and her tongue actually began to move with a reply, which would have sent his arm round her, and made them one for ever, but it did not come. Something fell and flashed before her, like lightning from a cloud overhead, divinely beautiful, but divinely terrible [ch. xxvii].

I don't think that Hale White can be accused of sentimentality there. The point is rather that because Clara envisages the 'little house' and its trappings, she understands it to be a trap – for her, at least. But understand is the wrong word, it suggests rational knowledge, and as the last sentence makes clear Clara isn't consciously in control of her decision. 'Something' controls her: the moment of revelation is veiled, dark; but it clearly has to do with Clara rejecting one kind of identity – companionship, a conventional woman's role – for another, which, for all her unconventionality, she feels to be 'terrible'. For after all the choice does require her to abandon all that can make for present comfort, in the possible interest of not wasting her human energy. And it should be noted that she doesn't as yet know how she is going to be able to expend that energy. Only after the rejection of Cohen does she meet Mazzini and decide to devote herself to his cause. So that her rejection of the man she loves really is terrible to her.

I see the last part of *Clara Hopgood* as an extraordinarily tactful and properly hesitant rendering of a woman's divided consciousness, of her struggle to discover her fullest identity, in and through choice, which requires the painful exclusion of other possible identities and, at the same time, as an unsettling, open-ended fiction in which important humanist affirmations are put disquietingly to the test: in which deliverance from self is itself a problem. *Clara Hopgood* isn't at all a novel one feels comfortable with (or about). Indeed, it is very nearly a darkly pessimistic novel, and although its bleakness is tempered by – among other things – Madge's arrowy passion, Clara's possible intuitive grasp of the transforming of energy and forces into selflessness as she watches the river, Mrs Caffyn's decency and Cohen's different kind of integrity, none the less its 'yes and no' anticipates Conrad every bit as much as recalling George Eliot. Only by radically distorting and sentimentalizing what it offers could Forster come up with the simple optimisms of *Howards End*. *Clara Hopgood* is a novel of ideas right enough, but in no sense is it a thesis novel, or one that turns up answers to or certainties about the questions and doubts that animate its pages. And in that it seems to me very much a novel of the late nineteenth century.

4

Hardy's Women

HARDY's novels are much concerned with the nature of change. Not merely change in a small, atypical manner, as some commentators have suggested, but change as the controlling factor in social life. As Raymond Williams in particular has remarked, we are certain to go badly wrong if we think of Hardy's Wessex as in any sense an isolated or a special case. Hardy, Williams remarks,

> . . . sees the harshness of the economic process, in inheritance, capital, rent and trade, within the continuity of the natural processes and persistently cutting across them. The social process created in this interaction is one of class and separation, as well as of chronic insecurity, as this capitalist farming and dealing takes its course. The profound disturbances that Hardy records cannot then be seen in the sentimental terms of a pastoral: the contrast between country and town. The exposed and separated individuals, whom Hardy puts at the centre of his fiction, are only the most developed cases of a general exposure and separation.[1]

This puts the point exactly. It is part of the argument of the present book that the social process of class and separation is something that the provincial novelist is supremely well equipped to handle, and I have noted the different ways in which Mrs Gaskell and Hale White achieve their successes and failures in the matter. Hardy, of course, has received far more attention than either of the other two novelists, and this is perhaps only right. After all, he is a greater writer. And it may well seem that there is no good reason for adding to the large and steadily growing number of commentaries that are now available on his fiction. Yet I do not think that much serious

attention has been paid to the ways in which he uses his fictional women to focus on precisely those issues of class and
separation which his novels explore, and which give them their
especial distinction. Which is why I want to write about them.

This is not to pretend that no other critic has had anything
worthwhile to say about Tess or Sue or Grace Melbury, for
example. On the other hand, I do think that one can see what
Hardy is up to if one focuses on these and other of his women in
a way that hasn't so far been done. And this means that among
other things one should try to see the later heroines in the
context of Hardy's development as a novelist (I take it for
granted that he did develop), and that it is worthwhile to try
to examine the complexity of their relationships with the
novel's men, rather than treating them as a matter of love, pure
and simple.

Hardy is, I think, unique in the *ways* in which he gives prominence to his women. In the early novels, up to and including
Far from the Madding Crowd, each heroine is contended for by
three men, after that matters become a good deal more complicated, but always choice and contention take in those
matters of class and separation which Williams rightly insists
on seeing as central to Hardy's fictional concerns.

And there is another point. Hardy often gives us our first
view of a heroine not through his eyes but through the eyes of
one of her lovers, so that we are given a vision of her that we
have to read as possibly ambiguous or as informative in ways
that the lover doesn't understand. And indeed, what happens
to the lover's vision, how it is sustained, modified or destroyed
is crucial to the meaning of Hardy's fictions because it is
crucial to the nature of the developing relationships through
which he dramatizes his exploration of the social process. Not
that Hardy actually sat down at his desk to 'dramatise an
exploration of the social process'. That's critic talk. But because
he writes about love in a social context he can't help but be
aware of the complexity of the issues he raises, and because he
was an unusually intelligent, sensitive and responsive man,
whose own involvement in the social process is both typical and
instructive (I think in particular of his evasions and conceal-
ments about his family, his 'raising' of his class status and
separation from those of his kin whom he felt to be beneath

him), his novels inevitably transform the clichés of romantic love relationships into something altogether more rich and disturbing.

II

Under the Greenwood Tree is the first of the Wessex novels and the first of Hardy's novels to be of any real interest. As the title implies it is in most respects an idyl: a holiday novel which banishes from its pages anything worse than winter and rough weather. And yet its idyllic quality is threatened by time – which sweeps away the Mellstock choir – and by Fancy Day who, as her name suggests, is at least a possible danger to the older, settled values of Dick Dewy, whom she eventually marries. Hardy divides the novel into four sections: 'Winter', 'Spring', 'Summer', and 'Autumn'; and there is as conclusion a short coda, 'Under the Greenwood Tree'. The seasonal cycle, so the novel suggests, is endlessly repeated. But set against this apparently ceaseless reiteration there is a sharp sense of time as the bringer of change, alterer of lives, of relationships, social structures. It is very lightly done. When all is said, the novel remains an idyl. And yet by the time it comes to its appointed end the choir has gone out of existence and the marriage of Dick and Fancy hints not so much at renewal within a stable community as at the real possibility of change.

I want to begin with our first view of Fancy Day. The Mellstock choir is on its customary round of carol singing on Christmas-eve night, and in due course the singers arrive at the school house. They sing their hymn, but there is no response. 'Perhaps she's just come from some noble city, and sneers at our doing', Reuben Dewy whispers. (She hasn't.) They call out a merry Christmas, and then a light makes itself visible in one of the windows of the upper floor.

> It came so close to the blind that the exact position of the flame could be perceived from the outside. Remaining steady for an instant, the blind went upward from before it, revealing to thirty concentrated eyes a young girl, framed as a picture by the window architrave, and unconsciously illuminating her countenance to a vivid brightness by a candle she held in her left hand, close to her face, her right hand being extended to the side of the window. She was wrapped in a white robe of some kind, whilst down her shoulders fell a twining profusion

of marvellously rich hair, in a wild disorder which proclaimed it to be only during the invisible hours of the night that such a condition was discoverable. Her bright eyes were looking into the grey world outside with an uncertain expression, oscillating between courage and shyness, which, as she recognised the semicircular group of dark forms gathered before her, transformed itself into pleasant resolution.

Opening the window, she said lightly and warmly:

'Thank you, singers, thank you!'

Together went the window quickly and quietly, and the blind started downward on its return to its place. Her fair forehead and eyes vanished; her little mouth; her neck and shoulders; all of her. Then the spot of candlelight shone nebulously as before; then it moved away.

'How pretty!' exclaimed Dick Dewy.

'If she'd been a rale waxwork she couldn't ha' been comelier,' said Michael Mail.

'As near a thing to a spiritual vision as ever I wish to see!' said Tranter Dewy, fervently.

'O, sich I never, never see!' said Leaf.

All the rest, after clearing their throats and adjusting their hats, agreed that such a sight was worth singing for [pt I, ch. v].

'Nebulous' is one of Hardy's favourite words. It crops up again and again in his writing, poetry and prose, and it nearly always accompanies or is related to a light that is visionary, to do with a loved woman. It hints at the unearthly, the unreal. Unreal, of course, can move in two different directions and it can engage both. On the one hand it is that which turns out to be a delusion, which has to fade into the common light of day; on the other it is that which suggests an incorporeal permanence of image. My feeling is that the latter possibility is one that is most fully explored in the poetry, though it is certainly there in the novels (especially *The Well-Beloved*).[2] The former is the one that customarily engages Hardy's concern in the novels. At all events one has to make a distinction between moments of vision – Hardy's own phrase – which represent or hint at a problematic permanence, and a vision such as the choir has of Fancy Day. For in this case vision fades as she becomes more substantial, comes down to earth.

There is much in the passage that repays attention. We note that the light she carries unconsciously illuminates her countenance. She allows her watchers to see more of her than she had planned. Unconscious suggests unguardedness – whereas Fancy is normally careful of her appearance; and it also suggests an absorbed absence of vanity such as sometimes attaches to her.

The light reveals a good deal about her. Not merely the disorder of her hair, the temporary failure of the respectability she wears as a badge, but the 'uncertain expression' of her eyes, with its hint that she doesn't understand the custom of the choir, nor how to respond to it. But not because she has come from some noble city, simply because the choir belongs to a moment in time that is remote from her. Yet she knows how to behave. Her response is one of pleasant resolution, not instinctive, but decisive.

To the choir, moreover, this makes her additionally unreal: waxwork – a spiritual vision. She isn't really flesh and blood to them, and the very fact that she is above them makes her a superior, unearthly image of beauty. As the novel progresses this image becomes stained with materiality, in particular for Dick, her lover.

He is not her only lover. After the choir have left the school house they move on to Farmer Shinar's, where they are told in no uncertain terms to shut up; and finally they go to the home of the new vicar, Mr Maybold, who calls out his thanks from bed. Fancy, Shinar and Maybold all have a part to play in the bringing down of the choir, all of them are socially superior to Dick and all of them are hostile or indifferent to the kind of customs with which he is identified. Yet his is a reluctant identification (there is a neatly emblematic moment in which the cart in which he and Fancy are jolting along is overtaken by a brand-new gig in which sits Shinar with a farmer-friend: Dick is immediately jealous). He is not to be mistaken for a farm labourer. His father the tranter is above that class of men, and approves of Fancy for Dick since 'her father being rather better in the world than we, I should welcome her ready enough if it must be somebody' (pt 2, ch. viii). His wife, indeed, wishes that the tranter would separate himself even more from the men with whom he daily and nightly mixes. 'Such a man as Dewy is! nobody do know the trouble I have to keep that man barely respectable. And did you ever hear too – just now at suppertime – talking about "taties" with Michael in such a labourer's way' (pt i, ch. viii). It is comic, yes, but it serves to remind us of just what a stickler for respectability Fancy herself is. To be respectable is to wish for social position or to wish to move up socially. When Dick takes the girl to Budmouth and orders tea

for them at an inn, she tells him that 'even if I care very much
for you, I must remember that I have a difficult position to
maintain. The vicar would not like me, as his school-mistress,
to indulge in *tête-à-têtes* anywhere with anybody' (pt 3, ch. 11).
At such a point we become aware that maintaining social
position quite literally demands separation – Dick ought to
take his tea elsewhere. As it happens, he stays, but Fancy's
words hint at the kind of concern that will become treated with
deadly seriousness in the later novels. Her desire for respectability looks towards Elizabeth-Jane and Grace Melbury,
where such a desire brings tragic possibilities in its wake. Not
here, to be sure: for in *Under the Greenwood Tree* respectability
can safely be laid aside or can be accommodated to a process of
inclusion rather than one of separation. At her wedding Fancy
doesn't want to walk two and two round the parish, as the
tranter takes for granted that they will. 'Respectable people
don't nowadays,' said Fancy. 'Still, since poor mother did, I
will' (pt 5, ch. 1). Poor mother. It reminds us that Fancy's
mother had married beneath her, just as Fancy is now doing.
Fancy's eyes are 'too refined and beautiful for a tranter's wife',
Hardy remarks; and then wrily adds, 'but, perhaps, not too
good'. At which point one recognizes how much he knows
about the history of the word 'refined' and the full extent of his
refusal to be taken in by it.[3]

Fancy's father is, however. When Dick comes to him, seeking
permission to marry her, Mr Day says:

'D'ye know what her mother was?'
    'No.'
    'A governess in a county family, who was foolish enough to marry
the keeper of the same establishment. D'ye think Fancy picked up her
good manners, the smooth turn of her tongue, her musical skill, and
her knowledge of books, in a homely hole like this? . . . Did ye know
that . . . she went to the training-school, and that her name stood
first among the Queen's scholars of her year? . . . and do ye know
what I live in such a miserly way for when I've got enough to do
without it, and why I make her work as a schoolmistress instead of
living up here?'
    'No.'
    'That if any gentleman, who sees her to be his equal in polish,
should want to marry her, and she want to marry him, he shan't be
superior to her in pocket. Now do ye think after this that you be good
enough for her?'

'No.'
'Then good-night t'ye, Master Dewy.'
'Good-night, Mr. Day' [pt 4, ch. ii].

It is worth noting that by now Dick has seen enough of Fancy
to know that she's 'perhaps, not too good' to be his wife. Her
flirtatiousness and possible vanity are lightly touched on, as is
Dick's unease about them (and after all they can be read as
tokens of her dissatisfaction with the restrictions and limitations
of Mellstock life). But he wants her because he aspires to her:
there is still something of vision that surrounds his view of her.
The nebulosity has faded, and with its going shadows and
complexities have become apparent. Yet again and again she
can return to the condition of vision. For example, after the
success of her trick to get her father to change his mind about
Dick's suitability as husband for her, Dick sees her as she comes
out of the school house, he himself being death-suited, returning
from a funeral. She is 'his goddess', and 'if ever a woman looked
a divinity, Fancy Day appeared one that morning as she
floated down the school steps, in the form of a nebulous collec-
tion of colours inclining to blue'. The meeting has its emblematic rightness, lightly and deftly touched on. Her ethereality,
his earthiness: blue against black. And then the vision fades.
'His first burst of delighted surprise was followed by less comfortable feelings, as soon as his brain recovered the power to
think.' She hasn't been thinking of him, has been absorbed in
self (just as on the night of his first vision of her she had been
'unconscious' of the effect she was producing on the choir).
  Hardy is making two points. One is that a man's vision of
woman often comes at the moment when she's least aware of
him, is, indeed, most mysteriously self-possessed, most looking
away. Second, the vision has to do with a sense that the woman
is beyond, not simply in being unattainable herself, but also
possibly unattainable because socially distanced. Fancy is not
thinking of Dick. She is, or may be, thinking (for we aren't given
her thoughts) that this morning she is to play the church organ.
For at Maybold's insistence, and with Shinar's approval, she is
at last to replace the choir, who as a result, 'Having nothing to
do with conducting the service for almost the first time in their
lives . . . felt awkward, out of place, abashed, and incon-
venienced by their hands' (pt 4, ch. v).

The moment of Dick's coming upon Fancy is therefore a
moment which in its small way dramatizes a crucial matter. It
looks before and after: to his involvement with the pattern of
life that she is indifferent to, and to his equal involvement with
what she stands for. He begins as a member of the choir and
her distant worshipper. He ends as her husband and the choir
is disbanded. But whereas he has made his choice, the choir has
no choice to make. Its members feel awkward and out of place
because they have been separated from their function; Dick's
vision of Fancy hints at a process of separation which is bound
up with change, aspiration, class status.

Fancy, for her part, nearly accepts Maybold's offer of marriage (he knows nothing of her relationship with Dick since the
demands of respectability have required her to conceal it –
that, and her hinted-at dissatisfaction with the tranter's son).
When she writes to Maybold to withdraw from her hasty
acceptance, she tells him: 'It is my nature – perhaps all
women's – to love refinement of mind and manners; but even
more than this, to be ever fascinated with the idea of surroundings more elegant and luxurious than those which have been
customary. And you praised me, and praise is life to me. It was
alone my sensations at these things which prompted my reply.
Ambition and vanity they would be called; perhaps they are
so' (pt 4, ch. vii). The candour of her letter saves her marriage
to Dick. It also tells something, no matter how fleetingly, of
him. For he, too, has been fascinated with an idea – the vision
of Fancy. What Hardy is saying, even in this fragilely beautiful
idyl, is that a man's vision of a woman has much to do with
issues that must finally be seen in terms of class and of change:
of the social process.

III

Under the Greenwood Tree was followed by *A Pair of Blue Eyes*, a
novel which has been badly underestimated by most of Hardy's
commentators. It has its flaws but it is also powerfully imagined.
The setting is, mostly, Cornwall and there can be no doubt that
the novel draws on Hardy's own experiences as the suitor of
Emma Gifford.

The novel's heroine, Elfride Swancourt, lives with her

widowed clergyman father in a remote Cornish village, and the epigraph for the first chapter is 'A fair vestal, throned in the west'. As that indicates, Elfride is from the first presented to us as a vision. Certainly that is how she appears to her lovers. Like Fancy, she has three of them. First of all, a young farmer who has loved her hopelessly, who is already dead, and whose mother is convinced that he moped himself to an early grave because of the girl's callous treatment of him. (It isn't true.) Then, when the novel opens, the young apprentice architect, Stephen Smith, comes on the scene. He falls in love with her and Elfride at first returns his love. But when he has gone away to India to make his fortune she meets an older man who, as it happens, is Smith's mentor, and this man, Henry Knight, fascinates the girl. Knight is shocked out of his bachelor ways and decides to marry her, but he learns about her earlier entanglement with Stephen, allows himself to be persuaded that she had flirted with the young farmer, and so leaves Elfride. At the end of the novel we learn that she has married the widowed Lord Luxellian, whose sickly wife and children she had become friendly with, as they were near neighbours. Not that we see anything of the marriage. Elfride has now been entirely distanced from us; and indeed, we discover what happened to her only after Knight's breaking off their affair because he accidentally discovers it himself, and discovers, too, that she is already dead. He and Stephen meet, acknowledge the fact that they were both Elfride's lovers and agree to go down to Cornwall together, where they learn her recent history. Knight tells Stephen: 'She is beyond our love, and let her be beyond our reproach. Since we don't know half the reasons that made her do as she did, Stephen, how can we say, even now, that she was not pure and true in heart.' Pure and true in heart. Knight's way of putting the matter indicates the sentimentality and rigid conventionality of his attitude to women, but the words also serve to remind us that the subtitle of *Tess of the d'Urbervilles* is 'A Pure Woman'. I wish to argue that in many ways *A Pair of Blue Eyes* tries out the subject that becomes central to Hardy's greatest novel: how male visions of a woman corrupt, compromise and finally destroy her. I do not suggest that Hardy is always in command of material or tone in the earlier novel, but for all that I think he is attempting something radical (and

which suggests a debt to Meredith a good deal more valuable
than the one he repayed him by writing *Desperate Remedies*).
Let's begin with Stephen's vision of Elfride.

> Miss Elfride's image chose the form in which she was beheld during
> these moments of singing, for her permanent attitude of visitation to
> Stephen's eyes during his sleeping and waking hours in after days. The
> profile is seen of a young woman in a pale gray silk dress with trim-
> mings of swan's-down, and opening up from a point in front, like a
> waistcoat without a shirt; the cool colour contrasting admirably with
> the warm bloom of her neck and face. The furthermost candle on the
> piano comes immediately in line with her head, and half invisible
> itself, forms the accidentally frizzled hair into a nebulous haze of light,
> surrounding her crown like an aureola. Her hands are in their place
> on the keys, her lips parted, and trilling forth, in a tender *diminuendo*,
> the closing words of the sad apostrophe:
>
> > O love, who bewailest
> > The frailty of things here,
> > Why choose you the frailest
> > For your cradle, your home, and your bier!
>
> Her head is forward a little, and her eyes directed keenly upwards
> to the top of the page of music confronting her. Then comes a rapid
> look into Stephen's eyes, and a still more rapid look back again to her
> business, her face having dropped its sadness, and acquired a certain
> air of mischievous archness the while; which lingered there for some
> time, but was never developed into a positive smile of flirtation [ch. 3].

Tom Paulin has pointed out how nearly this moment of vision
accords with Hardy's own recollection of Emma in the days
before their marriage. I think it important here, though, to
stress that the moment is fully part of the novel and in no way
intrusively autobiographical. The novelist tactfully separates
Stephen's vision of the girl from what he and we can see (the
shifts of tense in the last two sentences indicate something of the
way the separation is managed). Yet he does not pretend to
'read' Elfride in any way that will fix or type her. This is the
vision, not the portrait, of a lady. And of course the vision is
active on Stephen. He doesn't create it out of passive material.
'Miss Elfride's image chose the form. . . .' The apparently
clumsy syntax is in fact a sure lead to the way Hardy wants us
to regard the girl: as different images to different men, but only
because she contains multitudes, not because they invent her.
    Stephen's vision of Elfride is beautiful, but frailly dangerous.
One notes that the candle 'forms the accidentally frizzled hair

into a nebulous haze of light, surrounding her crown like an aureola'. It is reminiscent of the choir's vision of Fancy, it makes Elfride something of a goddess, and it alerts us to the fact that Stephen's vision of Elfride is bound up with attitudes to class. After all, she is socially above him. This is made very clear to Stephen by the girl's father, a snob with pretensions to gentility that Hardy very plainly dislikes (just as he disliked the Giffords' putting-on of airs). Swancourt mistakenly thinks that Stephen belongs to a family of landed gentry. In fact, his father is a stonemason, though Swancourt doesn't yet know it. So he tells the young man:

> 'You may be only a family of professional men now – I am not in-quisitive: I don't ask questions of that kind; it is not in me to do so – but it is as plain as the nose on your face that there's your origin! And, Mr. Smith, I congratulate you upon your blood; blue blood, sir; and, upon my life, a very desirable colour, as the world goes.'
> 'I wish you could congratulate me upon some more tangible quality,' said the younger man, sadly no less than modestly.
> 'Nonsense! that will come in time. . . . Ay, I'm a poor man – a poor gentleman, in fact: those I would be friends with, won't be friends with me; those who are willing to be friends with me, I am above being friends with' [ch. 2].

Stephen accepts Elfride's superiority as a matter of fact; and from what he says to his mother it becomes clear that his image of Elfride is radically conditioned by his view of her as above him. 'To marry her would be the great blessing of my life – socially and practically, as well as in other respects. No such good fortune as that, I'm afraid; she's too far above me. Her family doesn't want such country lads as I in it' (ch. 10). And his mother acknowledges that 'men all move up a stage by marriage. Them of her class that is, parsons, marry squires' daughters; squires marry lords' daughters; lords marry dukes' daughters; dukes marry queens' daughters.'

One can't necessarily blame Stephen for seeing Elfride in the way he does. My point is that Hardy is aware of the danger contained in such a vision. But here we come to something in *A Pair of Blue Eyes* that seems to me not quite satisfactory. In *Under the Greenwood Tree* Fancy had been presented as a girl who, while 'above' Dick socially, is flirtatious and touched with vanity. The irony of her not being too good for him is light enough. But it seems to me a simplification of matters to suggest

that Elfride, too, suffers from these same faults – and is therefore not too good for the men who fall in love with her. The
suggestion is intermittent and it doesn't do a great deal of
damage; but it allows Hardy to take a more sympathetic view
of one of her lovers than I think he deserves, or than we can
allow him.

I am not thinking of Stephen. Indeed, Hardy's treatment of
Elfride's relationship with him is near impeccable. One cannot
possibly complain, for example, of her 'certain expression of
mischievous archness', for it has exactly the right indefiniteness
and refusal to tip discernment into evaluation. And there is a
very considerable skill and tact in the way Hardy handles her
growing uncertainty about the young man's innocent youthful-
ness. I think particularly of a scene where they are out together,
she on horseback, he walking – it is the morning after he has
confessed his love for her – and she tells him that what is un-
usual in him is that his knowledge of certain things should be
combined with his ignorance of others. She cannot understand
why he has never learned to ride a horse.

> Stephen lifted his eyes to hers.
> 'You know,' he said, 'it is simply because there are so many other
> things to be learnt in this wide world that I didn't trouble about that
> particular bit of knowledge. I thought it would be useless to me; but
> I don't think so now. I will learn riding, and all connected with it,
> because then you would like me better. Do you like me less for this?'
> She looked sideways at him with critical meditation tenderly
> rendered.
> 'Do I seem like *La Belle Dame sans merci*?' she began suddenly,
> without replying to his question. 'Fancy yourself saying, Mr. Smith:
>
>>   I set her on my pacing steed,
>>   And nothing else saw all day long,
>>   For sidelong she would bend, and sing
>>   A faery's song. . . .
>>   She found me roots of relish sweet,
>>   And honey wild, and manna dew;
>
> and that's all she did.'
> 'No, no,' said the young man stilly, and with a rising colour:
>>   'And sure in language strange she said,
>>   "I love thee true." '
> 'Not at all,' she rejoined quickly. 'See how I can gallop. Now, Pansy,
> off!' And Elfride started; and Stephen beheld her light figure contract-
> ing to the dimensions of a bird as she sank into the distance – her hair
> flowing [ch. 7].

It is beautifully managed, this awareness of Elfride's that her flicker of impatience with Stephen partly suggests that she has trapped him where she herself doesn't want to be trapped (even the detail about her hair flowing suggests that it is her nature to be free – or perhaps pure. At all events, not fixed by a particular vision).

Emotionally and intellectually Elfride is a more mature person than her lover. So although when he is to go to India she agrees to elope with him to London and to marry in secret, their comic–sad journey there and back ends without the marriage taking place. She instinctively pulls back from commitment to him. And he becomes sadly aware that she can't be pinned down to his image of her. He accompanies her back to Cornwall and waits while she changes at a hotel. 'At length she came trotting round to him, in appearance much as on the romantic morning of their visit to the cliff, but shorn of the radiance which glistened about her then' (ch. 12). Stephen's knowledge of her, while by no means sufficient, has grown to the point where he recognizes her to be a good deal more troublingly complex than the fair vestal who had originally shone upon him.

All this part of the novel seems to me done with the kind of delicate tact for which Hardy is rarely given credit, but which is implicit in the good-byes that Elfride and Stephen say to one another. 'The boy and girl beguiled themselves with words of half-parting only.' 'Beguile': to cheat, to while away, to charm, to divert attention from; the word's multiple meanings are all caught up in the bitter–sweet experience which it records.

Unfortunately, the relationship of Elfride and Henry Knight isn't managed with entire success. It begins well enough. Knight has come to the Swancourt house because he is a relative of the rich widow whom Mr Swancourt has recently married, and there he meets Elfride and offends her because of the condescending manner with which he treats her.

> Elfride, in her turn, was not particularly attending to his words at this moment. She had, unconsciously to herself, a way of seizing any point in the remarks of an interlocutor which interested her, and dwelling upon it, and thinking thoughts of her own thereupon, totally oblivious of all that he might say in continuation. On such occasions she artlessly surveyed the person speaking; and then there was a time for a painter. Her eyes seemed to look at you, and past you, as you were

> then, into your future; and past your future and into your eternity –
> not reading it, but gazing in an unused, unconscious way – her mind
> still clinging to its original thought.
> This is how she was looking at Knight.
> Suddenly Elfride became conscious of what she was doing, and was
> painfully confused.
> 'What were you so intent upon in me?' he inquired.
> 'As far as I was thinking of you at all, I was thinking how clever you
> are,' she said, with a want of premeditation that was startling in its
> honesty and simplicity.
> Feeling restless now that she had so unwittingly spoken, she arose
> and stepped to the window. . . .
> Knight could not help looking at her. The sun was within ten
> degrees of the horizon, and its warm light flooded her face and
> heightened the bright rose colour of her cheeks to a vermilion red,
> their moderate pink hue being only seen in its natural tone where the
> cheek curved round into shadow. The ends of her hanging hair softly
> dragged themselves backwards and forwards upon her shoulders as
> each faint breeze thrust against it or relinquished it. Fringes and
> ribbons of her dress, moved by the same breeze, licked like tongues
> upon the parts around them, and fluttering forward from shady folds
> caught likewise their share of the lustrous orange glow [ch. 17].

This is very finely done. Elfride's rapt self-absorption, which
allows room for her absorption in another, is exactly caught and
it honours her inviolable strangeness. She exhibits here an unselfconscious concern to travel far into her own mind, to get
beyond respectabilities and conventions, and so to produce the
candour that startles both Knight and herself. 'How clever you
are.' As a result, she becomes a vision to Knight. But our vision
of her at this moment is not the same as his. The very fact that
Hardy uses the second person – 'her eyes seemed to look at
you' – suggests how he is setting down in an almost matter-of-
fact way a record of how it was. For him and for us. For Knight
it is different. 'He could not help looking at her.' Male vanity
has something to do with it, though he is certainly startled into
some kind of awareness of her strangeness. She can't be 'typed'
as this deeply conventional man would wish to type her. What
he notices are moments of tiny animation around her: the
moving ends of her hanging hair and of her fringes and ribbons.
She starts into life for him, but the life is somehow extrinsic to
her. His vision of her is, I think, condescending, limited in spite
of its genuineness.

Elfride, in her turn, has a vision of Knight. He reads the

lessons for Mr Swancourt at evening service: 'The sun streamed across the dilapidated west window, and lighted all the assembled worshippers with a golden glow, Knight as he read being illuminated by the same mellow lustre. Elfride at the organ regarded him with a throbbing sadness which was fed by a sense of being far removed from his sphere' (ch. 19). By now she is beginning to fall in love, and it is perhaps natural that she should think of him as being far removed from her sphere (that is how he regards the matter, after all). He is considerably older than she, is a city man, an intellectual and man of the world. She is in love with her vision of him.

Visions have to be undone. The trouble is that in Knight's case Hardy seems to go soft on the undoing. Indeed he often seems to endorse Knight's own sense of the gap between himself and Elfride. And this is not merely a matter of class or experience. Elfride is trivialized, she is made less not more complex: she becomes shallow and cheaply deceptive. It is done in order to make us sympathize with Knight, for when his vision of her fades because of his recognition of the 'truth', he will leave her, and that act needs a good deal of justifying. Hardy here seems to be struggling with material that is too close to him, he cannot treat it with the right kind of control.

Knight's vision of Elfride is held in his memory. 'Not till they had parted, and she had become sublimated in his memory, could he be said to have even attentively regarded her' (ch. 20, whose epigraph is 'A distant dearness in the hill'). Sublimed, sublimated. Hardyesque words. And the range of meanings for each is crucial to a full understanding of that little sentence. 'Exalted, elevated.' Yes, Elfride has been exalted by Knight. 'Raised to a high degree of purity or excellence.' Well, yes, Knight thinks of Elfride as a pure woman – in the sense of being entirely innocent of men. The word also means, when applied to physical things, 'purified, refined, rarified'. Exactly. She has become refined for him – the class meaning is important: Elfride has become possibly worthy of his affection. And in so doing has, of course, become unreal. And indeed the word also means 'that which is refined away into something unreal or non-existent'. How unreal Elfride has become in Knight's retained vision of her is made clear on the very same page where we read:

> He was intensely satisfied with one aspect of the affair. Inbred in him
> was an invincible objection to be any but the first comer in a woman's
> heart. . . . Knight's sentiments were only the ordinary ones of a man
> of his age who loves genuinely. . . .
>
> Knight argued from Elfride's unwontedness of manner, which was
> matter of fact, to an unwontedness in love, which was matter of
> inference only. Incrédules les plus crédules. 'Elfride,' he said, 'had
> hardly looked upon a man till she saw me.'

I wish I could detect a saving irony in the phrase about Knight's
sentiments being 'only the ordinary ones of a man of his age
who loves genuinely', but I can't. Hardy seems to me to be
excusing his conventionality, his innocence. 'He was intensely
satisfied with one aspect of the affair.' The irony doesn't seem
to me directed at him but at her. She is the cunning vixen who
lures him on? No, that is hardly fair, but there is no doubt that
Elfride at this point of the novel is made trivial in a way that
contradicts her earlier complexity. She simply becomes a
cowardly flirt. To put it another way. Hardy is here a good deal
closer to Knight than he will be to Angel Clare, although, as
we shall see, even Angel is treated with undue leniency. One
reason for this seems to be that Knight's disillusionment with
Elfride has something in common with Hardy's own experience
(with Emma?). Before he knows the worst, of her affair with
Stephen, Knight sits with Elfride on a high cliff where she and
her former lover had sat: 'Two or three degrees above that
melancholy and eternally level line, the ocean horizon, hung a
sun of brass, with no visible rays, in a sky of ashen hue. It was a
sky the sun did not illuminate or rekindle, as is usual at sunsets.
This sheet of sky was met by the salt mass of gray water, flecked
here and there with white' (ch. 31). It is an ominous and ill-
omened scene and immediately afterwards Elfride tells Knight
of her relationship with Stephen. Her candour puts an end to
Knight's love for her, and this is something that Hardy appears
to find natural and even proper, the more so as Knight thinks
that she and Stephen had probably enjoyed a full sexual
relationship. 'The scene was engraved for years on the retina of
Knight's eye: the dead and brown stubble, the weeds among it,
the distant belt of beeches shutting out the view of the house,
the leaves which were now red and sick to death' (ch. 34). Put
the two scenes together and it is obvious that we are in the
landscape of 'Neutral Tones'.[4]

We stood by a pond that winter day,
And the sun was white, as though chidden of God,
And a few leaves lay on the starving sod;
   – They had fallen from an ash, and were gray.

Your eyes on me were as eyes that rove
Over tedious riddles of years ago;
And some words played between us to and fro
On which lost the more by our love.

The smile on your mouth was the deadest thing
Alive enough to have strength to die;
And a grin of bitterness swept thereby
Like an ominous bird a-wing. . . .

Since then, keen lessons that love deceives,
And wrings with wrong, have shaped to me
Your face, and the God-curst sun, and a tree,
And a pond edged with grayish leaves.

It is a powerful, haunting poem, and it is so obviously close to
Hardy that discussion about a possible dramatic voice which
experiences the poem seems to me absurdly irrelevant. But the
anguish of the experience recorded in the poem has clearly
spilled over into the novel with unfortunate results, because it
means that Knight is treated with a great deal more sympathy
than he should be (after all, we don't know anything about the
woman in 'Neutral Tones', whereas we do know a lot about
Elfride, know above all that she doesn't deserve Knight's treatment of her). And because Hardy is also aware of this he has to
try to make Elfride much more trivial and immature than he
has earlier shown her to be. Hence the loss of focus.

Yet I don't want to make too much of this and suggest that
it is an especially serious matter. More important is that again
and again Hardy manages to show Elfride as a girl whose sense
of herself is threatened by the different men who love her. We
have already seen how she instinctively resents or tries to resist
Stephen's appropriation of her. It is also important to remark
that the young farmer's widowed mother, who obsessively
follows Elfride about, is a terrifying threat to her freedom (my
son loved you: he died, therefore you killed him. I will kill
you.). Being beautiful, becoming a vision to men, has dire
consequences. No wonder she should say to Knight:

> 'I almost wish you were of a grosser nature, Harry; in truth I do! Or
> rather, I wish I could have the advantages such a nature in you
> would afford me, and yet have you as you are.'
>   'What advantages would they be?'
>   'Less anxiety and more security. Ordinary men are not so delicate
> in their tastes as you; and where the lover or husband is not fastidious,
> and refined and of a deep nature, things seem to go on better, I fancy –
> as far as I have been able to observe the world' [ch. 30].

She puts the matter in words that show she is accepting him
at his own and others' evaluation. Delicate in taste. It is a
matter of refinement, of blood. Knight is 'above' her. Elfride,
in Cornwall, is the innocent country girl to be raised by his
love. But instinctively she reacts against this. 'I almost wish you
were of a grosser nature.'

Two moments in particular help us to see just how coercive
is Knight's romantic vision of Elfride. In the first we are told:
'Elfride, under Knight's kiss, had certainly been a very different
woman from herself under Stephen's. Whether for good or for
ill, she had marvellously well learnt a betrothed lady's part . . .'
(ch. 30). In the second, Knight is standing before Swancourt's
house, after Elfride has told him about her affair with Stephen.
He looks up to her dressing-room and, 'Elfride was there; she
was passing between the two windows, looking at her figure in
the cheval-glass. She regarded herself long and attentively in
front; turned, flung back her head, and observed the reflection
over her shoulder' (ch. 34). The impression this produces on
Knight is not, we are told, 'a good one'. To him it suggests
Elfride's vanity. But to us it can surely suggest that she is
studying herself in order to find out who she is, that she is trying
to recognize herself. That long attentive look seems to me to
have much to do with a desire to be able to acknowledge herself
as a pure woman, to resist the 'part' of the betrothed lady, or
perhaps to wonder whether she has the figure that men find
attractive. It is of course deeply ironic that at this moment when
she thinks she is most alone, most free to try to recognize herself,
she should in fact be watched by Knight, who has in his hand a
letter from the dead farmer's mother, which accuses Elfride of
all those things his conventional mind is quick to assume are
true and prove her unworthy of him. Even here she remains a
vision.

So that although there is an undeniable blurring of focus in the presentation of Elfride she is for the most part very well handled indeed. And she emerges as a convincing study of a girl struggling to realize her sense of herself, which means trying to keep it free from those coercive visions of her which her lovers have, which are intimately bound up with class assumptions, and which finally destroy her.

In the notes added to *Last Pages from a Journal*, Hale White notes: 'No matter how intimate you may be with your beloved, there is or ought to be in her a mystery, a something unpenetrated and impenetrable. It is as necessary as that which is known.'[5] As the pious sentimentality of Knight's last words to Stephen make clear, he cannot really understand that. His conception of women doesn't allow for the possibility of a something unpenetrated and impenetrable. He does not imagine – for his imagination deals only with what he 'knows' as conventional man – that Elfride can be pure and true in ways that have very little to do with what he means by the words. They are, however, ways in which Hardy continues to be passionately interested.

IV

When we come to *Far From the Madding Crowd* we encounter a heroine who is a good deal more difficult to place than is either Fancy or Elfride. For one thing Bathsheba has no living parents, and this is important because it means that she can have an independence of behaviour and action which is new among Hardy's women. For another, Hardy seems to me to be trying to do something far more ambitious with her than anything he had attempted with the earlier heroines. We can perhaps get some clue to what he has in mind if we ask what kind of a woman Bathsheba Everdene is (which includes asking what kind of a woman she thinks she is). What are her origins, where are her roots, what is her present social situation? Take the scene where she saves Gabriel from suffocating in his hut. He tells her:

'I believe you saved my life, Miss – I don't know your name. I know your aunt's, but not yours.'
'I would just as soon not tell it – rather not. There is no reason why I should, as you probably will never have much to do with me.'

'Still, I should like to know.'

'You can enquire at my aunt's – she will tell you.'

'My name is Gabriel Oak.'

'And mine isn't. You seem fond of yours in speaking it so decisively, Gabriel Oak.'

'You see it's the only one I shall ever have, and I must make the best of it.'

'I always think mine sounds odd and disagreeable.'

'I should think you might soon get a new one.'

'Mercy! – how many opinions you keep about you concerning other people, Gabriel Oak' [ch. III].

It may remind us of the great scene in *Our Mutual Friend*, where Eugene Wrayburn doesn't want to know Bradley Headstone's name, and reduces him to 'Schoolmaster'. Names suggest identity, so that to know the name is in some measure to know the person. Eugene doesn't want to know who Bradley is (his chosen ignorance produces, of course, disastrous consequences); and Bathsheba doesn't want to be known by Gabriel. 'You will probably never have much to do with me.' The voice of class speaks there as clearly as it does in Eugene's acceptance that Bradley's name doesn't 'concern' him. But the difference is that whereas Eugene chooses to have no doubts about his own identity, Bathsheba obviously has doubts about hers. It is hardly necessary to analyse in any detail that fragment of dialogue with Gabriel to recognize that she isn't entirely sure of herself or of her name. She thinks herself above him, wants to put him down, is warmed by his unshakeable self-reliance and composure to reveal something of herself and is then sufficiently discomposed by his familiarity to retreat into conventional flightiness and would-be acerbity. ('Mercy!' sounds to my ear slightly vulgar – as though Bathsheba isn't at all secure in the identity which she puts on when she tells Gabriel he will probably not have much to do with her.)

The point is that the impulsiveness and changes in manner of speaking that we can find in that dialogue point forward to such matters as the sending of the valentine to Boldwood and the elopement with Troy: they hint at Bathsheba's radical uncertainties about herself, which she tries to resolve by sudden action. To act is to discover herself. Or so she hopes. In short, Bathsheba offers Hardy a way of dramatizing the nature of social movement, and of how it works through individuals.

Jacob Smallbury says that her parents 'were townsfolk, and didn't live here. . . . I knowed the man and woman both well. Levi Everdene – that was the man's name, sure. "Man" said I in my hurry, but he were of a higher circle in life than that – 'a was a gentleman-tailor really, worth scores of pounds. And he became a very celebrated bankrupt two or three times' (ch. VIII). And a little later, commenting on the coolness of her manner to Oak, Hardy remarks that 'perhaps her air was the inevitable result of that social rise that had advanced her from a cottage to a large house and fields'. But Bathsheba herself doesn't find it easy to cope with that advancement, and although she can adopt the air of Mrs Charmond (shall we say), it never becomes natural to her. When, much later, she learns of Troy's affair with Fanny Robin, we are told: 'Her simple country nature, fed on old-fashioned principles, was troubled by that which would have troubled a woman of the world very little . . .' (ch. XLIII). 'Simple country nature' is perhaps over-doing it, but one sees what Hardy means.

It is in Bathsheba's relationship with the three men, however, that Hardy's meaning emerges at its richest. Risking over-simplification for the moment we might say that Oak appeals to Bathsheba's 'simple country nature', Boldwood to that air that accompanies her social rise 'from a cottage to a large house and fields', and Troy to the improbable romanticism of town-bred bankrupt gentlemen-tailors. Oak and Boldwood both have visions of Bathsheba, and she nurtures a vision of Troy. All three visions have to be shattered before Bathsheba can achieve anything like a firm sense of self.

Gabriel's first sight of her is when, imagining herself alone on a wagon, she takes out a looking-glass and studies her reflection. It is a device which Hardy has already used with Elfride and Knight and here as there the question is how to 'read' the incident.

> The picture was a delicate one. Woman's prescriptive infirmity had stalked into the sunlight, which had clothed it in the freshness of an originality. A cynical inference was irresistible by Gabriel Oak, as he regarded the scene, generous though he fain would have been. There was no necessity whatever for her looking in the glass. She did not adjust her hat, or pat her hair, or press a dimple into shape, or do one thing to signify that any such intention had been her motive in taking up the glass. She simply observed herself as a fair product of Nature

in the feminine kind, her thoughts seeming to glide into far-off though likely dramas in which men would play a part – vistas of probable triumphs – the smiles being of a phase suggesting that hearts were imagined as lost or won. Still, this was but conjecture, and the whole series of actions was so idly put forth as to make it rash to assert that intention had any part in them at all [ch. 1].

It is inevitable that Gabriel should interpret her actions as dictated by vanity, and right that Hardy should separate himself from that interpretation, and that we should therefore be left with an impression of Bathsheba that makes her something of a mystery: is she vain, shallow, coquettish; or is she trying to recognize, account for herself?

Gabriel creates her in his own image. His first vision of her is followed by another, at night, as she and her aunt tend a cow that has just given birth. He doesn't know it's her because of the 'hooding effect' of her cloak, and so, wanting

> ... to observe her features ... he felt himself drawing upon his fancy for their details. In making even horizontal and clear inspections we colour and mould according to the wants within us whatever our eyes bring in. Had Gabriel been able from the first to get a distinct view of her countenance, his estimate of it as very handsome or slightly so would have been as his soul required a divinity at the moment or was readily supplied with one. Having for some time known the want of a satisfactory form to fill an increasing void within him, his position moreover affording the widest scope for his fancy, he painted her a beauty.

The prose is pretty clumsy, but the reference to painting and the acceptance of the romantic credo about what we half-perceive and half-create make it clear that Hardy is drawing our attention to the inventiveness of Gabriel's vision. Immediately after this he recognizes who she is, and then she and her aunt 'took up the lantern, and went out, the light sinking down the hill till it was no more than a nebula' (ch. 11). That the word should make its appearance here is, I think, a clear indication of Hardy's interest in Oak's mental processes, and the fact that he has now his fixed vision of the girl. As with Dick's vision of Fancy and Stephen's of Elfride, it has to be decreated. Gabriel has to become an ignorant man again, in the sense in which Wallace Stevens meant the phrase.

It is Bathsheba, of course, who does most to shatter his vision. There is a brilliant moment – it comes after a very clumsy

description of her – when we are told of Gabriel's staring at her:
'Rays of male vision seem to have a tickling effect upon virgin
faces in rural districts; she brushed hers with her hand, as if
Gabriel had been irritating its pink surface by actual touch, and
the free air of her previous movements was reduced at the same
time to a chastened phase of itself' (ch. III). An acutely imagined
incident, and one that tells us much about the aggressive,
possessive nature of Gabriel's vision of Bathsheba, and against
which she fights back. Gabriel tells her he loves her and wants
to marry her.

> 'Mr. Oak,' she said, with luminous distinctness and common sense,
> 'you are better off than I. I have hardly a penny in the world – I am
> staying with my aunt for a bare sustenance. I am better educated than
> you – and I don't love you a bit: that's my side of the case. Now yours:
> you are a farmer just beginning, and you ought in common prudence,
> if you marry at all (which you should certainly not think of doing at the
> moment), to marry a woman with money, who would stock a larger
> farm for you than you have now' [ch. IV].

The direct practicality of this speech, and the toughness of
Bathsheba's spoken thoughts, effectively destroy Gabriel's
vision of her. She has broken free of him. And as a result he can
now deal with her at a practical level. There is a telling scene
where Gabriel rebukes her for sending the valentine to Boldwood. 'Bathsheba would have submitted to an indignant
chastisement for her levity had Gabriel protested that he was
loving her at the same time. . . . This was what she had been
expecting, and what she had not got. To be lectured because
the lecturer saw her in the cold morning light of open-shuttered
disillusion was exasperating' (ch. XX). The camera has replaced
the artist's eye. Vision cancelled by the truthful clarity of the
photograph: 'faithful as no art is'. Understandable, therefore,
that Bathsheba should feel pique at being exposed to an eye
'that will not censor blemishes'. And of course she knows she
has behaved badly to Boldwood. Self-reproach has much to do
with her exasperation.

But why send the valentine? It's part of her restlessness, her
impulsiveness, and of her desire for a full – equal – relationship.
Education and station prevent such a relationship with Gabriel,
whereas she learns that Boldwood is a squire and a man of
learning. And, as she tells Gabriel when she rejects him, she

also wants to be tamed, is almost frightened of her independence. The problem of finding herself, deciding who and what she is, tugs her in different directions. And is the cause of the valentine.

Unfortunately for her, Boldwood is very like Henry Knight in his romantic vision of women. Indeed, in many respects he is a rewriting of Knight. He doesn't like to think of Bathsheba in the market place: 'it was debasing loveliness to ask it to buy and sell, and jarred upon his conceptions of her' (ch. xvii). It is only when she is away from work that she becomes a vision to him: 'Boldwood, looking into the distant meadows, saw there three figures. They were those of Miss Everdene, Shepherd Oak, and Cainy Hall. When Bathsheba's figure shone upon the farmer's eyes it lighted him up as the moon lights up a great tower' (ch. xviii). It is an extraordinary image, and a considered one. Radiance positively flows from Bathsheba, bringing Boldwood into light. She has the power to illumine him and yet at the same time he creates the light, for in the market place she has no such effect on him.

When Boldwood proposes marriage, the decency and limitations of his view of her become obvious.

> 'I fear I am too old for you, but believe me I will take more care of you than would many a man of your own age. I will protect and cherish you with all my strength – I will indeed! You shall have no cares – be worried by no household affairs, and live quite at ease, Miss Everdene. The dairy superintendence shall be done by a man – I can afford it well – you shall never have so much as to look out of doors at hay-making time, or to think of weather in the harvest. . . . I cannot say how far above every other idea and object on earth you seem to me – nobody knows – God only knows – how much you are to me!' (ch. xix].

And there is the offer which will lead to her taming. Bathsheba is struck by it and entirely sympathetic to the 'deep-natured man who spoke so simply'. Left to herself, she muses that 'he is so disinterested and kind to offer me all that I can desire'. Yet she doesn't truly desire it. Though she may countenance this male vision of a woman's life she instinctively rebels against it, as Elfride had done. But where Hardy had occasionally cheapened Elfride in the interest of retaining our sympathy for Knight, he can now dramatize the tensions between Bathsheba and Boldwood without offending against the complexity of either. Both are treated with sympathy, and in the study of Bathsheba's agonized indecision over whether to accept or reject Boldwood's offer Hardy adroitly manages to reveal her struggle to keep free from a coercive vision of her that will separate her from herself. For the fact is that for her not to work amounts to self-separation. And indeed Boldwood's vision is of a woman parted from herself: 'you shall never have so much as to look out of doors at haymaking time, or to think of the weather in the harvest'.

Something of this comes out in the very beautiful chapter of the sheep-shearing supper, where the labourers are seated outside the house at a long table and 'an unusually excited' Bathsheba is inside the parlour window, facing down the table. The bottom place is left empty, until after the meal begins.

> She then asked Gabriel to take the place and the duties appertaining to that end, which he did with great readiness.
> At this moment Mr. Boldwood came in at the gate, and crossed the green to Bathsheba at the window. He apologised for his lateness: his arrival was evidently by arrangement.
> 'Gabriel,' said she, 'will you move again, please, and let Mr. Boldwood come there?'

It is an image of contained harmony and order such as one associates with a whole tradition of English literature going at least as far back as 'To Penshurst'. On a lower scale, it is true, but identical in its feeling of achieved repose. Except, of course, for the moving of Gabriel. And that tiny moment neatly emblematizes Hardy's refusal to be taken in by the myth of agreed order. Gabriel is shifted about at Bathsheba's whim; and is displaced by Boldwood, though he has a fuller understanding of her than the gentleman-farmer does. But she is the lady of the house, and her social position is one that makes it possible for her to deny him the right to be opposite her – to be her equal in love.

The twilight expands and, 'Liddy brought candles into the back part of the room overlooking the shearers, and their lively new flames shone down the table and over the men, and dispersed among the green shadows behind. Bathsheba's form, still in its original position, was now again distinct between their eyes and the light, which revealed that Boldwood had gone inside the room, and was sitting near her' (ch. XXIII).

The candle light shining out of the house and over Bathsheba's employees is like that of the lares and Penates: 'thy fires/Shine bright on every harth as the desires/Of the Penates had been set on flame,/To entertayne. . . .' And the singing of Coggan, Poorgrass and of Bathsheba herself remind us of that notion of social harmony and order implicit in the music which flows from the great house of Belmont: 'It is your music, Madam, of the house.' Hardy pays his tribute to the idea of achieved harmony, stability.

And at the same time he knows that it won't do. It is not merely the moving of Gabriel that reminds us that order depends on ordering; nor that Boldwood's going into the house can be seen as a dangerous invasion. There is also the threat implicit in the song Bathsheba sings. 'For his bride a soldier sought her,/And a winning tongue had he. . . .' It hints at Bathsheba's dissatisfaction with herself. As madam of the house she is separated from Gabriel; as madam she equally doesn't want Boldwood's appropriation of her.

What does she want, then? Well, what she thinks she wants turns up soon enough. The shearing-supper over, she walks round her estate and in the darkness collides with a man.

> The man to whom she was hooked was brilliant in brass and scarlet. He was a soldier. His sudden appearance was to darkness what the sound of a trumpet is to silence. Gloom, the *genius loci* at all times hitherto, was now totally overthrown, less by the lantern-light than by what the lantern lighted. The contrast of this revelation with her anticipations of some sinister figure in sombre garb was so great that it had upon her the effect of a fairy transformation [ch. xxiv].

This is her vision of Troy, a romantic one, of course, and one that she has painfully to undo. For Troy is as utterly conventional in his attitude to women as is Boldwood. This is revealed in the famous sword-exercise display, in which Bathsheba is quite passive, 'enclosed in a firmament of light, and of sharp hisses'; and it is also revealed in Troy's relationship with Fanny Robin, sentimental and brutal as that is by turns.

What Bathsheba thinks to find in Troy is a certain excitement which has to do with sexual abandonment: he is her folly, 'lymph on the dart of Eros'. It may seem that Hardy intends a reproof to Bathsheba's sexuality: 'though she had too much understanding to be entirely governed by her womanliness,

[she] had too much womanliness to use her understanding to the best advantage'. Yet I think that by womanliness Hardy means conventional 'romantic' femininity, which doesn't permit her to see that, like Isabel Archer, her choice of apparent unconventionality will lead her to be ground in the very mill of the conventional. We are told that after one meeting with Troy 'there burst upon [Bathsheba's] face when she met the light of the candles the flush and excitement which were little less than chronic with her now' (ch. xxx), and we need to recall that by the time Hardy came to use the word 'chronic' it meant not only constant, but bad, and was customarily applied to the condition of a disease (the word can be linked to the 'lymph on the dart of Eros' which Troy is for her). Troy's presence is an infection, a kind of sexual illness. It leads her to abandoning the affairs of her house, just as Boldwood's romantic love for her leads to the ruin of his harvests: between romantic love and the concerns of social life is another separation. What is apparently unconventional – the sexual excitement – is actually deeply conventional, and potentially disastrous to Bathsheba's full self-awareness.

Besides, it seems clear that she and Troy have no sexual life together. Later on we are told that Troy thought of how 'the proud girl . . . had always looked down upon him even whilst it was to love him . . .' and I detect there a hint that Troy feels himself incapable of sexual relationships unless he is the aggressor (as he certainly is with Fanny Robin).

Troy also threatens Bathsheba's social well-being, her being the madam of the house. And so we have the famous scene of the wedding-night drunkenness, and later we hear of Troy's gambling, which all but ruins her. Bathsheba's vision of him fades, and when that happens he disappears – for he is *only* vision, he himself recognizes that he can't survive once he can no longer be a vision to her. He takes off, and when he belatedly returns to Boldwood's house and Boldwood tells Bathsheba she must go to her husband, 'she did not move. The truth was that Bathsheba was beyond the pale of activity – and yet not in a swoon. She was in a state of mental *gutta serena*; her mind was for the minute totally deprived of light at the same time that no obscuration was apparent from without' (ch. LIV).

I think that such a moment shows beyond all reasonable

doubt how seriously Hardy took the psychological implications
of vision and its loss. For I do not think that he is playing with
words here. Bathsheba literally cannot see Troy because since
he is no longer a vision to her he is nothing. He has ceased to
have an identity which she can acknowledge.

By contrast, her relationship with Gabriel becomes anti-
visionary because it is anti-romantic. Each comes to accept the
other's social position, and their ripening friendship is dependent on the fact that Gabriel is once more a rising man, and
has money. The relationship is solidly bourgeois.

> He accompanied her up the hill, explaining to her the details of his
> forthcoming tenure of the other farm. They spoke very little of their
> mutual feelings; pretty phrases and warm expressions being probably
> unnecessary between such tried friends. Theirs was that substantial
> affection which arises (if any arises at all) when the two who are
> thrown together begin first by knowing the rougher side of each other's
> character and not the best till further on, the romance growing up in
> the interstices of hard prosaic reality. This good-fellowship – *cama-
> raderie* – usually occurring through similarity of pursuits, is unfor-
> tunately seldom superadded to love between the sexes, because men
> and women associate, not in their labours, but in their pleasures
> merely. Where, however, happy circumstance permits its development,
> the compounded feeling proves itself to be the only love which is
> strong as death – that love which many waters cannot quench, nor the
> floods drown, beside which the passion usually called by the name is
> evanescent as steam [ch. LVII].

Substantial: 'having a real existence'. Not a vision, not steam.
But such affection depends on 'happy circumstance' which, as
Hardy's fiction shows, is very rare indeed. Class differences,
expectation, change, the rise and fall of families and of individuals: all these matters typically forestall the circumstance
which allows for the growth of substantial affection between
Bathsheba and Oak. *Far From the Madding Crowd* is the last of
the novels to deal with a centrally successful relationship, one
in which both man and woman can allow for the substantiality
of the other's identity – simply because 'the mass of hard
prosaic reality' which largely forms their knowledge of one
another has to do with an attained, and a rare, balance of
social and economic quality as well as an unvisionary forbearance towards one another. (In the famous scene where
they work side by side to save the harvest, Gabriel is still Bathsheba's 'hand', their togetherness no more than an interlude.)

In implying, through a narrative which elaborates on their separations, how unlikely is their coming together, Hardy seems to me finely to recognize and explore a subject that is crucial to nineteenth-century experience, and in no way to be thought of as exotic, pastoral or escapist.

V

But it is with *The Return of the Native* that we can recognize in Hardy an undeniably major novelist. For it is with this novel that his imagination works at full pressure to create a fiction whose reverberations and meanings reach out disquietingly and, so it feels, in unavoidably upsetting ways. *The Return of the Native* is a tragic novel. By that I mean that its central figures – Eustacia and Clym – are defeated by social and circumstantial pressures which they heroically oppose, without ever fully understanding the hopelessly romantic nature of what they hope to set up as alternatives. It is of course a measure of their tragic stature that they should think in terms of opposition, should recognize the need for it; and should, individually, fail to make it a realizable possibility. For individual opposition is at once exotic and hopeless, is, in other words, tragic.

And also absurd. The title itself hints this much (Hardy hasn't, I think, been given the proper credit for his brilliant titles). *The Return of the Native*: it suggests a work of sentimental anthropology which is, of course, very different from what we actually get. And it prompts the obvious question – who is the native? Well, Clym of course. But Clym cannot defeat the social pressures he wants to batter down. He can't really go native. Whereas Diggory, who is a sort of parodic version of Clym, *does* go native. But he is only playing a game, assuming a role which he will throw off whenever it suits him. Eustacia also plays a part – as, for instance, when she dresses as a boy for the Mummer's Play, in which she is interested not for its own sake but because it is a means of getting to see Clym. And yet she does liken herself to the witch of Endor, Susan Nonesuch thinks that she really is a witch, and Hardy speaks of her 'Pagan eyes'. There are ways in which she would like to go native, others in which she wants to be the very opposite:

sophisticated, city-bound, class-conscious. And so with Wildeve, who has 'lowered' himself by his involvement with Tamsin, having once been 'started in that profession [of engineer] in an office at Budmouth, by those who had hoped much from him and had been disappointed' (bk i, ch. v). In short, we are confronted with a number of people who variously resist and/or cope with social pressures in ways that define how seriously they try to realize themselves, their identities and their natures. The seriousness has to do with the novel's tragic stature, just as the ways have to do with its countenancing of the absurd (though I know that this is a term Hardy wouldn't himself have used).

To say all this is to risk being ponderous, but I think it to be a necessary risk, for the *Return of the Native* is a more ambitious, deeper and stronger novel than anything that Hardy had previously attempted, and the fact needs to be stressed. I do not have the space in the present essay to deal with all the issues that the novel raises, but I want to focus particularly on Eustacia, since she herself is an important centre of interest in the novel, and also, I think, its most interesting figure. In her dark, passionate, frustrated energies she is not unlike Hedda Gabler or Turgenev's Irina Osinin, but Hardy manages marvellously to give her a uniquely stifled sense of being oppressed by the narrow cage of her existence: 'Egdon was her Hades, and since coming there she had imbibed much of what was dark in its tone, though inwardly and eternally unreconciled thereto. Her appearance accorded well with this smouldering rebelliousness, and the shady splendour of her beauty was the real surface of the sad and stifled warmth within her' (bk i, ch. vii). The title of the chapter from which those sentences come is called 'The Queen of Night', and I think it fair to admit that Hardy doesn't always avoid a sort of Swinburnian excess and silliness ('Her presence brought memories of such things as Bourbon roses, rubies, and tropical midnights; her moods recalled lotus-eaters and the march in "Athalie" '). But what he has in mind is so serious and intelligent that we have no excuse for relating his novel to those late-Victorian romances about women of dark, unholy passions (though they would repay study, and Mallock's *A Romance of the Nineteenth Century* could well be the place to start and Hardy, I think, wants to dare the comparison in order to show why it won't do). True, Eustacia's sexuality is extremely important, but it is so because it is part of a total identity that she struggles to identify and realize and which is largely frustrated by circumstance.

And this doesn't simply mean the circumstance of having to live with her grandfather ('she felt like one banished; but here she was forced to abide'). More important in the unfolding of her tragedy are the two men with whom she is involved. First, Wildeve. A man of brittle sophistication, shallow, whom she half despises and half desires (and despises herself for desiring), and whose utter conventionality abrades her. 'There isn't a note in you which I don't know', he tells her, and he speaks of her 'hot little bosom'. One can see why she both detests the trite sensuality of his words and yet responds to – or allows – his seductive mastery over her. After she has summoned him to her and he has left, Hardy notes:

> Eustacia sighed: it was no fragile maiden sigh, but a sigh which shook her like a shiver. Whenever a flash of reason darted like an electric light upon her lover – as it sometimes would – and showed his imperfections, she shivered thus. But it was over in a second and she loved on. She knew that he trifled with her; but she loved on. She scattered the half-burnt brands, went indoors immediately, and up to her bedroom without a light. Amid the rustles which denoted her to be undressing other heavy breaths frequently came; and the same kind of shudder occasionally moved through her when, ten minutes later, she lay on her bed asleep [bk 1, ch. vi].

Those sentences are not free of clumsiness. Anyone can see that. More important is to see how impressive is Hardy's attempted rendering of Eustacia's deep dissatisfactions. And how typical that he should reach for that simile of electric light to indicate the clarity of her unvisionary perception of Wildeve's worth.

Her dissatisfactions are emphatically not to be thought of simply in terms of frustrated sexuality. For that is bound up with her social awareness of herself. And it is here that Hardy seems to me to offer something piercing and original in his study of the girl. There is an especially important moment when she and Wildeve discuss in a desultory manner the probability of their running away to America (he is betrothed to Tamsin but not yet married to her), and she suddenly realizes: 'Her social superiority over him, which hitherto had scarcely ever impressed her, became unpleasantly insistent, and for the first time she felt that she had stooped in loving him' (bk 1,

ch. xi). That is the language of class. And Hardy makes us
realize how deeply Eustacia is affected by it, even to the point
of recognizing that Wildeve's notion of going to America is
vulgar rather than splendid: an escape from, rather than an
escape to. And so she murmurs: 'If it could be London, or even
Budmouth, instead of America.' Anywhere will do for a cheap
affair, anywhere that is not too far away. She doesn't really
want Wildeve.

But she does want to be away from the heath. Hence her
readiness to fall in love with Clym. For he comes from the great
world from which she had been banished on her parents' death,
and which has become in her mind a compound of 'romantic
recollections of sunny afternoons on an esplanade, with military
bands, officers, and gallants around' (bk 1, ch. vii). It is, of
course, a vulgar dream, and one that might seem to bring her
perilously close to Millicent Henning. The difference lies in the
fact that Hardy has a much stronger and surer sense of Eustacia's frustration than James does of Millicent, finely though he
manages with her. Even the vulgarity of her dream is poignant
rather than absurd. As Clym himself recognizes: 'In spite of
Eustacia's apparent willingness to wait through the period of an
unpromising engagement, till he should be established in his
new pursuit, he could not but perceive at moments that she
loved him rather as a visitant from a gay world to which she
rightly belonged than as a man with a purpose opposed to that
recent past of his which so interested her' (bk 3, ch. iv). Not
visitor, but visitant. Hardy's use of the word is obviously considered, because it includes among its meanings not merely 'a
stranger who spends a short time in a place' – though Eustacia
obviously hopes that Clym won't delay long in getting away
from the heath and taking her with him – but also, as applied
to supernatural beings or agencies, 'as revealing themselves to
mortals'. In other words, Clym recognizes that Eustacia sees
him as a kind of vision and that she is unwilling to perceive the
fact of his purpose.

No more is anyone else on the heath, it must be said. His
mother, 'a curate's daughter, who had once dreamed of doing
better things', unites with the locals in thinking him absurd or
perverse. So when Fairway wonders aloud to Clym what can
have kept him here, on the heath, Clym answers:

'I've come home because, all things considered, I can be a trifle less useless here than anywhere else. But I have only lately found this out. When I first got away from home I thought this place was not worth troubling about. I thought our life here was contemptible. To oil your boots instead of blacking them, to dust your coat with a switch instead of a brush: was there ever anything more ridiculous? I said.'

'So 'tis; so 'tis!'

'No, no – you are wrong; it isn't.'

'Beg your pardon, we thought that was your maning.'

'Well, as my views changed my course became more depressing. I found that I was trying to be like people who had hardly anything in common with myself. I was endeavouring to put off one sort of life for another sort of life, which was not better than the life I had known before. It was simply different.'

'True; a sight different,' said Fairway.

'Yes, Paris must be a taking place,' said Humphrey. 'Grand shop-winders, trumpets, and drums; and here be we out of doors in all winds and weathers – '

'But you mistake me,' pleaded Clym. 'All this was very depressing. But not so depressing as something I next perceived – that my business was the idlest, vainest, most effeminate business that ever a man could be put to. That decided me: I would give it up and try to follow some rational occupation among the people I knew best, and to whom I could be of most use. I have come home; and this is how I mean to carry out my plan. I shall keep a school as near to Egdon as possible, so as to be able to walk over here and have a night-school in my mother's house. But I must study a little at first, to get properly qualified. Now, neighbours, I must go.'

And Clym resumed his walk across the heath.

'He'll never carry it out in the world,' said Fairway. 'In a few weeks he'll learn to see things otherwise.'

' 'Tis good-hearted of the young man,' said another. 'But, for my part, I think he had better mind his own business' [bk 3, ch. i].

This mordant scene shows how impossible is Clym's dream of going native. And, anyway, the dream is much more class-bound than he is prepared to recognize – although shortly after this he tells his mother that he now plans to establish a 'good private school for farmers' sons' (bk 3, ch. iii).

Besides, Clym's purpose is naïve, even if he doesn't think so. When his mother rebukes him for his 'fancy', saying that she had always supposed 'you were going to push straight on, as other men do – all who deserve the name – when they have been put in a good way of doing well', he replies: 'Mother, I hate the flashy business. Talk about men who deserve the name, can any man deserving the name waste his time in that

effeminate way, when he sees half the world going to ruin for
want of somebody to buckle to and teach them how to breast
the misery they were born to?' (bk 3, ch. ii).

Hardy is not mocking Clym. The intensity of his idealistic
'purpose' is real enough. But very obviously his individualism –
somebody must buckle to – and his acceptance of the misery that
men are 'born to', mark him out as belonging to that line of
altruistic humanism tempered by a newer pessimism, which is
essentially a class response to a 'world view', which needn't be
pinned down to any particular decade in the nineteenth century
because it was a constantly recurring fact of all of them, and
which is ultimately divorced from the deepest understanding of
the nature of social change (though it is part of it).

There are times in the novel when Hardy himself appears to
share it. I think, for example, of that moment when, writing of
the moulding of Clym's face, he says:

> The view of life as a thing to be put up with, replacing that zest for
> existence which was so intense in early civilisations, must ultimately
> enter so thoroughly into the constitution of the advanced races that its
> facial expression will become accepted as a new artistic departure . . .
> [for] old-fashioned revelling in the general situation grows less and
> less possible as we uncover the defects of natural laws, and see the
> quandary that man is in by their operation [bk 3, ch. i].

But that nervelessly glum statement seems to me at odds with the
real strength of *The Return of the Native*. Hardy's unravelling of
the tragic consequences of Clym's involvement with Eustacia
is not, I think, to be seen as evidence of 'the effects of natural
laws', but as the result that accompanies the inevitable frustrations of any 'vision' which is romantic, possessive and therefore,
no matter how generously intended, finally corrupt.

I have already pointed out that Eustacia's vision of Clym is
of someone from a gay world who will return her to it. And of
course it has to be said that Clym's account of that world makes
clear the tawdriness of her dream, and also of the frustrations
that the dream implies (for it isn't that that she *really* wants, her
dreaming is as romantically inept as Clym's dream of 'purpose').
But it is important to note that Clym also has a vision of
Eustacia. And, as we might expect, it starts from his seeing her
at a window. She calls out to a group of men, Clym being one
of them, who are trying to rescue a bucket that has slipped to

the bottom of her grandfather's well: 'Everybody turned. The speaker was a woman, gazing down upon the group from an upper window, whose panes blazed in the ruddy glare from the west' (bk 3, ch. II). And so Eustacia becomes a fair vestal and Clym falls in love with her. And hard on this comes a crucial moment where Clym has a vision of a world freed from all social ills, which is linked to his vision of Eustacia. He goes up the barrow:

> He had often come up here without stating his purpose to his mother; but this was the first time that he had been ostensibly frank as to his purpose while really concealing it. It was a moral situation which, three months earlier, he could hardly have credited of himself. In returning to labour in this sequestered spot he had anticipated an escape from the chafing of social necessities; yet behold they were here also. More than ever he longed to be in some world where personal ambition was not the only recognised form of progress – such, perhaps, as might have been the case at some time or other in the silvery globe then shining upon him. His eye travelled over the length and breadth of that distant country – over the Bay of Rainbows, the sombre Sea of Crises, the Ocean of Storms, the Lake of Dreams, the vast Walled Plains, and the wondrous Ring Mountains. . . .
>
> While he watched the far-removed landscape a tawny stain grew into being on the lower verge: the eclipse had begun. This marked a preconcerted moment: for the remote celestial phenomenon had been pressed into sublunary service as a lover's signal. Yeobright's mind flew back to earth at the sight; he arose, shook himself, and listened. Minute after minute passed by, perhaps ten minutes passed, and the shadow on the moon perceptibly widened. He heard a rustling on his left hand, a cloaked figure with an upturned face appeared at the base of the barrow, and Clym descended. In a moment the figure was in his arms, and his lips upon hers [bk 3, ch. IV].

That seems to me imaginative writing of a very high order. Clym's almost Shelleyan-like desire is for an escape from life itself. Yeats thought of Shelley as one who hated life because 'he sought more in life than any understood' and that he would have 'wandered, lost in ceaseless reveries, in some chapel of the star of infinite desire'. Very 1890s, that prose, and yet it comes near to saying something about Clym that feels true to what Hardy is working towards in this scene. Clym is the romantic idealist, who can't accept the mess of life, who yearns towards some other world, and who has yet to learn the lesson implied in Cafavy's poem, 'The City'. 'You will not find new lands, not find another sea./The city will follow you.' The impossible vision fades, the eclipse begins, and his mind 'flew back to earth'. The cliché comes in with marvellous and telling irony, for of course Eustacia does – or should – represent the cancelling of Clym's vision, in favour of a more earthly contentment. If she doesn't it is simply because he refuses to abandon his vision of her, refuses to come fully down to earth.

He tells her that she must be his wife, and she answers by asking him to speak of Paris.

> 'Is there any place like it on earth?'
> 'It is very beautiful. But will you be mine?'
> 'I will be nobody else's in the world – does that satisfy you?'
> 'Yes, for the present.'
> 'Now tell me of the Tuileries and the Louvre,' she continued evasively.

She resists his pressurizing until he insists that he won't return to Paris because he hates his occupation there.

> 'But you can go in some other capacity.'
> 'No. Besides, it would interfere with my schemes. Don't press that, Eustacia. Will you marry me?'
> 'I cannot tell.'
> 'Now – never mind Paris; it is no better than other spots. Promise, sweet!'
> 'You will never adhere to your education plan, I am quite sure; and then it will be all right for me; and so I promise to be yours for ever and ever.'
> Clym brought her face towards his by a gentle pressure of the hand, and kissed her.

I think it proper to note here that he tells her that she mustn't 'press' him and uses 'gentle pressure of the hand' to bring her to him – having himself chosen to break off the discussion at that crucial point, since her promise to marry him depends on his giving up his 'scheme'. In short, she is made, no matter how gently, to act submissively, and his vision of her, tender and delighting though it undoubtedly is, cannot help but be coercive.

And one must also note that the vision is so powerful that he lives into it entirely, so that it obliterates everything else. There is a finely managed moment where they decide on the date of their wedding.

This was the end of their talk, and Eustacia left him. Clym watched her as she retired towards the sun. The luminous rays wrapped her up with her increasing distance, and the rustle of her dress over the sprouting sedge and grass died away. As he watched, the dead flat of the scenery overpowered him, though he was fully alive to the beauty of that untarnished early summer green which was worn for the nonce by the poorest blade. There was something in its oppressive horizontality which too much reminded him of the arena of life; it gave him a sense of bare equality with, and no superiority to, a single living thing under the sun [bk 3, ch. v].

It is of course reminiscent of Crabbe's *Lover's Journey*, but the potential is here tragic rather than comic. Clym has invested everything of significance to himself in his vision of Eustacia, and it is as though she takes all life and meaning with her, leaving him appallingly blank and vulnerable. And the intense romanticism of his vision carries the seeds of tragedy just because he does not see her as part of 'the arena of life'. She is to be apart from that, linked with 'some world' of moonscape. This vision is not to be mocked at or belittled; and I intend no demeaning criticism of it when I compared Clym with Yeats's version of Shelley; but there can be no doubt of the dangers that his vision represents.

There are hints of what is to follow in the wonderful description of the honeymoon period (from which Lawrence surely took something when he came to write of Will and Anna's honeymoon in *The Rainbow*, just as he seems to me to have found a source for his opening chapter, which explores the tensions between the Brangwen men and women in the tensions set up between Clym and Eustacia).

The heath and changes of weather were quite blotted out from their eyes for the present. They were enclosed in a sort of luminous mist, which hid from them surroundings of any inharmonious colour, and gave to all things the character of light. . . . They were like those double stars which revolve round and round each other, and from a distance appear to be one. The absolute solitude in which they lived intensified their reciprocal thoughts; yet some might have said that it had the disadvantage of consuming their mutual affections at a fearfully prodigal rate [bk 4, ch. i].

They are like Donne's planetary lovers, but they have to fall back into the world of men. And when they do there is an inevitable retreat from vision, signalled by Clym's loss of sight as he pores over his books, anxious to advance his 'scheme' (the irony of this requires no comment). As a result he must work as a furze-cutter (it is the nearest he comes to going native); and the work soothes him. In the self-absorption of the labour he is 'cheerfully disposed and calm'.

Not so Eustacia. For his work excludes her, and is moreover an affront to her vision of him. 'To hear him sing and not rebel against an occupation which, however satisfactory to himself, was degrading to her, as an educated lady-wife, wounded her through. . . . It was bitterly plain to Eustacia that he did not care much about social failure; and the proud fair woman bowed her head and wept in sick despair at thought of the blasting effect upon her own life of that mood and condition in him' (bk 4, ch. II). As with Fancy, Elfride and Bathsheba, Eustacia is agonized by thoughts of her lover's social inferiority; but where in the earlier novels the problem had been resolved it is not to be so here. And in his refusal to soften, deflect or dissolve the problem, Hardy seems to me to be offering a fiction that drives straight to the heart of the social process, and is necessarily more sombre than his previous novels had been.

Eustacia's frustrations lead her back to Wildeve. She goes to a village dance, meets him there and they find that 'the dance had come like an irresistible attack upon whatever sense of social order there was in their minds, to drive them back into old paths which were doubly irregular' (bk 4, ch. III). Eustacia has, in a sense, gone native at this point (Hardy has said of the dancers that 'for the time Paganism was revived in their hearts'), and yet the grip of social circumstance has her firm. Yeobright comes to meet her, Venn at his side, and she suspects that Diggory's keen eye 'had discerned what Yeobright's had not' – Wildeve withdrawing from her. Venn, the social outsider, the most 'native' of all the main characters has, in fact, a keen eye for social proprieties (it is another aspect of the irony implicit in the novel's title).

Clym's vision of Eustacia finally collapses when he sees her face in the mirror and reads there her guilty acknowledgement of the part she has played in his mother's death (although I think the slow piecing together of the manner of that death to be overdone and that Clym's priggishness is not treated as ruthlessly as it should be): 'the carmine flush with which warmth and sound sleep had suffused her cheeks and neck, dissolved from view, and the death-like pallor in his face flew across hers. He was close enough to see this, and the sight instigated his tongue. "You know what is the matter," he said huskily. "I see it in your face" ' (bk 5, ch. III). What he now sees cancels any previous vision of her, just as she now sees him in a bleak, unvisionary way, and one which I find much more sympathetic and convincing. We are asked to feel more for Clym than he deserves. Why should we be expected to sympathize with him? (But then who would dare to show a hero unrepentant over his mother's death?) Eustacia sees his face in the glass. 'It was ashy, haggard, and terrible.' The finality of this reminds us of 'Neutral Tones'. No wonder she should feel that 'the glory which had encircled him as her lover was gone now' (bk 5, ch. VII).

In destroying their visions of one another they destroy themselves. For it is in the nature of things impossible that they should be able to sustain an unvisionary relationship. Clym and Eustacia both have a vision, flawed, tawdry, honourable, but out of focus. A blurring of actuality. And the bleak pitilessness of the novel insists that only in death can Eustacia return to a visionary loveliness, in Clym's eyes at least. 'Pallor did not include all the quality of her complexion, which seemed more than whiteness: it was almost light' (bk 5, ch. IX).

There is something very terrible in the exacerbating energies and frustrations which finally destroy Eustacia and defeat Clym. And against this we are offered only the ordinary, muffled satisfactions of those who accept an unvisionary reading of life and so survive. And it is here that Diggory becomes of great importance. Hardy himself made it clear that he had at first intended that Venn should 'have retained his isolated and weird character to the last, and . . . have disappeared mysteriously from the heath, nobody knowing whither – Thomasin remaining a widow' (footnote to end of bk 6, ch. III). But no matter how apparently powerful such an ending would have been, its pessimism would actually have been facile compared with what we now have. For in the received ending Diggory achieves a typicality that is part of the novel's strength, its attentiveness to the nature of social change. He has after all been doing no more than slum, has in fact played the part of the 'native'. Yet as he himself says (and the remark is solidly commonsensical, who can deny it?): 'I have got so mixed up with business that my soft sentiments are gone off in vapour like. Yes, I am given up body and soul to the making of money. Money is all my dream' (bk 6, ch. II). Of course, he is partly joking, but it is a complacent joke, because he also means what he says. How else, after all, can he hope to get Tamsin? For Clym – the returned native – doesn't think him to be worth her. (Clym comes close to telling his cousin that Venn isn't quite gentleman enough for her.)

But Venn triumphs. Soft sentiments can go off like 'vapour' (like the luminous mist which had wrapped the newly-married Clym and Eustacia about). What we have left is a hard-headed, decent commonsense attitude which allows for cooperation with the social process. It is a more bluntly optimistic version of that view which comes to Mrs Yeobright when, alone, heart-wounded and ill, she watches a colony of ants who have 'established a thoroughfare across the way, where they toiled, a never-ending and heavy-laden throng. To look down upon them was like observing a city street from the top of a tower. She remembered that this bustle of ants had been in progress for years at the same spot – doubtless those of old times were the ancestors of these which walked there now' (bk 4, ch. VI). Life as ceaseless struggle – an arena of unrelieved horizontality – is what, in their different ways, both Clym and Eustacia fight against; but for both the fight ends in defeat. Victory, the novel suggests, can go only to the individual who does not fight but who cooperates. Or who lacks, or chooses to do without, vision. Vision is corrupt and corrupting, but only the visionary can be a hero. Who would be a hero on such terms?

VI

The women of Hardy's next major novel, *The Mayor of Casterbridge*, are inevitably of less interest than Eustacia. Her very independence and enforced isolation had forced choice upon her: how to live, who to live with. But the three women of the *Mayor* have no such possibilities of choice. In different ways they are all victims of their menfolk. That is one reason why it is absurd to think of *The Mayor of Casterbridge* as somehow about past versus present. It is about change all right, but in no simple way, and certainly not one that can resolve itself into opposites. It is in fact a very subtle novel and if I have comparatively little to say about it that is because I think it possible to be brief in indicating how Hardy handles its women.

We begin with a view of Henchard and Susan, walking along a highway 'and the woman enjoyed no society whatever from his presence . . . she seemed to have no idea of taking his arm, nor he of offering it; and far from exhibiting surprise at his ignoring silence she appeared to receive it as a casual thing'. And Hardy then adds that 'she had the hard, half-apathetic expression of one who deems anything possible at the hands of Time and Chance except, perhaps, fair play'.

Such a statement doesn't come from Hardy the fatalist, however. For he immediately adds that Susan's expression is probably the work of 'civilization' (ch. 1). In the context of the novel civilization means what men make of women: how they regard them, judge them and what they expect of them; and in its concern with these matters *The Mayor of Casterbridge* is very much a novel of the late nineteenth century.

It is set back much earlier, of course. Hence, the possibility of the wife sale. Henchard and Susan reach the fair, go into the furmity tent and Henchard quickly becomes drunk. He speaks of his wife in a particularly brutal manner – which she accepts – and then, drunk, brutish and evidently tired of her, he offers her for sale to the highest bidder. It is appallingly vicious, this bartering of the bride; but Susan joins in, for as she says, 'Her present owner is not at all to her liking.' That is her one assertion and she holds to it through the shocking nature of what follows (when somebody bids five shillings for her and there's laughter, Henchard says, 'No insults. . . . Who'll say a guinea?').

Hardy went out of his way to insist that such wife sales had happened in parts of Dorset early in the nineteenth century, and one shouldn't think of that as a kind of equivalent of Dickens's defence of Krook's death by spontaneous combustion. As far as Hardy is concerned the bare fact matters, because he isn't writing fable or allegory. On the contrary, actuality is all important. This is how men treated women and how women expected to be treated. Maybe not all of them, maybe not so

extremely. But the wife sale typifies the man–woman relationship. And to call up such a fact about the nature of the relationship is very late Victorian, is to think in a certain way
about 'civilization'.

Moreover, Hardy doesn't separate this episode off from the
rest of the novel. It is in no sense a detachable prelude. True,
after the wife sale we jump forward in time about eighteen
years, but, as we shall see, women still expect no 'fair play'
from their menfolk or from social attitudes; or rather, they
expect to have to subdue their identities to the wishes and
apparently just needs of the men. To see this we can look
briefly at the part Elizabeth-Jane is made to play (especially
by Henchard and by her borrowed notions of what is expected
of her).

Elizabeth-Jane is obsessed with the notion of 'respectability'.
'Don't speak to her,' she begs her mother, who has recognized
the old, and by now shabby, furmity woman and wants to
inquire whether she's seen or heard anything of Henchard.
Why not? 'It isn't respectable.' When they come to Casterbridge she suggests that they should lodge at The Three
Mariners, because she has just seen a young man go in there (it
is in fact Farfrae) and 'he is respectable'. Installed in the inn,
she doesn't mind helping to pay for their board by waiting on
him. 'He's so respectable and educated far above the rest of 'em
in the inn' (ch. viii). And when, after the débâcle of Henchard's
fair, the mayor rebukes her for dancing amid 'such a mixed
throng' as Farfrae's successful entertainment, she senses that 'her
tastes were not good enough for her position, and would bring
her into disgrace' (ch. xvii).

On this last occasion, her sense of having fallen short of what
respectability demands is doubly important, because the girl is
desperately keen to improve herself and also because Henchard
is, she knows, keen that she should do so. Keen is perhaps
hardly the word, obsessed is more like it; and that this should be
so again indicates why one can't see the novel in terms of
simplistic oppositions between past and present, since Henchard
as 'rising man' is determined to keep up with what he thinks to
be proper social form and behaviour (and in this he anticipates
Melbury's relationship with Grace). It is Henchard who, on
his first meeting with his former wife and her daughter, sees

Elizabeth-Jane's clothes as 'a respectable suit of black, and her very best [but] decidedly old-fashioned even to Casterbridge eyes' (ch. x). She must learn to keep up with fashion.

Later, he rebukes her for using dialect words. 'Good god, are you only fit to carry wash to a pig-trough, that ye use such words as those?' (ch. xx), and when she sadly decides to leave him because of his coldness towards her, he is softened by going into her room and discovering 'evidences of her care, of her endeavours for improvement' (ch. xxi). Hardy notes that her mind 'ran on acquirements to an almost morbid degree', and she constantly worries about failing to achieve respectability. So, when Lucetta says to her that her father seems distant with her, Elizabeth-Jane replies: 'It is because he does not think I am respectable. I have tried to be so more than you can imagine, but in vain' (ch. xxiv).

There is an irony here of which she is unaware, for by now Henchard has discovered that she is not his daughter but Newson's, the sailor who had bought his wife from him. She is therefore disreputable, not merely because she has failed, or so he thinks, to 'improve' herself sufficiently, but because he knows that he cannot regard her as his property. And property is how he has wanted to regard her (and again we sense here an anticipation of Melbury's attitude to Grace and, for that matter, Durbeyfield's attitude to his daughter). Henchard has made Elizabeth-Jane take his surname: 'usage is everything in these matters', he tells her; and he has also taken it as his right to decide whether she shall be courted by Farfrae. At first he prohibits it and then writes to Farfrae to say that he's changed his mind.

Everything that Elizabeth-Jane does or does not do is conditioned by her desire to please her father rather than herself; she hopes for nothing better than to become a fixed image that will answer to his aggressive proprietorial attitude towards 'his' women. This conditioning emerges most forcefully when she tells Lucetta that she shouldn't marry anyone but Henchard.

'I think when any one gets coupled up with a man in the past so unfortunately as you have done, she ought to become his wife if she can, even if she were not the sinning party. . . .'

Any suspicion of impropriety was to Elizabeth-Jane like a red rag to a bull. Her craving for correctness of procedure was, indeed, almost

> vicious. Owing to her early troubles with regard to her mother a
> semblance of irregularity had terrors for her which those whose names
> are safeguarded from suspicion know nothing of [ch. xxx].

Her attitude represents an awful triumph of respectability (and
at the same time provides evidence of Hardy's acute psychological understanding of the kind of person he's created in
Elizabeth-Jane).

Lucetta is also all for respectability, and Hardy is finely
sympathetic to her difficult situation, as he will be to Mrs
Charmond's, although it has to be said that the latter is by far
the more impressive achievement. This is because he hasn't
really very much to say about Lucetta beyond showing her to
be the bored woman, looking away from the enforced tedium
of her life. She is of good family, well bred, and well educated,
we are told, and Henchard tells Farfrae that his affair with her
'did me no harm, but was of course ruin for her' (ch. xii). Of
course.

And so Lucetta comes to Casterbridge. And falls in love with
Farfrae. A neat little scene shows how she has moved beyond
Henchard. He comes in to see her – Farfrae is already there –
and 'she seemed so transubstantiated by her change of position,
and held out her hand to him in such cool friendship, that he
became deferential, and sat down with a perceptible loss of
power. He understood but little of fashion in dress, yet enough
to feel himself inadequate in appearance beside her whom he
had hitherto been dreaming of as almost his property' (ch.
xxv). 'Position', 'power', 'property'. The words point to Hardy's
concern with the nature of the relationship between Henchard
and his women. And so he can be callously cruel to Lucetta
when she reveals the fact of her marriage to Farfrae. 'I've a
mind to punish you as you deserve! One word to this brand-
new husband of how you courted me, and your precious happiness is blown to atoms!' (ch. xxix). And yet Henchard can also
struggle free of the conventionality such words imply. That is
one of the reasons why he is a man of character and not mere
circumstance. He repents his vicious treatment of Susan, is
appalled at what happens to Lucetta as a result of the skimmity
ride, and he even – and almost selflessly – grows towards loving
Elizabeth-Jane. Hardy doesn't sentimentalize this: 'In the
midst of his gloom [Elizabeth-Jane] seemed to him a pin-point

of light. He had liked the look of her face as she answered him from the stairs. There had been affection in it, and above all things what he desired now was affection from anything that was good and pure. She was not his own; yet, for the first time, he had a faint dream that he might get to like her as his own, – if she would only continue to love him' (ch. XLI). The liking will be his, the love must be hers. And of course her love is crushed by her discovery of how he had lied to Newson. Only in his 'will' therefore can he behave selflessly to her, and decree: 'That Elizabeth-Jane Farfrae be not told of my death, or made to grieve on account of me.' His determined use of her surname spells out Henchard's pain. Farfrae has by now taken both 'his' women from him.

And this is where we reach the heart of Henchard's tragedy. For he had inclined to Lucetta as a lady well bred and well educated and she, in turn, had inclined to a man whom Elizabeth-Jane had described to her mother as being respectable and educated (more so than Henchard, it goes without saying). Lucetta and Farfrae go together. When Farfrae brings into town the 'new-fashioned agricultural implement called a horse-drill' Lucetta takes Elizabeth-Jane to look it over, and 'among the agriculturalists gathered round the only appropriate possessor of the new machine seemed to be Lucetta, because she alone rivalled it in colour' (ch. XXIV). Henchard's dream of improvement ends with himself being left behind, abandoned by former lover, by daughter and by befriended manager. He cannot continue as master of 'his' women because new means of mastery declare themselves.

But there is an implicit tragedy for the women as well. For in choosing Farfrae they choose a new form of submissiveness. Lucetta herself realizes that 'the curious double strand of Farfrae's life – the commercial and the romantic – were very distinct at times. Like the colours in a variegated cord those contrasts could be seen intertwisted, yet not mingling' (ch. XXIII). And there is a pointed incident in a novel which perhaps more than most of Hardy's fictions works by means of the near-epigrammatic scene in which Lucetta and Elizabeth-Jane watch Farfrae on market day: 'Both stole sly glances out of the window at Farfrae's shoulders and poll. His face they seldom saw, for, either through shyness, or not to disturb his mercantile mood, he avoided looking towards their quarters' (ch. XXIV). We are a long way now from the shared, unromantic and un-visionary life of Gabriel and Bathsheba – which is not to suggest that Hardy criticizes Farfrae ever. Simply, this is the way it is. Sharing becomes increasingly an impossibility in a love re-lationship (and, as we shall see in his next novel, loneliness and separation become a norm).

We should not put this down to the fact of the 'newer' world, even though the process of separation is emphasized there. We need to recall our first view of Susan and Henchard and of his 'ignoring silence'. The sense of ownership that implies separa-tion – because there is no companionship – is present from the very beginning of the novel; and indeed Farfrae is more of a companion to his women than Henchard ever was. And the life of settled respectability that Elizabeth-Jane attains with Farfrae forbids our mockery. Better that than an ignoring silence. But there is a necessary wryness in Hardy's final comment that Elizabeth-Jane's position 'was, indeed, to a marked degree one that, in the common phrase, afforded much to be thankful for'. Position: the wife of Farfrae. That is what her struggle for respectability and acquirement has brought her to. And it is significant that in the novel's last paragraph Hardy should speak of her as a person on her own, Farfrae never being mentioned. Separateness is the condition of their marriage, of her 'position'.

VII

We come now to *The Woodlanders*, which seems to me Hardy's most perfect fiction and one in which he hardly ever puts a foot wrong. It is necessary to say that much at the beginning of my discussion because what follows is an inevitably partial account in which many of the novel's greatest virtues have simply to go unremarked. But the title deserves comment. It surely suggests that we shall be dealing with a small, isolated, remote com-munity or even tribe (for there is a hint of the social-anthro-pological about *The Woodlanders*, as about *The Return of the Native*)? Certainly the novel's opening sentences look to claim a kinship with the writings of George Borrow or W. H. Hudson.

The rambler who, for old association's sake, should trace the forsaken coach-road running in a meridional line from Bristol to the south shore of England, would find himself during the latter part of his journey in the vicinity of some extensive woodlands, interspersed with apple-orchards. . . . The spot is lonely, and when the days are darkening the many gay charioteers now perished who have rolled along this way, the blistered soles that have trodden it, and the tears that have wetted it, return upon the mind of the loiterer.

But though Hardy allows for the dream of this world as immemorially ancient, settled, rooted, a world of soft primitivism, he knows that it is a dream. For although we can name some intruders who represent a threat to the apparent settled calm of the woodlanders' society – Percomb, Mrs Charmond, Fitzpiers – the settled calm is itself an illusion. At the beginning of the novel Percomb arrives in the woodlands of Little Hintock in order to bribe Marty South to part with her hair. Mrs Charmond, the lady of the great house, has taken a fancy to it, and Percomb is prepared to pay Marty two guineas for it. A straightforward case of the girl's exploitation by, and vulnerability to, the outside world, or so it may seem. But what makes Marty finally accept his money is the fact that she *is* exploited – and the word is exact even though she wouldn't think of using it – by Melbury, the timber dealer. For each thousand spars she can make for him he pays her eighteen pence, which means, as Percomb tells her, that in a day and a half's work she can earn two shillings and threepence. Her selling her hair to Percomb is a direct result of Melbury's dealings with her. And Melbury is an integral part of the woodlanders' community.

In fact, Melbury has dealings with nearly everyone, and especially with his daughter, Grace. A glance at the language he uses when talking to or about her quickly reveals that he regards her as valuable property. Indeed he speaks of her in ways that bring to mind Dickens's handling of the Veneerings, the Lammles, Silas Wegg. And to say even that is to make plain how *The Woodlanders* rejects that myth of settled community, of contentment among people far from the madding crowd, which it apparently sets out to celebrate. Melbury doesn't want his daughter to marry Giles, the man to whom she's been promised, because 'since I have educated her so well, and so long, and so far above the level of the daughters hereabout, it is *wasting her* to give her to a man of no higher standing than he' (ch. III).

The very fact that Hardy chose to italicize 'wasting her' shows how he wants us to regard the pressures that dictate or underlie Melbury's choice of words. Later, telling Giles of Mrs Charmond's request that Grace should go over to her great house and spend some time with her, he says: 'that freemasonry of education made 'em close at once. Naturally enough she was amazed that such an article – ha – ha! should come out of my home' (ch. VII). The interjected laugh hints, I think, at Melbury's startled embarrassment at finding himself prepared to use such a word of the daughter he loves. But love is corrupted by being called into the service of 'improving' her. When she 'sorrily' remarks that she seems to cost him a great deal he replies: 'never mind. You'll yield a better return' (ch. XII). And when she asks him whether he really wants to lead Fitzpiers on to propose marriage, Melbury tells her that he does: 'Haven't I educated you for it?' (ch. XXI).

Such interchanges remind us of Papa Meagles and his attitude to Pet, and indeed what happens to Fitzpiers and Grace, and Fitzpiers's attitude to the Melburys, recall what had happened between Gowan and Pet and Gowan's attitude to the Meagles. And it is all part of the social process, of separation and regrouping and of loneliness. (Even Melbury's 'touching faith in members of long-established families. . . . His daughter's suitor was descended from a line he had heard of in his grandfather's times as being once among the greatest . . . how then could anything be amiss in this betrothal' – even this reminds one of Meagles's delighted readiness to work out and recite the entire Barnacle family tree.)

Melbury even takes a perverse delight in thinking himself inferior to his daughter. He tells Giles that it's a year 'since she was in this old place, and naturally we shall look small, just at first. . . .' And Hardy notes that, 'Mr. Melbury's tone evinced a certain exultation in the very sense of inferiority that he affected to deplore . . .' (ch. IV). He repeatedly discovers snubs or slights to her. So when Giles arranges a party for the Melburys, the timber dealer is furious to discover that among the other guests are men whom he thinks unsuitable to be found in Grace's presence. 'That's the sort of society we've been asked to meet!' he says to his wife. 'For us old folk it didn't matter; but for Grace – Giles should have known better!' (ch. X). And he worries that, 'Grace will gradually sink down to our level again, and catch our manners and way of speaking, and feel a drowsy content in being Giles's wife. But I can't bear the thought of dragging down to that old level as promising a piece of maidenhood as ever lived – fit to ornament a palace wi', that I've taken so much trouble to lift up' (ch. xi). And there is a neatly emblematic moment when a gentleman-farmer speaks rudely to her. Melbury is mortified.

> 'He ought not to have spoken to 'ee like that!' said the old man in the tone of one whose heart was bruised, though it was not by the epithet applied to himself. 'And he wouldn't if he had been a gentleman. 'Twas not the language to use to a woman of any niceness. You so well read and cultivated – how could he expect ye to go shouting a view-halloo like a farm tomboy! Hasn't it cost me near a hundred a year to lift you out of all that, so as to show an example to the neighbourhood of what a woman can be? Grace, shall I tell you the secret of it? 'Twas because *I* was in your company. If a black-coated squire or pa.son had been walking with you instead of me he wouldn't have spoken to you so' [ch. xii].

Sad ironies. For of course gentlemen do speak like that, as Melbury will discovery after his daughter's marriage to Fitzpiers; and at the same time we note that the old man would have seen nothing wrong in such language being used to a farm tomboy (just as he sees nothing wrong in the amount of money he pays Marty South for her back-breaking work). And how dreadful that he should wish himself out of his own daughter's company, or her out of his. And yet that is the consequence of cultivation. For at the centre of the experience which *The Woodlanders* explores is not the contentment of a settled community but the fact of loneliness and separation.

Wherever you look in the novel you find the process of separation at work. When Giles fetches Grace home he recognizes how she has grown away from her native place. 'It seemed as if the knowledge and interests which had formerly moved Grace's mind had quite died away from her' (ch. vi). When the Melbury family arrive too early for Giles's party, the father and mother set to to help him, but Grace 'pottered idly'. She has no function now in the community, and indeed she finds that she cannot even join in the party dances: 'Grace had been away from home so long, and was so drilled in new dances, that she had forgotten the old figures . . . she was thinking, as

she watched the gyrations, of a very different measure that she
had been accustomed to tread with a bevy of sylph-like creatures
in muslin in the music-room of a large house, most of whom
were now moving in scenes widely removed from this, both as
regarded place and character' (ch. x). Not very good, I grant;
and Grace's thoughts are sketched-in as a reach-me-down
cliché. But the point is that she now finds life at Hintock no
more than 'quaint'. That she should do so is in the nature of
things, is the way of social change. And the interlocking defeated love relationships all echo the fact. Marty loves Giles
who aspires to Grace who aspires to Fitzpiers who aspires to
Mrs Charmond. For them all loneliness and separation mark
the outcome of their love affairs.

The most significant relationship is perhaps that of Grace
and Fitzpiers. The girl is pushed towards him by her father,
but why does Fitzpiers choose her? After all he condescends to
her quite as much as Mrs Charmond does. But the condescension is mostly directed at Melbury himself. Fitzpiers is frankly
disappointed when he discovers who Grace's father is: 'I didn't
anticipate quite that kind of origin for her', he tells Giles (ch.
xvi), but he none the less goes ahead and flirts with her. For he
thinks of Grace as a holiday romance (rather as Holdsworth
thinks of Phillis), and his view of Hintock life is that of the
city-dweller, for whom the county is a quaint retreat. And so
he is able to tell himself: 'This phenomenal girl will be the
light of my life while I am at Hintock; and the special beauty
of the situation is that our attitude and relations to each other
will be purely casual. Socially we can never be intimate. Anything like matrimonial intentions towards her, charming as she
is, would be absurd.' Yet shortly afterwards: 'The thought that
he might settle here and become welded in with this sylvan
life by marrying Grace Melbury flitted across his mind for a
moment. Why should he go further into the world than where
he was? The secret of happiness lay in limiting the aspirations;
these men's thoughts were conterminous with the margin of the
Hintock woodlands, and why should not his be likewise limited
– a small practice among the people around him being the
bound of his desires?' (ch. xix). As that language makes plain,
Fitzpiers is indulging a familiar enough townsman's sentimentality for 'sylvan life' which is quite divorced from any

real insight into it. Indeed, sylvan life would be a peculiarly inappropriate phrase for the hardships that Marty and her father endure, or for the vulnerability of Giles (all of them are exploited, their livelihoods threatened and indeed made forfeit to the whims of Mrs Charmond). And Melbury's aspirations are certainly not conterminous with 'the margin of the Hintock woodlands', certainly not as far as Grace is concerned. In short, although Fitzpiers's vision of the woodlanders is one that Hardy's critics have occasionally imagined to be Hardy's own, the doctor is quite simply inventing a world that never was. The nearest he comes to the truth of the matter is when he discovers that he is bored with the place. Fitzpiers lacks the knowledge of the area which Melbury, Winterborne and Grace have.

> They are old association – an almost exhaustive biographical or historical acquaintance with every object, animate or inanimate, within the observer's horizon. He must know all about those invisible ones of the days gone by, whose feet have traversed the fields which look so grey from his windows; recall whose creaking plough has turned those sods from time to time. . . . The spot may have beauty, grandeur, salubrity, convenience; but if it lack memories it will ultimately pall upon him who settles there without opportunity of intercourse with his kind [ch. xvii].

The passage is reminiscent of that famous remark where Hardy notes that cloud and landscapes are unimportant compared with the wear of a foot on a threshold; and it also reminds us of the associations out of which many of his greatest poems are written.

Because Fitzpiers has no associations he is forced to invent; and among the things he invents is the 'sylvan life' with a visionary Grace at its centre. For she is visionary to him, as we can tell from that extraordinary moment when she goes to the house where he lodges, enters the room where he lies asleep and sees him in the glass: 'An indescribable thrill passed through her as she perceived that the eyes of the reflected image were open, gazing wonderingly at her. Under the curious unexpectedness of the sight she became as if spell-bound, almost powerless to turn her head and regard the original. However, by an effort she did turn, when there he lay asleep the same as before' (ch. xviii). Hardy offers an explanation for this phenomenon (and of course one remembers Bathsheba's mental state

when she is belatedly confronted with her returned husband);
but the point surely is that Fitzpiers only 'sees' Grace in a kind
of waking trance?

There is a tremendous and compelling drive about the ironies
that follow each other at this point in the novel. Fitzpiers indulges his fancy about the sylvan life while sitting in the woods
reading. About him are Melbury's men, hard at work (the
doctor looks on them as 'the scene and the actors'). He lingers
until nightfall, becoming more and more attracted to the
notion of a life of 'calm contentment'. He then accidentally
comes upon Grace, discovers that she has been loved by and
has rejected another man and, thoroughly in the grip of his own
fancy, begs 'now that he is gone from the temple, that I may
draw near?' The sentimentality, and possible archness of his
words suggest that he still half-recognizes the fact that he is
playing the role of lover, is taking part in his own fiction. And
then comes a diversion when two birds fall in front of Grace and
him, 'engrossed in a desperate quarrel'. ' "That's the end of
what is called love", said someone' – who turns out to be
Marty. The blunt sense of her words banishes the sylvan scene.
And immediately after this comes the midsummer-eve game in
which Fitzpiers first claims Grace – 'You are in my arms,
dearest,' said Fitzpiers; 'and I am going to claim you, and
keep you there all our two lives!' – and then seduces Suke
Dawson. The sylvan scene allows for that, of course. Gentlemen
can behave as they like to farm tomboys.

What strikes me as so fine about all this is the way in which it
dramatizes Hardy's sense of the social process: of Fitzpiers's
involvement in a world he can casually raid because it is all
unreal, a game; and of the way in which that world is in fact
appallingly vulnerable to him and to what he stands for. And so
Melbury encourages the wedding between his daughter and the
young doctor, and immediately Fitzpiers begins to separate her
from her family and friends. He won't, he tells her, marry in
church?

> 'O,' she said with real distress. 'How can I be married except at
> church, and with all my dear friends round me!'
> 'Yeoman Winterborne among them?' [ch. xxiii].

The contempt rings out there, as it does when, in words that
directly recall Gowan, Fitzpiers says to her:

'I daresay I am inhuman, and supercilious, and contemptibly proud of my poor old ramshackle family; but I do honestly confess to you that I feel as if I belonged to a different species who are working in that yard.'

'And from me, too, then. For my blood is no better than theirs.'

He looked at her with a droll sort of awakening. It was, indeed, an anomaly that this woman of the tribe without should be standing there beside him as his wife, if his sentiments were as he had said. In their travels together she had ranged so unerringly at his level in ideas, tastes and habits, that he had almost forgotten how his heart had played havoc with his ambition in taking her to him.

'Ah, *you* – you are refined and educated into something quite different,' he said self-assuringly.

'I don't quite like to think that,' she murmured with regret [ch. xxv].

It is a crucial interchange because it marks Fitzpiers's 'awakening' from his vision of Grace, and of hers, too. In many ways he is separated from her (and his self-assuring words won't long convince him otherwise), but she is also now separated from her family, and her regret cannot change the situation back. 'If we continue to live in these rooms,' Fitzpiers tell her when the couple have taken up quarters in Melbury's house, 'there must be no mixing in with your people below. I can't stand it, and that's the truth' (ch. xxv). It is a separation which Melbury has accepted, of course, but for Grace now there are 'little carking anxieties; a curious fatefulness seemed to rule her, and she experienced a mournful want of someone to confide in' (ch. xiv).

Her experience is one that feels central to the novel and central to the kinds of process which Hardy's novel dramatizes and, for that matter, central to the nature of social change. *The Woodlanders* is not an exotic novel but an eloquent exploration of concerns that run right through the nineteenth and twentieth centuries.

Indeed, it has about it something of that feeling of relentless forward movement, of irreparability of action and decision, that help to make *Great Expectations* at once so great and so central. What is done can't be undone. I think, for example, of the beautiful and touching moment when Melbury tells Winterborne that he thinks Grace's disastrous marriage can be dissolved, and adds: ' "My boy, you shall have her yet – if you want her." His feelings had gathered volume as he said this, and the articulate sound of the old idea drowned his sight in mist' (ch. xxxvii).

Those last words carry the resonance that often attaches itself to Hardy's finest poetry. They tell not merely that Melbury is near to tears but that his wish to undo the past has clouded his gaze. He cannot now see clearly, cannot see that there can be no undoing of the past (which is not to say that Grace couldn't have left Fitzpiers, but that had she done so she would have ceased to be representative in the way that obviously engages Hardy's attention).

The sad, elegiac rhythms of the novel insist on the facts of separation and of loss. And this is particularly true of the way in which Hardy handles the developing relationship between Giles and Grace after Fitzpiers's elopement with Mrs Charmond. Grace may think of Giles that 'her early interest in [him] had become revitalised into growth by her widening perceptions of what was great and little in life' (ch. xxx), but the growth is imperfect, peters out. For she cannot undo her education, her upbringing, her social sense of self. Two delicately judged moments show how this is and must be so. The first comes when she sees Giles as 'Autumn's very brother' and they walk together in the peaceful evening.

> Her abandonment to the seductive hour and scene after her sense of ill-usage, her revolt for the nonce against social law, her passionate desire for primitive life may have showed in her face. Winterborne was looking at her, his eyes lingering on a flower that she wore in her bosom. Almost with the abstraction of a somnambulist he stretched out his hand and gently caressed the flower.
>   She drew back. 'What are you doing, Giles Winterborne?' she exclaimed, with severe surprise [ch. xxviii].

The lovely, tactful symbolism of that moment of unselfconscious abandonment on Winterborne's part is broken by Grace's sharp use of his surname. We are returned to social actualities, the grip of convention. Their rare mood of accord broken, they know that they are still apart. Knowledge defeats their vision of one another, of his somnambulistic behaviour (how often in Hardy's fiction the visionary perception of the loved one happens in a sort of trance), and of her extraordinarily moving vision of him, his face 'sunburnt to wheat-colour, his eyes blue as corn-flowers, his sleeves and leggings dyed with fruit-stains.

. . . Her heart rose from its late sadness like a released bough; her senses revelled in the sudden lapse back to Nature unadorned. The consciousness of having to be genteel because of her husband's profession, the veneer of artificiality which she had acquired at the fashionable schools, were thrown off. . . .' But such a lapse cannot last, there is no going back; and so: 'What are you doing, Giles Winterborne?'

That is one moment. The other comes after Melbury tells Giles that he wishes he could bring Grace to him, and Giles replies: 'She would hardly have been happy with me. . . . I was not well enough educated: too rough in short. I couldn't have surrounded her with the refinements she looked for, anyhow at all' (ch. XXXI). And afterwards Grace is able to feel glad that Giles and her father are once more friends.

'And then they stood facing each other, fearing each other, troubling each other's souls. Grace experienced acute regret at the sight of these wood-cutting scenes, because she had estranged herself from them . . .' (ch. XXXIII). It comes when Giles accompanies her to Sherton market and suggests that they dine together. Her marriage to Fitzpiers has, she acknowledges, 'brought her deeper solitude than any she had known before', and she is deeply grateful to Giles to find herself 'the object of thoughtful care'. Yet she cannot be happy with his proposal. 'How could she have expected any other kind of accommodation in present circumstances than such as Giles had provided? And yet how unprepared she was for this change! The tastes that she had acquired from Fitzpiers had been imbibed so subtly that she hardly knew she possessed them till confronted by this contrast . . . she felt humiliated by her present situation, which Winterborne had paid for honestly on the nail' (ch. XXXVIII). It is therefore only when Giles and Grace are somehow 'outside' society, lapsing back to nature, that they can establish a closer identification. Yet even there, in the weeping woods that are Giles's death place, we find a necessary distance-keeping, and not because Hardy chooses to bow to novelistic conventions but because Giles treats her as 'a lady'. And even after his death Grace wants her father to know 'the true circumstances of my life here' (ch. XLIII).[6]

Fitzpiers returns to claim her and they go away. And leave behind them death and decay. In particular the death of

Winterborne and, one feels, the moment of history with which
he was associated: 'The whole wood seemed to be a house of
death, pervaded by loss to its uttermost length and breadth.
Winterborne was gone, and the copses seemed to show the
want of him' (ch. XLIII). It is without doubt an intensely moving
moment, as are the words of Marty South with which the novel
ends, and which remind us that she and Giles have a quite
unvisionary perception of one another, a sense of sharing that
looks back to Gabriel and Bathsheba but which here is defeated
because other pressures intervene to separate them, so that
although Grace has a sudden awareness of their shared 'clear
gaze' and a realization that Marty 'had formed [Winterborne's]
true complement in the other sex, had lived as his counterpart,
had subjoined her thoughts to his as a corollary' (ch. XLIV), the
fact remains that Giles aspires to Grace. The inevitable defeat
of his aspiration has much to do with his death, and that it
should typifies something about the social process.

But it is not only Winterborne's death which establishes the
feeling of the inevitability of change, decay, breakdown. I
think of that sad/comic episode of the mantrap, of Tim Tangs's
desire to revenge himself on Fitzpiers, of his justified rage and
of the outcome of it which merely bring Fitzpiers and Grace
together again (Tangs's grotesque plan becomes not a real
threat but a joke, he is that much relegated to quaintness, to a
past moment). Even more eloquent is the moment at the end
of the novel when Melbury's men, searching for Grace, turn up
outside Sherton's finest hotel, just after her father has found her
with Fitzpiers.

> He left the hotel, not without relief, for to be under the eyes of strangers
> while he conversed with his lost child had embarrassed him much. His
> search-party, too, had looked awkward there, having rushed to the
> task of investigation some in their shirt-sleeves, others in their leather
> aprons, and all much stained – just as they had come from their work
> of barking, and not in their Sherton marketing attire; while Creedle,
> with his ropes and grapnels and air of impending tragedy had added
> melancholy to gawkiness [ch. XLVIII].

The collision of those two worlds ends, inevitably, with the
retreat of Melbury's, while Grace stays, to be identified with
Sherton and the hotel which had been 'rebuilt contem-
poraneously with the construction of the railway'. In a novel

where the mode of travel has conspicuously been that of the horse and horse-drawn vehicles, Hardy's sudden mention of the railway cuts deep. It, too, is part of the process, of change and separation with which *The Woodlanders* is so finely concerned and in which the women have so important a part to play.

Which leads me to Mrs Charmond. Like Grace when she is 'pottering idly', Mrs Charmond is a functionless person. She can make or destroy lives, but she is separated from any real relationship with those she hurts, just as she is separated from the labour on which her wealth depends. She is the very opposite of Marty South: her emptiness, sense of desolate ennui, is reminiscent of Lady Dedlock down at Chesney Wold.

> 'O', she murmured . . . 'the world is so dreary outside! Sorrow and bitterness in the sky, and floods of agonized tears beating against the panes. I lay awake last night, and I could hear the scrape of snails creeping up the window glass; it was so sad! My eyes were so heavy this morning that I could have wept my life away. I cannot bear you to see my face; I keep it away from you purposely. O! why were we given hungry hearts and wild desires if we have to live in a world like this? Why should Death alone send what life is compelled to borrow – rest? . . .
>
> Then, when my emotions have exhausted themselves, I become full of fears, till I think I shall die from very fear. The terrible insistencies of society – how severe they are, and cold, and inexorable – ghastly towards those who are made of wax and not of stone. O, I am afraid of them; a stab for this error, and a stab for that – correctives and regulations pretendedly framed that society may tend to perfection – an end which I don't care for in the least. Yet for this all I do care for has to be stunted and starved' [ch. xxvii].

She is play-acting, of course; and it is difficult to know what she might really care for. Yet it will not do to write her off as a fraud. Hardy does not mock her or treat her dismissively. On the contrary, he is sympathetic to her loneliness, boredom, the sheer pointlessness of her life. And one sees why she and Fitzpiers appeal to one another. For he is a welcome relief from her isolation, while she represents for him a release from the cripplingly boring world of Little Hintock. But since each is using the other, the relationship is hardly likely to prosper. That is disturbing enough. More disturbing is the fact that Grace is moving in Mrs Charmond's direction. Not willingly, perhaps, but it is what cultivation will do; what the desires of her father and the marriage to Fitzpiers threaten to bring about. She, too, could if she wished, speak of the 'terrible insistencies of society', and she, too, knows what it is to find that all she cares for 'has to be stunted and starved'. The meaning of separation from self, the denial of identity, is one of the terrible separations that *The Woodlanders* explores. But to see Hardy at full stretch with this matter we have to turn to his greatest novel, *Tess of the d'Urbervilles*.

VIII

It isn't a faultless novel. There are some serious flaws and I suspect that most of them spring from the revisions that Hardy made to the book, all of them in the interest of 'purifying' Tess, thereby making it less possible for a critical hue and cry to be raised over it. The process of revision has been very well discussed by J. T. Laird in *The Shaping of 'Tess of the d'Urbervilles'*, and there is no point in my going over ground he has already covered. But there are some matters he doesn't touch on or about which I find myself in disagreement, and it is worth making something of these since I think that they do some damage to the novel.

In the first place, it needs to be said that in the revised version Alec comes out as an altogether 'blacker' figure and as a result seems a cruder figure. Indeed he seems to me to be something of a conventionally melodramatic villain. 'He had an almost swarthy complexion, with full lips, badly moulded, though red and smooth, above which was a well-groomed black moustache with curled points, though his age could not be more than three-or-four-and-twenty. Despite the touches of barbarism in his contours, there was a singular force in the gentleman's face, and in his bold rolling eye' (phase one, v).

Second, I think Hardy is far too lenient in his treatment of Angel, especially after his discovery of Tess's seduction by Alec. It's as though he anticipates a conventional response from his readers and goes halfway to meet it. And so he writes of Angel:

> He was embittered by the conviction that all this desolation had been brought about by the accident of her being a d'Urberville. When he found that Tess came of that exhausted ancient line, and was not of the new tribes from below, as he had fondly dreamed, why had he not stoically abandoned her, in fidelity to his principles? This was what he had got by apostasy, and his punishment was deserved.

> Then he became weary and anxious, and his anxiety increased. He
> wondered if he had treated her unfairly. . . .

Well, 'yes', is the obvious answer to that, but Hardy doesn't
get there for another five lumbering pages, when he finally
brings himself to say:

> . . . with all his attempted independence of judgment this advanced
> and well-meaning young man, a sample product of the last five-and-
> twenty years, was yet the slave to custom and conventionality when
> surprised back into his early teachings. No prophet had told him, and
> he was not prophet enough to tell himself, that essentially this young
> wife of his was as deserving of the praise of King Lemuel as any other
> woman endowed with the same dislike of evil, her moral value having
> to be reckoned not by achievement but by tendency [phase five, xxxix].

It is a soggy piece of writing and one that offers to protect
Angel more than feels right. It reminds me of the unduly
generous treatment of Henry Knight, of Clym after his banishment of Eustacia and of the fact that John Loveday is positively
applauded for scaring off his brother's intended wife, having
recognized in her an actress and camp follower (for this see
The Trumpet Major, ch. xviii).

A partial explanation for Hardy's soft attitude to Angel must
lie, I think, in Angel's own 'conviction that all this desolation
had been brought about by the accident of her being a d'Urberville'. Of course, we want to take that ironically; but what
prevents us from confidently doing so is that Hardy himself
makes so much of the heredity theme – far more than he had
originally planned. And I am thinking here less of the novel's
clumsily comic opening (although I do think that the tone of
the opening pages is misjudged) than of those moments when
Hardy intrudes into his novel in order to 'explain' Tess in
terms of her d'Urberville blood. As for example, when he notes
that she is 'an almost standard woman, but for the slight in-
cautiousness of character inherited from her race' (phase two,
xiv), or when, Angel having decided to leave Tess, she submits
to his conditions, and Hardy writes: 'Pride, too, entered into
her submission – which perhaps was a symptom of that reckless
acquiescence in chance too apparent in the whole d'Urberville
family . . .' (phase five, xxxvii); or when, after her murder of
Alec and her confession to Angel, he is amazed at her affection
for himself 'which had apparently extinguished her moral sense

altogether. Unable to realise the gravity of her conduct she seemed at last content; and he looked at her as she lay upon his shoulder, weeping with happiness, and wondered what obscure strain in the d'Urberville blood had led to this aberration – if it were an aberration' (phase seven, LVII).

I don't think that those last few words really do much to save the situation. And I doubt if they are meant to. For Hardy seems to have taken quite seriously the 'blood taint' of the d'Urbervilles (just as he will take seriously the curse of the Fawleys). I suppose he hopes by means of it to exonerate Tess, but it has the opposite effect, since it makes her less of a free moral agent and more of a hunted animal, which imagery is made much more of in the revised version. So the impact of her being a pure woman is muffled and indeed there are moments when it feels as though Hardy intends the phrase to be applied in a thoroughly demeaning sense. On more than one occasion he refers to Tess, the 'standard woman', as a vehicle for sensations rather than thoughts. Oh, *that's* what women are like. Of course the phrase can demean, as in the way in which Angel thinks of Tess as pure and as a result of which he is absurdly condescending to her (before the marriage, anyway). True, he tells himself that Tess is 'no insignificant creature to toy with and dismiss; but a woman living her precious life – a life, which, to herself who endured or enjoyed it, possessed as a great a dimension as the life of the mightiest himself' (phase four, xxv), but as the tone of that suggests, Angel has difficulty realizing Tess as woman. And in fact she is much nearer a toy to him: 'You are a child to me, Tess,' he says, and throughout his courtship of her he finds it almost impossible to take her seriously. And we should note that Alec finds Tess attractive partly because she is pure; deflowering a virgin counts for more.

They demean, Hardy shouldn't. Yet the heredity theme runs the risk of doing precisely that. But having said that much I want to add that for the most part Hardy keeps clear of unfortunate generalizations and explanations. Simply, Tess is a pure woman. And this is where we come to the heart of the matter. For in spite of its flaws *Tess of the d'Urbervilles* is a great novel about a girl who tries to discover, and live into, a secure identity, a sense of self that shan't be fixed for her, shan't deny her her own sense of integrity. And of course the whole relentless pressure of the novel is towards showing how again and again she has to struggle free of various 'fixed' images of purity and womanhood, how she desperately tries not to be 'owned', 'possessed', how the men in the novel – Alec, Dairyman Crick, Angel, Farmer Groby – do in different ways 'own' her, and how finally they defeat her struggles, so that at the end, when she lies asleep on Stonehenge, her breathing comes quick and small, 'like that of a lesser creature than a woman', words which are heartbreaking in their sad, grieving eloquence. Even the fact that she lives by sensations rather than thoughts may not be totally demeaning – though I think that Hardy puts the matter badly and that it occasionally allows him to condescend to her. More justifiably, however, it implies that Tess tries to intuit rather than rationalize or arrive by intellectual means at her sense of self, that she has no words to compete with the men's sense of her, only a determination to live – if she possibly can – from some centre, some awareness of herself as pure woman, purely a woman. 'I know if you don't ask me,' St Augustine famously said when he was asked to explain time; and in a way the words apply to Tess's sense of self. If the centre will not hold it is because of the ways in which it is constantly denied, as men think of her in their terms as pure or impure and try to fix her identity. Hence of course the sombre irony of the novel's title. Almost from the first Tess has an identity pinned to her.

At the very beginning of the novel Hardy makes some attempt to show Tess as a girl looking away, caught between two worlds, speaking two languages, 'the dialect at home; ordinary English abroad and to persons of quality', dissatisfied with the 'dreariness' of her home life, glimpsing the possibilities of a better life in her first view of Angel. 'She had no spirit to dance again for a long time, though she might have had plenty of partners; but ah! they did not speak so nicely as the strange young man had done' (phase one, III). But the theme is not much developed, for although Hardy is concerned in this novel as always with separation from family and community what really engages his interest is separation from self, and the ways in which Tess's sense of selfhood is denied her.

First by her parents, who want her to claim d'Urberville connections. And then by Alec. For she reluctantly agrees to go

to the d'Urberville mansion and see if something can be done
to help her parents' dismal fortunes. She discovers that the
great house is not a 'manorial home' but 'a country-house built
for enjoyment pure and simple, with not an acre of trouble-
some land attached to it beyond what was required for resi-
dential purposes, and for a little fancy farm kept in hand by the
owner, and tended by a bailiff. . . . Everything on this snug
property was bright, thriving, and well kept. . . . Everything
looked like money, like the last coin issued from the Mint'
(phase one, v).

The Stoke d'Urbervilles represent just one moment in that
constant appropriation of land and property which, because its
intrusiveness is obvious, is thought of as somehow different
from the 'manorial home' which 'naturally' belongs. Certainly, the emphasis on new money is of real importance: it
suggests the power and attractiveness that can go with being
up-to-date, and which has much to do with the process of social
and communal separation. What matters most here, though, is
the fact that the Stoke d'Urbervilles are indulging a pastoral
fancy, and not just with their 'little fancy farm'. For Tess comes,
unwillingly and at first unknowingly to play her part in this
fancy. When she arrives she meets Alec who gives her straw-
berries to eat and then 'he filled her little basket with them;
and then the two passed round to the rose trees, whence he
gathered blossoms and gave her to put in her bosom. She
obeyed like one in a dream, and when she could affix no more
he himself tucked a bud or two into her hat, and heaped her
basket with others in the prodigality of his bounty' (phase one,
v). Apart from the obvious symbolism of the rose picking (and
one of the roses will later prick her) what matters here is that
Tess is reduced to a townsman's cliché of a pastoral shepherdess.
As pretty as a picture. And as unreal. And reminiscent of Mrs
Skewton's dream of pastoral delight: 'I assure you, Mr.
Dombey, nature intended me for an Arcadian. I am thrown
away in society. Cows are my passion. What I have ever sighed
for, has been to retreat to a Swiss farm, and live entirely
surrounded by cows – and china' (*Dombey and Son*, 21).

But Alec's fancy is a possible one because of his money and
Tess's mistaken belief about his lineage. The power he exercises
over her is material, which is what gives the special edge to her

desperate struggle to resist him (how desperate, and how committedly Hardy is writing here, can be gauged by comparing the entire sequence with the crass comedy of Festus's attempts to seduce Anne, in *The Trumpet Major* [chs vii and xxvii]). There is a revealing moment when he tells her that he has been sending presents to her family and she replies: 'I almost wish you had not. . . . It – hampers me so' (phase one, xi). The stumbling, hesitant phrase finely catches her sense that he is pinning her down, taking possession of her. So that sexual possession is for her only one aspect of his attempt to own her, and not the single decisive act that he takes it for. Which is why Hardy is right, I think, to make little of it. Of course, the demands of publishers' and readers' tastes had something to do with the matter, but undoubtedly the novel gains considerably from the discretion forced oṇ it at this moment. From Tess's point of view Alec's seduction, for all its apparently showing that he has finally mastered her (and indeed there are hints that the act is nearer to rape), still won't persuade her to accept that he now owns her.

And it is her point of view which matters. Thus, when she tells him that 'my eyes were dazed by you a little, and that was all', she is admitting that her vision of him as a possible lover led to her seduction, that she was herself partly responsible – in other words, acted freely – and that she now chooses to leave him. And it doesn't matter whether she's telling the truth or not, whether she had chosen or had been 'in a dream'. All that counts is her determination to stay free. 'I have said I will not take anything more from you and I will not – I cannot. I *should* be your creature to go on doing that, and I won't!' And again: ' "I have never really and truly loved you, and I think I never can." She added mournfully, "Perhaps, of all things, a lie on this thing would do the most good to me now; but I have honour enough left, little as 'tis, not to tell that lie. If I did love you I may have the best of causes for letting you know it. But I don't" ' (phase two, xii). That is surely totally convincing? Her strong struggle to stay free of him and of his 'fixing' her doesn't exclude an inevitable acceptance of conventional standards ('I have honour enough left, little as 'tis'), which imply their own kind of fixing, but still she can't submit to them. And so she rallies when her mother tells her that after

what has happened between her and Alec she should have got
him to marry her:

> 'Any woman would have done it, but you. . . .'
> 'Perhaps any woman would except me.'

It makes its point. And her spirit recovers even after the birth
and death of her infant. 'Some spirit within her rose auto-
matically as the sap in the twigs. It was unexpended youth,
surging up anew after its temporary check, and bringing with
it hope, and the invincible instinct towards self-delight' (phase
two, xv).

And so she sets out for her new life and her meeting with
Angel Clare. And once again has to struggle against being
'fixed' by his vision and version of her. I have to say that I find
much of the writing about Angel unsatisfactory, not simply
because Hardy takes him more seriously than feels justified, but
also because his condescension to Tess is not nearly so well
managed as that of Fitzpiers's towards Grace and the 'sylvan
life'. By comparison with Hardy's handling of that, Clare's
speculations about the 'unpractised mouth and lips' of such 'a
daughter of the soil' seem almost parodic and dangerously to
threaten the kind of man Hardy wants us to believe in.

But this criticism cannot possibly apply to the account of
their early-morning walks through the meadows, which is
Hardy at his very greatest.

> The spectral, half-compounded, aqueous light which pervaded the
> open mead, impressed them with a feeling of isolation, as if they were
> Adam and Eve. . . .
> Whilst the landscape was in neutral shade his companion's face,
> which was the focus of his eyes, rising above the mist stratum, seemed
> to have a sort of phosphorescence upon it. She looked ghostly, as if
> she were merely a soul at large. In reality her face, without appearing
> to do so, had caught the cold gleam of day from the north-east; his
> own face, though he did not think it, wore the same aspect to her.
> It was then . . . that she impressed him most deeply. She was no
> longer the milkmaid, but a visionary essence of woman – a whole sex
> condensed into one typical form. He called her Artemis, Demeter, and
> other fanciful names half teasingly, which she did not like because she
> did not understand them.
> 'Call me Tess,' she would say askance; and he did.
> Then it would grow lighter, and her features would become simply
> feminine; they had changed from those of a divinity who could confer
> bliss to those of a being who craved it [phase three, xx].

The writing here is so rich, so intensely imaginative, that any commentary is bound to feel hopelessly clumsy. But it is necessary to make a few points. And first, we note that they feel isolated, apart from and somehow outside society: like Adam and Eve. Such paradisal imaginings prefigure a descent into a fallen world. And there is the dangerous loveliness of Tess as vision to Angel, requiring that Hardy add the prosaicism which tells us of 'the cold gleam of day' on her face, and therefore subtly and movingly alerts us to the fading of vision and the fact that for all his name-calling she wants to be herself, to be called Tess. And the word 'then' which begins the next paragraph is perfectly positioned to hint at the fact that as a result of her wanting him to recognize who she is the visionary gleam fades and her features become 'simply feminine'.

There has been a previous adjustment between vision and reality, on the occasion when Angel watches Tess at her milking: '. . . and the sun chancing to be on the milking-side it shone flat upon her pink-gowned form and her white curtain-bonnet, and upon her profile, rendering it keen as a cameo cut from the dun background of the cow.' As pretty as a picture. Hardy surely intends us to notice the cliché, and also the fact that a cameo is a particularly stylized, flat form, for he immediately adds: 'How very lovable her face was to him. Yet there was nothing ethereal about it; all was real vitality, real warmth, real incarnation' (phase three, XXIV). All was real vitality. I think that Hardy enters the novel in his own right there, correcting Angel's vision of Tess, offering a muted rebuke to the notion of her as 'ethereal' – or, as he will later think of her, 'a visionary essence of woman'. ('Ethereal' means not only light, airy, but also 'celestial', 'spirit-like, impalpable'.) It is when one thinks of that and of her imploring 'Call me Tess', that one realizes just how finely and attentively Hardy's imagination is working.

This entire section of the novel is, of course, very beautiful, charged with fullness of feeling for the present loveliness of Tess and Angel's relationship and its future dangers, the 'cold gleams of day'. For they are living in a holiday world, Adam and Eve, from which they descend jarringly to the actualities of social life (as when they visit the railway station, or when he visits home and comes up against the facts of class snobbishness and prejudice). Still, for the most part they are cocooned against them, and this helps to allow for Angel's condescension towards Tess, his refusal really to understand that she is 'a woman living her precious life'.

It is Tess who is fearful about the unreality of their love, and this comes out in a moment of quite extraordinary delicacy, when Hardy writes of their marriage ceremony: 'At a pause in the service, while they were kneeling together, she unconsciously inclined herself towards him so that her shoulder touched his arm; she had been frightened by a passing thought, and the movement had been automatic, to assure herself that he was really there, and to fortify her belief that his fidelity would be proof against all things.' And hard on this comes the terrible, aching moment when she comes to accept that Angel's vision of her makes no contact with reality: 'O my love, my love, why do I love you so!' she whispered there alone; 'for she you love is not my real self, but one in my image; the one I might have been!' (phase four, xxxiii). 'She whispered there alone.' There are very few novelists who could make that insignificant phrase carry so much meaning, could give it so powerful, sad a charge.

And then follows her attempts to tell Angel about herself and his rejection of her: 'Don't Tess, don't argue. Different societies, different manners. You almost make me say you are an unapprehending peasant woman, who have never been initiated into the proportions of social things' (phase five, xxxv). The point is obvious, but it cuts deep. And it doesn't, I think, involve any parodic 'blacking' of Angel. Quite simply Tess is being denied her sense of self by the man who knows 'the proportion of social things'. As she says, hopelessly: 'I thought, Angel, that you loved me – me, my very self! If it is I you do love, O how can it be that you look and speak so?' And Angel replies: 'I repeat, the woman I have been loving is not you.' She is no longer a vision to him, and he cannot cope with the cold gleam of day. 'She knew that he saw her without irradiation.' Obvious again, perhaps, but perfectly judged.

As is the moment when he walks out of their room and she follows him with 'dumb and vacant fidelity'. That phrase is screwed up to much more tautness than might at first seem likely. 'Dumb.' Like an animal, reduced to helpless stupidity;

and words, of course, won't reach to where the tragedy is and won't give Tess back herself, now that Angel has drained happiness and the rising sap from her. Fidelity. But this is a mockery of the married state. And of course she is faithful, but in his mind hasn't been so, which is what appals him, she has been 'owned' by someone else. Vacant. I suspect that the word has lost much of the power it still had when Hardy made use of it. Right through the nineteenth century it seems to have meant not only empty, but devoid of all identifiable energy. That is how I think Wordsworth used the word in 'I wandered lonely as a cloud' (although of course for him it's akin to wise passiveness, is a necessary emptiness), and it is how Shelley used it when he wrote at the end of 'Mont Blanc':

> And what were thou, and earth, and stars, and sea,
> If to the human mind's imaginings
> Silence and solitude were vacancy?

The same meaning attaches to the use of the word in Lucy Ashton's song in the *Bride of Lammermoor*, 'Vacant heart and hand and eye/Easy live and quiet die', though here it is bitterly ironic (don't bother with life and life won't bother you). And finally we may notice Dickens's use of the word when he describes Mr Dombey watching Florence with the infant Paul in her arms, 'toiling up the great, wide, vacant staircase'. There, all energy has been drawn into the figure of Florence, and all love and human relationship too, leaving Dombey's splendid house and its great wide staircase a pathetic shell, dehumanized by his refusal to accept that girls have anything to do with Dombey and Son. I know of no greater use of the word than Dickens's, but Hardy's is not far behind. And in his case of course it also includes the older use, often linked with shepherds or country people, as where Thomson speaks of 'vacant shepherds piping in the Dale' (*The Castle of Indolence*, stanza IV). Vacant as silly as shepherd: Tess has almost been reduced to that, one feels, because she has now become a 'daughter of the soil'. (Different societies, different manners.)

And so after Angel leaves her she tries to obliterate her identity (the phrase occurs in chapter XLI) by snipping off her eyebrows; and she wishes that 'the time would come when [her brow is] bare'. She wants death, almost. For she cannot even find a secure identity in work. Alec's pursuit of her alienated the other women at the d'Urberville estate, Dairyman Crick has turned her off – and, as she rightly says to Angel, 'I don't think you ought to have felt glad, Angel. Because 'tis always mournful not to be wanted, even if at the same time 'tis convenient.' Convenient for Angel, that is, because it is a way of 'forcing your hand' (phase four, XXXII). And now work degrades her, pushing her beyond her limit, forcing her to suffer loss of wages and physical exhaustion. (A quite separate essay could and should be written on Hardy's study of the treatment of women at work.)

This brings us of course to the famous episode of the 'red tyrant' threshing-machine, that 'the women had come to serve', which further humiliates Tess – 'Groby gave as his motive in selecting Tess that she was one of those who best combined strength with quickness in untying, and both with staying power' (phase six, XLVII) – and which leads to her last desperate struggle to realize herself. For Alec has by now reappeared and offers her a way out of the appalling work to which she has been condemned; and she slaps his face, tries to finish her work. 'But Tess still kept going: if she could not fill her part she would have to leave; and this contingency, which she would have regarded with equanimity and even with relief a month or two earlier, had become a terror since d'Urberville had begun to hover round her.' But he will not leave her.

> Tess untied her last sheaf; the drum slowed, the whizzing ceased, and she stepped from the machine to the ground.
> Her lover, who had only looked on at the rat-catching, was promptly at her side.
> 'What – after all – my insulting slap, too!' said she in an under-breath. She was so utterly exhausted that she had not strength to speak louder [phase six, XLVIII].

It is a terrible trap: on the one hand a life of dehumanizing labour; on the other an equally dehumanizing (or from her point of view depersonalizing) life with Alec.

What finally decides her to go back to him is the fact that her mother and the children have been made to leave the cottage at Marlott. Tess can never really get away from economic pressures. They led her to Alec in the first place, they 'forced her hand' with Angel, they made for her degradations at Flintcomb Ash; and now they lead to her final, weary acceptance of Alec's offer that she become his mistress, cease to struggle to be herself. Hardy is quite explicit about the reason for the Durbeyfield removal from Marlott, and the way he spells it out ought to prevent any critical nonsense about 'traditional values versus the new intrusive forces'. For the Durbeyfields are not denied their home because of some sudden cataclysmic event; it is part of the social process: '. . . as the long holdings fell in they were seldom let again to similar tenants, and were mostly pulled down, if not absolutely required by the farmer for his hands. Cottagers who were not directly employed on the land were looked upon with disfavour, and the banishment of some starved the trade of others, who were thus obliged to follow' (phase six, LI). And so the Durbeyfield family has to seek a fresh home, and because the father is dead they are at a particular disadvantage: 'But to Tess and her mother's household no . . . anxious farmer sent his team. They were only women; they were not regular labourers; they were not particularly required anywhere; hence they had to hire a waggon at their own expense, and got nothing sent gratuitously' (phase six, LII). The unremitting misery of their journey, of their attempts to find lodgings, and of the hopelessness of their situation – in short of a whole series of inescapable actualities, the culmination of so many others – these are what force Tess back to Alec.

When Angel eventually finds her, 'he had a vague consciousness of one thing, though it was not clear to him till later; that his original Tess had spiritually ceased to recognise the body before him as hers – allowing it to drift, like a corpse upon the current, in a direction dissociated from its living will' (phase seven, LVI). If one thinks of her previous resilience, of her surgings of desire to become and sustain a sense of self, of the intensity of her struggles to resist the various selves given her, then that moment is both acute and terrible. And the direction dissociated from a living will leads to the pathos of her and Angel's brief escapade, as though all can now be made right by romantic conventionalities. When they are discovered asleep in an empty house: 'The caretaker was so struck with their innocent appearance, and with the elegance of Tess's gown hanging across a chair, her silk stockings beside it, the pretty parasol, and the other habits in which she had arrived because she had nothing else, that her first indignation at the effrontery of tramps and vagabonds gave way to a momentary sentimentality over this genteel elopement, as it seemed' (phase seven, LVIII). It is a final terrible taunt, a cosy fiction that denies her her identity.

IX

It remains to say something about *Jude the Obscure*. A few words will do because the novel seems to me to be something of a muddle, at least as far as Sue is concerned. The trouble is not simply that she is irritating, although she certainly is, but that Hardy himself is unable to make up his mind about her, so that it becomes almost impossible to know how one is supposed to take her. (With Arabella there is no such problem, but she is perfunctorily sketched in, part of the 'problem' of the marriage tie which novels of the 1890s take up and about which I have something to say in the next chapter.)

At first glance it may look as though with Sue we are dealing with a subject familiar enough from Hardy's earlier fiction. She is a woman in pursuit of her own identity, her sense of self; and encountering various kinds of self-separation. She is at different times an artist and a trainee teacher; and even a wife. And she is not happy in any of these roles, for they all impose upon her, constrict her. Much of this is well done and there is a particularly good moment when she writes to Jude asking him to give her away when she marries Phillotson. 'I have been looking at the marriage service in the Prayer-book, and it seems to me very humiliating that a giver-away should be required at all. According to the ceremony as there printed, my bridegroom chooses me of his own will and pleasure; but I don't choose him. Somebody *gives* me to him, like a she-ass or she-goat, or any other domestic animal' (part third, VII). And she later remarks to Jude: 'When people of a later age look back upon the barbarous customs and superstitions of the times that we have the unhappiness to live in, what *will* they say!' (part fourth, II).

She doesn't want to marry Jude, even after Phillotson has let her go (Hardy is very good on the schoolmaster). 'I think I should begin to be afraid of you, Jude, the moment you had contracted to cherish me under a Government stamp, and I was licensed to be loved on the premises by you . . .' (part fifth, 1).

So far, so good. Sue isn't a 'standard woman' because she's too articulate, too quiveringly ready to insist on her independence. But she sees herself as a representative woman, and that matters. 'Fewer women like marriage than you suppose,' she tells Jude, 'only they enter into it for the dignity it is assumed to confer, and the social advantages it gains them, sometimes – a dignity and an advantage that I am quite willing to do without' (part fifth, 1). The trouble is that Hardy also introduces the idea that it isn't the social process that makes women into victims, it's the nature of women themselves. This may not matter so much when Jude thinks to himself that he's been checked in moving towards his own ideal – and sense of self – by two women and wonders whether 'the women are to blame . . . or is it the artificial system of things, under which the normal sex-impulses are turned into devilish domestic gins and springes to noose and hold back those who want to progress' (part fourth, III). There, he is reflecting on his own bad luck and we can understand that he is hampered much more by the artificial system than by 'women'. But what are we to make of a passage in which Hardy speaks in his own person and, writing of the girl student teachers in their dormitory, says that every face bears 'the legend "The Weaker" upon it, as the penalty of the sex wherein they were moulded, which by no possible exertion of their willing hearts and abilities could be made strong while the inexorable laws of nature remain what they are' (part third, III). As soon as Hardy introduces that phrase about 'the inexorable laws of nature' we are bound to be in something of a muddle. For at the very least we would need more in the way of women than the novel actually gives us before we could begin to sort nature's laws from 'the artificial system of things', whereas all we actually get are Sue and Arabella, and the latter is so simply treated that she can count for very little.

Sue, then? But here another difficulty presents itself. For in many ways, and they be the most important ones, Sue isn't representative at all, and this seems to me very unfortunate and something for which she can't be blamed, although Hardy does, I think, feel that she can be. It isn't just that she is irritating but that she irritates him. And yet she didn't choose her surname, he did; and uses it as an indication of her essential sexlessness. *That's* her trouble! And so she is petulant and tearful: 'I *wish* I had a friend here to support me; but nobody is ever on my side!'; and at the same time wanting to be on nobody's side herself. She has an 'epicene tenderness' and when she is asleep looks as 'boyish as Ganymedes'.

It seems to me one thing for Sue to be appalled at the thought of sex with Phillotson (he is old and why should she have to submit to him) and another for her to be frightened of sex with Jude. Yes, it can represent an act of oppression, of ownership – but then that is, or ought to be, mutual. She doesn't see it like that, ever. As Jude points out it is by her wish that they are friends, not lovers; and in a moment of bewildered affection and frustration he calls her a 'spirit, you disembodied creature, you dear, sweet, tantalizing phantom – hardly flesh at all; so that when I put my arms round you I almost expect them to pass through you as through air! Forgive me for being so gross, as you call it!' (part fourth, v). If Sue fights shy of Jude she becomes interesting as a pathological case but she can hardly be thought of as a representative woman, although that is precisely how Hardy seems to want to take her elsewhere in the novel.

And that leads to another point, which is that I suspect he makes this conflation as a way of trivializing Sue – and therefore trivializing the complex of issues that the greater side of him struggles to make her represent. For there can be no doubt that a number of passages in the novel do trivialize her, make her *merely* silly, petulant, childish, irritating (as though this is what Hardy thinks the 'woman question' itself is). I think for example of her near-fainting when she discovers during the course of her teaching at Phillotson's school that she is being studied by a school inspector (part second, v), or of her prattle about liking reading 'and all that' but craving to get back to 'the life of my infancy and its freedom' (part third, II). And I think in particular of the passage where Hardy writes of her after an especially painful meeting with Jude: 'Then the slim little wife of a husband whose person was disagreeable to her, the ethereal, fine-nerved, sensitive girl, quite unfitted by temperament and instinct to fulfil the conditions of the matrimonial relation with Phillotson, possibly with scarce any man, walked fitfully along, and panted, and brought weariness into her eyes by gazing and worrying hopelessly' (part fourth, III). Hardy is doing his best to be fair to her, but I simply do not believe that he writes out of any deep feeling of respect or affection for the person he has imagined (as he certainly does for Eustacia and Tess, say). And indeed for *him* to call her ethereal suggests that she's something of an unreal vision as far as he, the novelist, is concerned.

This is not to deny that in many ways *Jude the Obscure* is a fine novel, nor even that its treatment of Sue is altogether awry. There are strong, sure moments and many have to do with her struggle to stay free, to be, as Jude puts it, 'dear, free Sue Bridehead'. But the fact is that the total effect is muddled and therefore her tragedy is muffled, so that her eventual defeat – 'can this be the girl who brought the Pagan deities into this most Christian city? . . . quoted Gibbon, and Shelley, and Mill?' – (part sixth, III), feels somehow inauthentic, especially if you compare it with Tess's. And I suspect that Hardy knew as much. At all events, *Jude the Obscure* was his last novel.

5

A Note on the Treatment of Love and Marriage in Later Victorian Fiction

In November 1895 the *Athenaeum* carried a review of *Jude the Obscure*. 'A titanically bad book', the reviewer called it, and he spelt out his reasons for finding it such a disaster.

> Sue and Jude may have been right in their detestation of the marriage tie – that is not the question: the point is that if they act as they did with their eyes open, it is absurd of them to repine because Society and Destiny do not accept their conduct in the same way that they do. . . . There is no tragedy in the foolish weakness of their behaviour as displayed here – it is merely ludicrous. . . .
> [Mr. Hardy should not have written about] the marriage tie and its permanence. Not that the subject is in itself out of place in fiction; Mr. Meredith has triumphantly shown that it is in place; but lately so many of the inferior writers of novels have stirred up the mud with this controversy, that one would have been content if so great a writer as Mr. Hardy had not touched it, if he was not going greatly to dignify it.[1]

To some extent I share the reviewer's irritation with the 'foolish weakness' of Sue and Jude, but that is not why I quote him. No, the reason for looking at what the *Athenaeum* has to say about late-nineteenth-century novels is that it can fairly be taken as a representative voice; it reflects current thinking while attempting a decent impartiality (which doesn't mean that it always achieves it); and as the reference to 'inferior writers of novels' hints, the *Athenaeum* is a good place to start if you want to get some idea of the subjects that interested novelists at any particular point in time. Not many slip through its net. And although I am not going to offer anything like a survey of all novelists, good, bad or indifferent, who wrote about the 'marriage tie and its permanence' during the last decades of the nineteenth century, it is important to note that many did.

In this respect the reviewer's reference to Meredith is crucial.

It is hardly too much to say that Meredith becomes a sort of touchstone for the *Athenaeum* during the 1890s. Hardly surprising, perhaps, seeing that this was the time of the enormous rise in his reputation (which as one might expect the magazine reflected rather than helping to create).[2] But one should note that Meredith is mostly invoked whenever women or love relationships are under discussion. In the review of *Tess of the d'Urbervilles* we are told of Tess herself: 'It is impossible not to feel for her as we feel for the most lovable of Mr. Meredith's women.'[3] And the reviewer of *Clara Hopgood* notes: 'The description . . . of Madge's gradual perception of the superficiality, mental and moral, of her first lover, is done with much subtlety, and even faintly suggests Mr. Meredith's penetrative glance into the emptiness of the conventional man.'[4]

Tess of the d'Urbervilles was published in 1891, *Jude the Obscure* in 1895, and *Clara Hopgood* a year later.[5] If we add to these an appallingly bad novel, *The Woman Who Did*, by Grant Allen, also published in 1895, we have a spread of late-Victorian novels dealing with the 'marriage tie and its permanence'. The Meredith novel that the *Athenaeum* had in mind when making comparison with Jude and Clara Hopgood would almost certainly have been *The Amazing Marriage* (1895) and just possibly *Lord Ormont and his Aminta* which had appeared the previous year and which had caused Henry James to note: 'It fills me with a critical rage, an artistic fury, utterly blighting in me the indispensable principle of respect' – a remark that has since been used as a trap door through which to drop Meredith into the flames.

I am not going to defend *Lord Ormont and his Aminta*. James was perfectly right to detest it. It is a very bad novel. *The Amazing Marriage* is, however, a different matter. It is a very good novel and Barbara Hardy has written very well about it.[6] It is one of those complex and deeply imaginative studies of marriage for which Meredith had first shown his genius in the great poem, *Modern Love*. If I say nothing more about it here it is not because I think it can be ignored but because I hope its virtues can be taken for granted and because I want to say something about an earlier and far from successful novel of Meredith's. I don't mean to be perverse in doing this. The point

is that it links up with a novel of Gissing's, *The Odd Women*,
which was published in 1892. Gissing was a great admirer of
Meredith: 'George Eliot never did such work', he told his
brother, 'and Thackeray is shallow in comparison. . . . For the
last thirty years he has been producing work unspeakably above
the best of any living writer. . . .'[7] The heroine in *The Odd Women*
is called Rhoda Nunn. How Gissing came by her surname is
obvious enough. She renounces men and marriage and devotes
herself to a lonely life of service to women. And her Christian
name? It surely recalls the eponymous heroine of Meredith's
Rhoda Fleming?

Rhoda Nunn isn't *like* Rhoda Fleming. That isn't the point.
But Meredith's novel ends with the famous words, spoken by
Rhoda's dying sister, Dahlia: 'Help poor girls.' And that *is* the
point. For though the words are spoken with Dahlia's own
plight in mind they also refer to Rhoda. *She* is to help poor girls,
and be helped.[8]

Robert Louis Stevenson praised *Rhoda Fleming* very highly.
He told an American reporter that the novel was 'the strongest
thing in English letters since Shakespeare died, and if Shakespeare could have read it he would have jumped and cried
"here's a fellow" '. To which one can only reply, oh no, he
wouldn't. *Rhoda Fleming* is a poor novel. Yet it is of interest to
us mostly because of the two sisters and the contrasting ways in
which they live and move (this use of sisters is a major struc-
tural device of the English novel from *Heart of Midlothian* and
Sense and Sensibility through to *Howards End* and *Women in Love*).
They are daughters of a hard-up Kent farmer. Rhoda is the
girl of iron principle, Dahlia the weaker and more attractive
one, who falls in love with Edward Blancove, son of Sir William
Blancove. Her father has indeed hoped that her face would be
her fortune – and the cause of mending his. But Edward is
intended for higher things in life than marriage to the daughter
of a penniless farmer. So he makes her his mistress and they go
to France. Much of the novel is tediously taken up with the
hunt for Dahlia. It is spearheaded by Robert Eccles, a reformed
drunkard and a Tom Jones kind of character (Meredith at his
worst) who loves Rhoda and eventually marries her.

The prolepsis of Dahlia's fate occurs in chapter one when the
two sisters befriend a girl with 'a spotted name' and earn their

father's displeasure. They are brought to realize that 'the kindest of men can be cruel, and will forget their Christianity towards offending and repentant women'. The sisters take it for granted that it is the woman who offends and who has to be repentant.

When Edward and Dahlia meet he sets out to train her in the ways of an ideal mistress. (A mistress has to be groomed to be socially acceptable every bit as much as a wife.) Dahlia writes to Rhoda from France:

> Persuade – do persuade father that everything will be well. . . . I know that I am life itself to Edward. He has lived as men do, and he can judge and he knows that there never was a wife who brought a heart to her husband like mine to him. He wants to think, or he wants to smoke, and he leaves me; but, oh! when he returns, he can scarcely believe that he has me, his joy is so great. . . .
>
> But you must be beautiful to please some men. You will laugh – I have really got the habit of talking to my face and all myself in the glass. . . .
>
> A spot on my neck gives me a dreadful fright. If my hair comes out much when I comb it, it sets my heart beating; and it is a *daily* misery to me that my hands are larger than they should be, belonging to Edward's 'resplendent wife.' I thank heaven that you and I always saw the necessity of being careful of our finger-nails. My feet are of moderate size, though they are not *French feet*, as Edward says. No: I shall never dance. He sent me to the dancing-master in London, but it was too late. He does not dance (or mind dancing) himself, only he does not like me to miss one perfection. It is his love. Oh! if I have seemed to let you suppose he does not love me as ever, do not think it. He is most tender and true to me [ch. IX].

Dahlia, of course, isn't Edward's wife, and as is clear from that letter, she cannot even manage to be a perfect mistress. Her pathetic dependence on him, her complete subservience to him, means that she has to turn herself into a beautiful doll. But it isn't enough.

> . . . when he was by himself, Edward pitched his book upon the floor and sat reflecting. The sweat started on his forehead. He was compelled to look into his black volume and study it. His desire was to act humanely and generously; but the question inevitably recurred: 'How can I utterly dash my prospects in the world?' It would be impossible to bring Dahlia to great houses; and he liked great houses and the charm of mixing among delicately-bred women. On the other hand, lawyers have married beneath them – married cooks, housemaids, governesses, and so forth. And what has a lawyer to do with a dainty

> lady, who will constantly distract him with finicking civilities and
> speculations in unprofitable regions? What he does want is a woman
> amiable as a surface of parchment, serviceable as his inkstand; one
> who will be like the wig in which he closes his forensic term, disreput-
> able from overwear, but suited to the purpose.
>   'Ah! if I meant to be nothing but a lawyer!' Edward stopped the
> flow of this current in Dahlia's favour [ch. xxi].

The near-Dickensian language of the last sentences is given a
special twist, one that Meredith often employs. Even Edward's
favourable thoughts of Dahlia make her utterly subservient to
him. At her best she will be suited to his purpose. Meredith
shares with Dickens a keen sense of how society encourages the
idea of taking possession of individuals, of turning them to
objects of use, and that such individuals accept this as right;
and we might note that at precisely the moment that Meredith
was allowing Edward to muse on the fact that lawyers married
beneath them, Eugene Wrayburn was marrying Lizzie Hexam.
But of course Lizzie has resisted being an object of use to
Eugene, whereas Dahlia hasn't made such resistance to
Edward.

Dahlia, indeed, is utterly conventional. She accepts that her
face should be her fortune, accepts Edward's use of her, accepts
that she is a fallen woman – she begs Robert Eccles to carry a
message to Rhoda saying: 'Dahlia was false, and repents, and
has worked with her needle to subsist, and can, and will, for her
soul strives to be clean' (ch. xxx – called, significantly, 'The
Expiation'). She even accepts that she must be made fit to face
her father, which means accepting marriage to a lumpish brute
called Sedgett so as to protect Farmer Fleming's name.

And Rhoda is equally conventional, accepting that Dahlia
is right about herself. After Dahlia's reluctant agreement to the
marriage with Sedgett, she and Rhoda talk together.

> Dahlia said, as she swept her brows, 'I am still subject to nervous
> attacks.'
>   'They will soon leave you,' said Rhoda, nursing her hand.
>   Dahlia contracted her lips. 'Is father very unforgiving to women?'
>   'Poor father!' Rhoda interjected for answer, and Dahlia's frame was
> taken with a convulsion.
>   'Where shall I see him to-morrow?' she asked; and, glancing from
> the beamless candle to the window-blinds: 'Oh! it's day. Why didn't
> I sleep! It's day! Where am I to see him?'
>   'At Robert's lodgings. We all go there.'

'We all go? – *he* goes?'

'Your husband will lead you there.'

'My heaven! my heaven! I wish you had known what this is, a little – just a little.'

'I do know that it is a good and precious thing to do right,' said Rhoda [ch. xxxv].

The point of this and much else in the novel is surely to give authority to the novel's last words? 'Help poor girls' must mean helping Rhoda to see the vicious absurdity of those conventions by means of which Dahlia is condemned and which she herself endorses. Had Dahlia kept her honour intact Edward might have married her, and that would have been a good thing. Good for Farmer Fleming's bankrupt estate, good for family pride. Attractive girls should marry above them, what else are they for? (Think of Pet Meagles, Rosamund Vincy, Tess – even of Catharine Earnshaw.) What they are *not* for is sexual freedom, the right to choose, reject, make their own discoveries. Certainly not according to any of the characters in *Rhoda Fleming*, anyway. And not according to the *Athenaeum* either. The reviewer of the novel remarked: 'All that concerns Dahlia's sacrifice of womanly honour is the least satisfactory part of the book, – her fall being a case of sin and suffering wrought through woman's heedlessness and passion rather than man's design, and her seducer having for his palliation the excuse of the boy who, on being charged with stealing his master's fruit, pleaded that the pear fell into his open hand.'[10]

There would be little point in spending time on the ludicrous double-standard morality of this were it not for two things. One, that the reviewer has to twist matters violently in order to make Dahlia appear sexually licentious, since Meredith makes it clear that she isn't particularly passionate (it's the dark-haired Rhoda who has the greater sexual vitality), so that she accepts a sexual relationship with Edward because it's part of the role of being the ideal mistress. *He* controls it, not her. The other matter of interest is the image of Dahlia as a pear that fell into Edward's open hand. Whether this was a cliché by the 1860s I don't know, but it certainly seems to have become one by the 1890s, at least if we may take *Jude the Obscure* as evidence. After Sue has returned to Phillotson, his friend Gillingham says to him: 'Well: you've all but got her again at last. She can't very

well go a second time. The pear has dropped into your hand'
(part sixth, ch. v). There are some obvious connections between
Sue and Dahlia, and Hardy knew his Meredith. But he also
knew his Browning, and it is more likely his use of the phrase
goes back to Browning's great poem 'A Light Woman', first
published in *Men and Women* (1855). It is about an honourable,
deeply conventional man who desires to save his young friend
from a sexually experienced woman who will, he assumes, add
'just him/To her nine-and-ninety other spoils,/The hundredth
for a whim!' And so 'I gave her my own eyes to take . . . and
[she] gave me herself indeed.' Naturally, his friend hates him
for what he's done. But what of the woman herself?

> And she – she lies in my hand as tame
>   As a pear late basking over a wall;
> Just a touch to try and off it came;
>   'Tis mine, – can I let it fall?
>
> With no mind to eat it, that's the worst!
>   Were it thrown in the road, would the case assist?
> 'Twas quenching a dozen blue-flies' thirst
>   When I gave its stalk a twist.
>
> One likes to show the truth for the truth;
>   That the woman was light is very true:
> But suppose she says, – Never mind that youth!
>   What wrong have I done to you?

I quote these stanzas because in them Browning allows us to
see how the man who speaks the poem, honourable, apparently
kindly intended, is in fact troubled at the probable implications
of his conventionality. We cannot know if he's telling the truth
about the woman, but we can know that he's fearful of her
sexuality. The horrific image of her 'quenching a dozen blue-
flies' thirst', tells us much more about him than it does about
her. And the anxious 'That the woman was light is very true' is
an attempt to shift the blame for his half-fascinated, half-
appalled involvement with her, before he comes to acknowledge
that she has claims on him which in his male conventionality he
dare not meet. 'What wrong have I done to you?' What wrong,
indeed.

To answer that question opens up important areas on Victorian – and not just Victorian – attitudes to female sexuality.

I have tried to show something of the ways in which Hardy, with Tess, and Hale White, with Madge Hopgood, write with intelligent sympathy about this problem, for a problem it is, or is seen to be. That is what *Rhoda Fleming* partly reveals, both in itself and in the reception given it. And it is what 'A Light Woman' is about. Browning's speaker betrays his fear of woman's sexuality, of her ripeness. So by a contradictory turn of phrase she is made 'light' when in fact she is heavy with full life. He uses language to try to tame his awareness of the fact. The language rightly betrays him. (I take it for granted that Browning recognized what was exploitable in the cliché phrase, 'a light woman'.)[11]

Farmer Fleming, the *Athenaeum* reviewer, the speaker of Browning's poem: they all have one thing in common, a desire to forbid women their sexual identity. Their concern is to desexualize them, to keep them in a state of passivity, submissiveness: subjection. I use that word deliberately, of course, because it reminds us of John Stuart Mill's great essay, *The Subjection of Women*, which he wrote in 1861, published in 1869, and which, predictably, was more unpopular with his contemporary audience than anything else he wrote. Mill anticipated this when, at the beginning of the essay, he notes that he can hardly expect to convince many people of the rightness of his arguments, for 'even if I could . . . leave the opposite party with a host of unanswered arguments against them, and not a single unrefuted one on their side, I should be thought to have done little; for a cause supported on the one hand by universal usage, and on the other by so great a preponderance of popular sentiment, is supposed to have a presumption in its favour, superior to any conviction which an appeal to reason has power to produce in any intellects but those of a high class.'[12] How right he was. As St John Packe shows in his *Life*, nearly all Mill's male contemporaries were scandalized by the essay. Fitzjames Stephen said that it provided 'the strongest distinct illustration known to me of what is perhaps one of the strongest, and what appears to me by far the most ignoble and mischievous of all popular feelings of the age'. And Mill's friend, Alexander Bain, remarked in wonder and consternation: 'He leads us to suppose that the relations of men and women between themselves may work on a purely voluntary level.'[13]

I do not think it necessary to repeat Mill's argument in any great detail, but it will perhaps help if I set down its leading ideas. He begins by noting that in the present state of society women are bred up for marriage. 'All women are brought up from the very earliest years in the belief that their ideal of character is the very opposite to that of men; not self-will, and government by self-control, but submission and yielding to the control of others. . . . It would be a miracle if the object of being attractive to men had not become the polar star of feminine education and formation of character' (p. 444). Pet Meagles, Dahlia Fleming, Rosamund Vincy, Tess: the list of fictional women who testify to their creators' awareness of the truth of what Mill is saying could be extended, but this will do to be going on with.

Since women are to be trained for marriage it is important that laws be set up that guarantee that 'they shall never in all their lives be allowed to compete for certain things' (p. 448). Which means above all else that they cannot enter the professions. Mill is obviously thinking of middle-class women, and it is one of the weaknesses of his essay that he more or less confines himself to that class. Its strengths are more important, however. He makes a particularly good point when he notes that although men will argue that women aren't fitted for the professions the truth is that they are usually ignorant of women. 'It is only a man here and there who has any tolerable knowledge of the character even of the women of his own family' (p. 454). And indeed men will remain ignorant 'until women have told all that they have to tell' (p. 456). In a sense this can be interpreted as a call for serious fiction by women, rather than a multiplication of 'Silly Novels by Lady Novelists' (the title of one of George Eliot's most trenchant essays). Yet if we except George Eliot herself, the fact is that it is male novelists who in the years after Mill's essay do their best to tell all that they have to tell about women. They are in a tiny minority, however, and Mill is in the right of it when he remarks that men are by and large content to think that 'the natural vocation of a woman is that of a wife and mother' (p. 458).

The whole drift of the first section of the essay is to establish the fact: 'What is now called the nature of women is an eminently artificial thing – the result of forced repression in some directions, unnatural stimulation in others. It may be asserted without scruple, that no other class of dependents have had their character so entirely distorted from its natural proportions by their relations with their masters . . .' (p. 451). In short, women are slaves, and of a particularly unfortunate kind. 'No slave is a slave to the same lengths, and in so full a sense of the word, as a wife is' (p. 463). Since this is so, Mill wittily suggests that 'since her all in life depends upon obtaining a good master, she should be allowed to change and change again until she finds one' (p. 464). No wonder Mill's contemporaries were shocked. And many would clearly be horrified by his next move, which is to argue that as far as the man is concerned a family is all too often 'a school of wilfulness, overbearingness, unbounded self-indulgence, and a double-dyed and idealised selfishness' (p. 469). It is to this ideal that women are sacrificed.

Mill proposes that it should be replaced by 'a voluntary association between two people' in which neither is master; and at the very end of the essay he argues that men require the lesson 'not to add to the evils which nature inflicts, by their jealous and prejudiced restrictions on one another' (p. 548). But it will be difficult to achieve this, since men can't bear the idea of women as equals and so pretend that they are intellectually and in most other ways inferior. It is a pretence which the educational and social systems of the country nourish. A boy is brought up differently from a girl. As a result, 'how early the notion of his inherent superiority to a girl arises in his mind; how it grows with his growth and strengthens with his strength; how it is inoculated by one schoolboy upon another; how early the youth thinks himself superior to his mother, owing her perhaps forbearance, but no real respect; and how sublime and sultan-like a sense of superiority he feels, above all, over the woman whom he honours by admitting her to a partnership in his life' (p. 523). And Mill concludes the essay with an eloquent passage in which he outlines the emptiness in the lives of women who have failed to achieve what society demands of them: 'What of the greatly increasing number of women, who have had no opportunity of exercising the vocation which they are mocked by telling them is their proper one?' And what of others, 'many of whom pine through life with the consciousness of thwarted vocations, and activities which are not suffered to expand . . .' (p. 545).

Meredith shares Mill's appalled sense of the tyranny of the man's knowing what is good for woman. When Dahlia finally breaks down because of Edward's easy indifference towards her:

> 'Ah, poor thing!' ejaculated the young man, not without an idea that the demonstration was unnecessary. For what is decidedly disagreeable is, in a young man's calculation concerning women, not necessary at all – quite the reverse. Are not women the flowers which decorate sublunary life? It is really irritating to discover them to be pieces of machinery that, for want of proper oiling, creak, stick, threaten convulsions, and are tragic and stir us the wrong way. However, champagne does them good: an admirable wine – a sure specific for the sex! [ch. xi].

What could look like muddled language is appropriate here. Dahlia – the name implies as much – should be a flower. To Edward's surprise and discomfort she turns out to be more complicated than that, though even then she can be accommodated to the language of use: she is a piece of machinery (it is worth noting that at the same time as Meredith was writing this passage Dickens was using strikingly similar language to characterize the relationships of individuals in *Our Mutual Friend*). Finally, she becomes humanized, is tragic. But that awareness is far too uncomfortable for Edward to accept and so Dahlia is once again reduced to cliché, to 'the sex'.

Mill and Meredith are very important in the challenge they offer to conventional high-Victorian notions of woman, love and marriage, and their championing of women's rights is of obvious importance to later generations of writers concerned with woman's role in society. Chief among these are, of course, Hardy and Hale White, but Gissing's *Odd Women* is another text that repays examination – whereas Grant Allen's absurd *The Woman Who Did* certainly does not. As the *Athenaeum* reviewer remarked, the novel 'reads more like a somewhat broken-winged manifesto from a few extremists against marriage as an institution than a sensational work of fiction. . . .'[15] I do not even know whether Allen is being serious. *The Women Who Did* might almost be a spoof or a way of cashing in on a fashionable subject (and of course it was itself the cause of the spoof *The Woman Who Didn't* by 'Victoria Cross').

Gissing, on the other hand, is deadly serious, and the *Athenaeum* reviewer was willing to recognize as much. The novel is

> . . . intensely modern, actual in theme as well as in treatment. Amidst the vexed social questions that surround us on all sides, and seem to defy solution, he has chosen one of real interest, and has turned it to clever and original purpose. The problem of the odd woman and what is to be done with her presents, in truth, a grim enough aspect. As treated by Mr. Gissing the interest is of almost too painful a character; yet it is full of suggestion and significance.

It is a sombre book, and yet 'latent in it all is an element of hope, a something that encourages the idea that with time and effort the baffling problem of the odd women may be success-fully solved'.[16] It seems from this as though the phrase 'the odd women' must have had some currency in the 1890s, though I have been unable to track it down. But certainly it raises a very important question. Just who *are* the odd women? The *Athenaeum* reviewer doesn't tell us, either because he assumes we know or because he thinks the phrase self-explanatory. Yet the fact is that in different ways all the women of the novel are odd. To be a woman is to be odd. Or so it seems. But let us have the main characters of the novel before us.

First, the Madden sisters. There are three of them, and they are left almost penniless when their father suddenly dies. They are also more or less without resources, it having been his plan that they should either marry or devote themselves to looking after him in his old age. Alice, the oldest, is a weak, ineffectual drudge who keeps up a pathetic pretence that she will one day open a school for young ladies and who in the meantime descends from one shabby-genteel lodging house to another, living on tinier and tinier amounts of money. Gissing is good on her, just as he is on the middle sister, Virginia, who is attractive but becoming too old for marriage, and who anyway is caught in the classic knot of the shabby-genteel-girl-becoming-mature-woman: not prepared to marry the kind of man who would have her, not a financially attractive proposition to the kind of man she would like to marry. In her increased loneliness she takes to secret drinking and becomes an alcoholic.

The youngest sister, Monica, is determined to escape from the kinds of lives her elder sisters live. She goes to work at a

milliners' and allows herself to be courted by a much older man
whom she marries though she feels a physical revulsion from
him. Gissing is excellent on both of them, on Monica's fierce
determination not to go down with Alice and Virginia, and on
Widdowson's unthinking kindness, sexual timidity and jealousy,
and his tyranny over the girl. For Widdowson is a domestic
tyrant, who suffocates Monica with his pressing love and need
to be loved. And with his determination to decide everything
for them both. Gissing resists satirizing him, but Widdowson is
a bleak and ruthless study of male conventionality.

> Monica soon found that his idea of wedded happiness was that they
> should always be together. Most reluctantly he consented to her going
> any distance alone, for whatever purpose. Public entertainments he
> regarded with no great favour, but when he saw how Monica enjoyed
> herself at concert or theatre, he made no objection to indulging her
> at intervals of a fortnight or so; his own fondness of music made this
> compliance easier. He was jealous of her forming new acquaintances;
> indifferent to society himself, he thought his wife should be satisfied
> with her present friends, and could not understand why she wanted to
> see them so often.
>   The girl was docile, and for a time he imagined that there would
> never be a conflict between his will and hers. Whilst enjoying their
> holiday they naturally went everywhere together, and were scarce an
> hour out of each other's presence, day or night. In quiet spots by the
> seashore, when they sat in solitude, Widdowson's tongue was loosened,
> and he poured forth his philosophy of life with the happy assurance
> that Monica would listen passively. His devotion to her proved itself
> in a thousand ways; week after week he grew, if anything, more kind,
> more tender; yet in his view of their relations he was unconsciously
> the most complete despot, a monument of male autocracy. Never had it
> occurred to Widdowson that a wife remains an individual, with rights
> and obligations independent of her wifely condition. Everything he
> said presupposed his own supremacy; he took for granted that it was
> his to direct, hers to be guided. A display of energy, purpose, ambition,
> on Monica's part, which had no reference to domestic pursuits, would
> have gravely troubled him; at once he would have set himself to
> subdue, with all gentleness, impulses so inimical to his idea of the
> married state [ch. xv, 'The Joys of Home'].

That spells it out, and in the way Gissing shows Widdowson
taking for granted his male supremacy and becoming terrified
at his wife's struggles to free herself from his grip he goes far
towards creating the kind of character who becomes treated
again and again in fictions of the next decade or two. I think

for example, of Henry Mynors in Bennett's *Anna of the Five Towns*, of John Stanway in his *Leonora* and of Laurence Riddaway in his *Whom God Hath Joined*; and of Ann Veronica's father; and of Henry Wilcox in *Howards End*.

Trying to escape Widdowson, Monica meets and falls in love with a much younger man, Bevis. He is well meaning, mildly vain, flattered to be given the chance of flirting with Monica and panic-stricken when he discovers that she's serious, and wants to run away with him.

> He embraced her with placid tenderness, laying his cheek against hers, kissing her hands.
> 'We must see each other again,' he continued. 'Come on Sunday, will you? And in the meantime find out some place where I could address letters to you. You can always find a stationer's shop where they will receive letters. Be guided by me, dear little girl. Only a week or two – to save the happiness of our whole lives.'
> Monica listened, but with half-attention, her look fixed on the floor. Encouraged by her silence, the lover went on in a strain of heightening enthusiasm, depicting the raptures of their retirement from the world in Bordeaux. How this retreat was to escape the notice of his business companions, through whom the scandal might get wind, he did not suggest. The truth was, Bevis found himself in an extremely awkward position, with issues he had not contemplated, and all he cared for was to avert the immediate peril and public discovery. The easy-going, kindly fellow had never considered the responsibility involved in making mild love – timorously selfish from the first – to a married woman who took his advances with desperate seriousness [ch. xxii, 'Honour in Difficulties'].

Bevis looks back to Edward Blancove and forward to, among others, Frank Palmer of *Clara Hopgood*, Charlie Fearns of *Whom God Hath Joined*, and Paul Wilcox of *Howards End*. He is appalled that Monica shouldn't answer to his cliché version of her and thoroughly discomposed by what Gissing allows us to recognize as her sexual fierceness and her wish to decide freely who shall be her sexual partner. She shrinks from Widdowson not because she is sexually frigid but because she simply doesn't want him sexually.

Monica's problem is that she wants economic, social and sexual independence, yet can hope to achieve it only through a marriage which turns out to be a trap. In walking into a trap she earns herself the disapproval and even scorn of Rhoda Nunn and Miss Barfoot, who have set up a school for typists in a

determination to make chosen girls thoroughly independent of
men. I use the phrase 'chosen girls' deliberately, because both
women have a debased Darwinian attitude to their own sex (an
attitude which almost certainly has Gissing's approval). Only
the fittest will and should survive, and they survive by learning
to do without men. True, Rhoda falls in love with and comes
close to marrying Miss Barfoot's cousin, but at the last she
resists the temptation, settling instead for her life of service to
the cause for which she and the other women fight.

It isn't a cause for all. Rhoda tells Miss Barfoot that she
thinks it important not to help girls who rush into marriage,
and Miss Barfoot replies:

> 'We differ a good deal, Rhoda, on certain points which as a rule would
> never come up to interfere with our working in harmony. You have
> come to dislike the very thought of marriage – and everything of that
> kind. I think it's a danger you ought to have avoided. True, we wish
> to prevent girls from marrying just for the sake of being supported, and
> from degrading themselves . . . but surely between ourselves we can
> admit that the vast majority of women would lead a wasted life if they
> did not marry.'
>
> 'I maintain that the vast majority of women lead a vain and miser-
> able life just because they *do* marry.'
>
> 'Don't you blame the institution of marriage with what is chargeable
> to human fate? A vain and miserable life is the lot of nearly all mortals.
> Most women, whether they marry or not, will suffer and commit
> endless follies.'
>
> 'Most women – as life is at presently arranged for them. Things are
> changing, and we try to have our part in hastening a new order.'

But the new order is delayed because of women's sexual
natures, or so Rhoda argues. Miss Barfoot disagrees. 'The girls
of our class', she tells Rhoda, 'are not like the uneducated, who,
for one reason or another, will marry almost any man rather
than remaining single.' But that is no reason to insist on sexual
celibacy. Rhoda disagrees.

> 'Women's battle is not only against themselves. The necessity of the
> case demands what you call a strained ideal. I am seriously convinced
> that before the female sex can be raised from its low level there will
> have to be a widespread revolt against the sexual instinct. . . .'
>
> 'I can't declare that you are wrong in that. Who knows? But it isn't
> good policy to preach it to our young disciples.'
>
> 'I shall respect your wish; but – '
>
> Rhoda paused and shook her head.

'My dear,' said the older woman gravely, 'believe me that the less we talk or think about such things the better for the peace of us all. The odious fault of working-class girls, in town and country alike, is that they are absorbed in preoccupation with their animal nature. We, thanks to our education and the tone of our society, manage to keep that in the background. Don't interfere with this satisfactory state of things. Be content to show our girls that it is their duty to lead a life of effort – to earn their bread and to cultivate their minds. Simply ignore marriage – that's the wisest. Behave as if the thing didn't exist. You will do positive harm by taking the other course – the aggressive course' [ch. VI, 'A Camp of the Reserve'].

In some ways this foreshadows Hardy's handling of Arabella and Sue in *Jude* and certainly the terms of the discussion between Rhoda and Miss Barfoot suggest affinities with issues that Hardy's novel raises. Which is not to deny that there are differences. Hardy, after all, is a great novelist even if *Jude the Obscure* is far from being his best novel, whereas Gissing at best is a good novelist and no more. But in both *Odd Women* and *Jude the Obscure* we are dealing with odd women, since to be a woman is to be in an odd position; and in both cases the women try to help themselves, either through marriage or in defiance of it. And behind both one can hear the echo and import of Dahlia Fleming's dying words: 'help poor girls'.

Notes

Chapter 1

1   John Lucas, *Tradition and Tolerance in Nineteenth Century Fiction* (1966).
2   William Myers, *Literature and Politics in the Nineteenth Century* (1971), pp. 119–20.

Chapter 2

1   Friedrich Engels, *The Condition of the Working Class in England in 1844* (London). I use the text of the Institute of Marxism–Leninism, Moscow, as published by Panther and introduced by Eric Hobsbawm. As Steven Marcus has pointed out in his *Engels, Manchester and the Working Class* (1974), we still have no reliable edition of Engels's great work. The Panther text is the best I know.
2   For this and the previous quotations see Asa Briggs, *Victorian Cities* (London 1963), pp. 86–8.
3   Briggs, *Victorian Cities*, pp. 110–11.
4   Henry Colman, *European Life and Morals* (1849).
5   Briggs, *Victorian Cities*, pp. 112–13.
6   River pollution especially shocked the Victorian consciousness and one can see why: fresh running water has obvious symbolic connotations – I think of Blake's innocent chimney sweeper, of *The Water Babies* – and to be deprived of it was deeply horrifying. Pollution signified a final loss of innocence, of being washed clean, of restorative possibilities, which must have set up wounding reverberations. (See, for example, Ruskin's descriptions of his approach to Bradford in *The Two Paths* [1859]. And see ch. 47 of *David Copperfield*.)
7   Quoted by A. B. Reach in his *Manchester and the Textile Districts in 1849*, ed. C. Aspin (1972), p. 25.
8   Reach, *Textile Districts*, p. 32.

9 For a detailed discussion of the reception of Mrs Gaskell's novel, see my essay in *Tradition and Tolerance in Nineteenth Century Fiction.*

10 *Westminster Review*, LI (July 1849).

11 Marcus, *Engels*, p. 49.

12 Marcus, *Engels*, pp. 145–53.

13 Marcus, *Engels*, p. 168. Engels remarks that the conditions in the towns amount to warfare and this war grows from year to year, as the criminal tables show, more violent, passionate, irreconcilable. The enemies are dividing gradually into two main camps – the bourgeoisie on the one hand, the workers on the other (p. 162).

14 Quoted in Briggs, *Victorian Cities*, p. 109.

15 It is worth comparing Engels on Manchester with Orwell on working-class people who want, among other things, 'a bath once a day'. That has much more to do with Orwell's own middle-class hatred of smells and dirt than with working-class desires. See *Looking Back on the Spanish War.*

16 Reach, *Textile Districts*, p. 4.

17 Reach, *Textile Districts*, p. 5.

18 For example, the autobiographies of Thomas Cooper, Samuel Bamford, Joseph Arch, W. E. Adams and the biographies of Tom Mann and John Burns; and one might also look at the monograph by Stan Shipley on 'Club Life and Socialism in Mid-Victorian London', *History Workshops Pamphlets*, 5. It is, however, worth noting that Reach devotes sizeable sections to 'The Quest for Knowledge', and 'Sunday Schools' and that he points out how socially advantageous schools in Manchester are; how they provide companionship and *some* pleasure-giving activities and relief from the hard grind of work. He is not naïve about this: 'I believe that we must have a comfortable and a cleanly living people before we have an educated or a moral people' (Textile Districts, p. 43).

19 The kind of distinctions that Engels was incapable of making are also brought out in an interesting moment in *Deliverance* where Mark Rutherford and his journalist friend, M'Kay are walking through Drury Lane, and Mark becomes aware of the horrors of life in this spot.

> The desire to decorate existence in some way or other with more or less care is nearly universal. The most sensual and the meanest almost always manifest an indisposition to be content with mere material satisfaction. . . . The instinct, even in its lowest forms, is divine. . . . In the alleys behind Drury Lane this instinct, the

very salt of life, was dead, crushed out utterly, a symptom which
seemed to me awful in the last degree. The only house in which
it survived was in that of the undertaker, who displayed the
willows, the black horses, and the coffin. These may have been
nothing more than an advertisement, but from the care in which
the cross was elaborated, and the neatness with which it was made
to resemble a natural piece of wood, I am inclined to believe that
the man felt some pleasure in his work for its own sake, and that
he was not utterly submerged [p. 26].

20 Some indication of Mrs Gaskell's knowledge of working-class
literature can be found in an article by Michael D. Wheeler,
'The Writer as Reader in *Mary Barton*', *Durham University
Journal* (December 1974).

Chapter 3

1 W. Hale White, *Letters to Three Friends* (1924), pp. 170 and 180.
2 W. Hale White, *Last Pages from a Journal* (1915), p. 133.
3 It is, of course, true that one can find Mark's kind of melancholy at large in writings of the 1840s, but Hale White does not
see it as typical of the earlier decade, whereas he certainly *does*
see it as typical of the 1880s.
4 Hale White, *Pages from a Journal* (1900).
5 There is a useful account of Hale White's use of Spinoza in
Clara Hopgood by Linda K. Hughes, *Victorian Studies*, XVIII: 1,
though it is spoilt by her mechanistic application of Spinozistic
ideas to the novel's two sisters.
6 James Thomson, 'The City of Dreadful Night' (1880).
7 It is significant that Mark Rutherford's encounter with the
Lyrical Ballads while he is a theological student is said to produce
a change in him that 'could only be compared with that which
is said to have been wrought on Paul himself by the Divine
apparition'. And the older Mark accounts for this, at least
partly, by saying that Wordsworth's real God was the God of
the hills and that 'to this [i.e. Nature] my reverence was trans-
ferred . . . he re-created my Supreme Divinity' (*Autobiography*,
Ch. 2). One inevitably recalls J. S. Mill's famous statement in
his Autobiography (1873) about the *Lyrical Ballads* having helped
him out of the nervous breakdown which his early education
had led him into.
8 Hale White, *Last Pages from a Journal*.
9 Whether this failure is to be attributed to Hale White or to the
'author', Mark Rutherford, is a complex question. Certainly

Mark is allowed to voice an essentially Romantic wish for the reintegration of self and natural world – a shared purposiveness – that Hale White would be too diffident to express *in propria personas.*

10 Joseph Jacobs, *Jewish Ideas and other Essays* (1896), p. xii.

11 For a detailed account of novels of the 1880s that deal with the possibilities of social revolution, see my essay 'Conservatism and Revolution in the 1880's', in *Literature and Politics in the Nineteenth Century*, ed. John Lucas (1975).

12 Hale White, *Pages from a Journal.*

13 E. P. Thompson, *The Making of the English Working Class* (1963), p. 193. It is worth noting that Jean Caillaud, a friend of the Major's who becomes deeply friendly with Zachariah, is a shoemaker – as the famous Thomas Hardy had been.

14 The Club is held in Red Lion Street, which was, and continued to be, famous for its association with radical societies.

15 Hale White is heavily dependent on Samuel Bamford's *Autobiography*, which Mark quotes without comment but with obvious approval (ch. XI), though the precise reference to Bamford's experience of London clubs is 1817 – and Bamford is writing out of a mood of disenchantment. After saying something of the then 'most influential leaders of the London operative reformers', Bamford comments, 'the blind were then leading the blind'. See W. H. Chaloner (ed.), *Passages of the Life of a Radical* (1967), pp. 23–5.

16 Thompson, *English Working Class*, p. 608. It is proper to remark that Thompson pays tribute to Cartwright as being 'more interested in the principle of the men with whom he worked than in their income or occupation'. See his chapter 'Demagogues and Martyrs'.

17 Thompson, *English Working Class*, p. 646.

18 E. Halevy, *The Liberal Awakening* (1961), p. 27.

19 Bamford, *Autobiography*, I: *Early Days*, p. 328. It is worth noting an episode when Zachariah is on the run, after the collapse of the march; he takes shelter in a pub and witnesses a parson, a farmer and an overseer spurn the desperate request for food from a starving weaver. It no doubt takes something from Bamford on the Rotten Boroughs, but still more from a desire to expose the enemies of the people – once the march had failed.

20 Thompson, *English Working Class*, p. 646.

21 I should say that in *Everywhere Spoken Against: Dissent in the Victorian Novel* (1975), Valentine Cunningham will not allow the accuracy of Mark's diagnosis of this decay. Unfortunately

Mr Cunningham's book came out too late for me to make use
of it – or to take issue with his interesting but questionable
argument.

22 *Miriam's Schooling* is not divided into chapters. I therefore give
page references from the collected edition.

23 Hale White on more than one occasion in the *Journals* has tales
of bitterly unsatisfactory marriages, in which the wife is the
sufferer, the victim of her husband's coldness and intellectual
incuriosity, and is removed from her friends. See, for example,
'Esther', an epistolary tale, in which letters between Esther and
her mother effectively chart the breakdown of the girl's marriage (*More Pages from a Journal*). Also the anecdotal 'James
Forbes', in which the free-thinking James breaks off his engagement to the religious 'Elizabeth' because 'a marriage which is
not a marriage of minds is no marriage' (*Pages from a Journal*).
In this case, James lives to repent his decision, which links the
tale to the *Autobiography* and also to *Miriam's Schooling*.

24 Arthur Symons, *London: A Book of Aspects* (1909), p. 66. This
passage was written in the 1890s. I owe my discovery of it to
Martin Wood's as yet unpublished thesis on 'Darwinism and
Pessimism in Late-Victorian Life and Literature'.

25 One might in this context note the emblematic figure, a walking
cadaver, whom Zachariah meets in the workhouse hospital in
Liverpool and whose blank lifelessness is truly appalling.

26 For more on this see Ch. 5 of this book.

27 The near echo of *Rasselas* is unlikely to be accidental. Hale
White was a keen admirer of Johnson and in 1907 brought out
a selection from the *Rambler*.

28 The text says Longland. It may either be a joke in not very
good taste ('that's all they know about poetry') or a misprint.

29 For a discussion of some of these novels see Ch. 5 of this book.

30 The phrase comes from the *Athenaeum* review of *Jude the
Obscure*, 2252 (23 November 1895), pp. 709–10.

31 *Athenaeum*, 3590 (15 August 1896), p. 220.

32 Hughes, *Victorian Studies*, p. 72.

33 Mazzini's reputation had sunk very low by the 1890s, so that
readers of the novel could hardly be expected to think Clara's
sacrifice unambiguously noble.

Chapter 4

1 R. Williams, *The English Novel from Dickens to Lawrence* (1974),
pp. 93–4.

2 For a fuller discussion of Hardy and vision, see Donald Davie's 'Hardy's Virgilian Purples', in the special Hardy issue of *Agenda*, 10: 2 (1972) and Tom Paulin's brilliant *Thomas Hardy: the Poetry of Perception* (1975).

3 I have traced something of the word's history during the nineteenth century in *The Melancholy Man: A Study of Dickens's Fiction* (1970). See especially the chapter on *David Copperfield*.

4 Tom Paulin touches on this though his interests lead him in a different direction – and he uses only the second scene in relation to the poem. The first may be less of a parallel but its kinship seems to be beyond dispute.

5 Hale White, *Last Pages from a Journal*, p. 317.

6 The words call to mind Dahlia Fleming and her determination to appease her father, for which see Ch. 5 of this book.

Chapter 5

1 *Athenaeum*, 3552 (23 November 1895), pp. 709–10.

2 For the rise in Meredith's critical fortunes, see my essay on his reputation in *Meredith Now*, ed. Ian Fletcher (1971).

3 *Athenaeum*, 3350 (9 January 1892), p. 49.

4 *Athenaeum*, 3590 (15 August 1896), p. 220.

5 These dates refer to first book publication.

6 See her essay in *Meredith Now*.

7 *Letters of George Gissing to Members of his Family* (1927), pp. 170–2.

8 The point is made by David Howard in his subtle essay on the novel in *Meredith Now*.

9 In L. Stevenson, *The Ordeal of George Meredith* (1954), p. 277.

10 *Athenaeum*, 1781 (14 October 1865), p. 495.

11 The image of the sexually alert woman as a pear seems to be a traditional one in English. It certainly goes as far back as Chaucer's Alison, whom the Miller describes as 'full moore blisful on to see/Than is the newe pere-jonette tree'. Still, Alison's early ripeness is regarded quite without disapproval. Indeed, the Miller's frank admiration of her sexuality is in marked contrast to the way the speaker of Browning's poem regards his light woman. But it is worth noting that male fear of female sexuality is often heightened – or explored and ridiculed – by having an old man marry a young woman. The Carpenter, Phillotson, and Widdowson of the *Odd Women* are all much older than their wives, and are all repulsive to them (as for that matter is January to May in the Merchant's Tale; and of

course Damyon and May have sex in a pear tree). Browning's very subtle poem takes up the idea of the older man 'saving' the young one from a mature woman: i.e. the speaker thinks that he's sexually more qualified to deal with her than is his friend. It's another kind of sexual jealousy and typically has to put the blame on the woman.

12 John Stuart Mill, *Three Essays*, introduced by Richard Wolheim (1975), p. 429.

13 Michael St John Packe, *The Life of John Stuart Mill* (1954), p. 495. Stephen is using the word 'popular' in its familiar nineteenth-century sense of 'radical'.

14 For a detailed discussion of this see my chapter on the novel in my study, *Dickens, The Melancholy Man.*

15 *Athenaeum*, 3514 (2 March 1895), p. 277.

16 *Athenaeum*, 3422 (27 May 1893), p. 667.

Index